THE FRAGRANT PATH

香り高い道

日本の香道への案内

The Fragrant Path
A GUIDE TO THE JAPANESE ART OF INCENSE

Michael J. Cousineau

KIKOH INCENSE
CHICAGO • 2024

ISBN hardback: 979-8-9916529-2-6
ISBN paperback: 979-8-9916529-1-9
ISBN ebook: 979-8-9916529-0-2

Library of Congress Control Number: 2024922695

Kikoh Incense, LLC
757 DuPage Blvd. #3210
Glen Ellyn, Illinois 60137
www.kikohincense.com

Cover and interior design by Michael Cousineau
Illustrations by Michael Cousineau
Frontispiece calligraphy by Kisyuu Calligraphy

ACKNOWLEDGMENTS

*Tamaki Tiballi for her encouragement and generous sharing
of her time and knowledge of the Japanese language.*

*Dr. Phillip Moscatel for his chiropractic skills, his inspiration
and insights into writing a book, and his friendship.*

*My wife, Linda, for listening to me talk
about Japanese incense every day,
month after month, for years on end,
yet loving me anyway.*

CONTENTS

INTRODUCTION
Welcome to the Fragrant Path

Whether you've just lit your first stick of incense or burned ten thousand, each journey exploring the Japanese art of incense is as unique as it is fragrant. Ancient in its origin, incense was first burned in ritual and spiritual practice in Egypt and India over four thousand years ago. From there, it traveled to China as the embodiment of the Buddha's words, continuing its journey east to arrive in Japan in the sixth century. There, for over 1,400 years, the Japanese art of incense has painted the air, its fragrant wisps of smoke like the soft monochromatic hues of a sumi ink painting.

More than a utilitarian commodity, incense is one of Japan's most comprehensive art forms—an expression of Japanese culture and a reflection of the poetic, literary, spiritual, and historic events that shaped its refinement. When we "listen" to Japanese incense, we listen to the whispers of nature and engage with emperors and shōguns, samurai and tea masters, merchants and courtiers through a shared experience that transcends time. The beauty of the Japanese art of incense lies in this ability to transport us in ways that are as inspiring as they are fragrant. Allowing us to touch the wisdom of nature directly, Japanese incense is capable of teaching us not only about its rare and fragrant ingredients but about ourselves as well.

My journey along the Fragrant Path began by accident. Like most in the West, I enjoyed the typical bamboo-cored incense found in specialty stores whose air was thick with jasmine and Eastern spirituality. I delighted in the smokey scents of thick sticks of lavender, sandalwood, and "frankincense." One holiday season, I ran out of incense, and a trip to restock revealed that my source had gone out of business. It was the early days of the internet, and the only nearby store I could find online was also going out of business. All they had left were bundles of Japanese incense. I had never heard of Japanese incense, let alone its ritual appreciation, but one bundle included a frankincense blend. Even at 50 percent off, it was expensive, but it seemed worth the risk, so I ordered it. I had no idea what was in store for me.

After the package arrived and the boxes were freed from their bubble wrap straitjackets, I was disappointed how small the incense was. Unlike the familiar foot-long lollipops of plump incense on red bamboo sticks, the Japanese incense was short and thin, barely the size of a pencil lead, and less than six inches long. Concerned, I lit a stick and found myself wondering if the purchase was a bust. There was no blast of fragrance nor the billowing smoke I was accustomed to. Instead, there was only a thin wisp of smoke and a subtle fragrance. *No wonder this incense shop is going out of business,* I thought.

Then it happened. Where my old incense screamed "Frankincense!" through a cloud of smoke, the Japanese incense whispered to me of the true nature of *real* frankincense. Slowly, over several minutes, a beautiful redolence filled the space with nuanced notes of woody sweetness mixed with citrus, soft and light. The Japanese incense was alive, notes rising and falling in a fragrant dance that enchanted and soothed, its much greater dynamic range effortlessly moving from low whispers of woody bass to boisterous fruity highs.

But what really astonished me was the feeling that the incense created a space around me. Its fragrance encircled me like a warm blanket on a cold winter night. Feelings of peace, calm, and relaxation surrounded me like a gentle embrace. Transported from my daily life by the beauty of nature's gift of fragrance, I was at peace.

There was no going back. My journey on the Fragrant Path had begun.

It is no wonder that Japanese incense manufacturers display such artistry in their creations. Many prominent incense houses trace their origins back over five centuries, with even modern companies having a lineage of one hundred years or more. The manufacture of Japanese incense is not merely a means of commerce for these companies. As skilled artisans, their ability to work fragrant notes back and forth, into and out of awareness, using a limited number of woods and aromatics, allows them to create an almost-unlimited range of fragrances. With roots in a time ruled by the samurai, Japanese incense houses have a lineage they honor and seek to continue in today's world.

More than simply an object of utility, incense, or kō (香), is deeply embedded in Japanese culture. Refined through the practices of imperial courtiers and shōguns alike, it has been used as a means of relaxation, purification, protection, and entertainment as well as a method of displaying refinement, social status, and power. The influential nineteenth-century writer Lafcadio Hearn, one of the first to introduce Japanese culture to the West, wrote of the prevalence of incense in Japan in his book *In Ghostly Japan:*

> It is almost ubiquitous,—this perfume of incense. It makes one element of the faint but complex and never-to-be-forgotten odor of the Far East. It haunts the dwelling-house not less than the temple,—the home of the peasant not less than the yashiki of the prince.

This prevalence of incense represents the embodiment of centuries of rich cultural heritage. The refined arts of Chadō, or the Way of Tea (more commonly known as the tea ceremony), and Kadō, or the Way of

Flowers (more well known as ikebana), are familiar to us in the West. But sitting at the pinnacle of the Japanese art of incense is Kōdō, the Way of Fragrance. The least known of Japan's refined arts, Kōdō developed alongside the tea ceremony and the arrangement of flowers over five hundred years ago. As a comprehensive art, Kōdō draws upon not only expertise with rare and fragrant woods, but also a knowledge of classical poetry, literature, history, and choreography that was originally taught in tandem with the tea ceremony. Taking over thirty years to master, the incense ceremony is a rich cultural experience unique to the Japanese that goes well beyond the mere smelling of incense.

Arising from its spiritual roots imported with Buddhism, incense also embodies the Japanese spirit. Infused with Zen and a poetic reverence for the seasons, the Japanese art of incense transcends fragrance, opening us to a dialogue with the natural world. Produced by only 1 to 2 percent of a handful of tree species and taking over a hundred years to form, aloeswood—known in Japanese as *jinkō*—is considered a fragrant miracle of nature, prized for its spiritual significance as much as for its exceptional fragrance. Japanese incense is not smelled or sniffed; like the words of the Buddha, it is "listened" to with one's whole being. Similar to the experience of sitting in meditation, listening to the rare and fragrant woods at the heart of the Japanese art of incense can open us to insights only nature can provide.

The sublime fragrance of Japanese incense started me on my journey, but the farther I traveled along the Fragrant Path, the more my reverence grew for the traditions that transformed Japanese incense into an art form. Like the other refined arts of Japan, the art of incense can be studied for a lifetime. It is said that to lose yourself in incense is to find your true nature. To me, this is what makes the Japanese art of incense so special and keeps me traveling along the Fragrant Path.

So, light some incense, make yourself comfortable, and together let's explore the Japanese art of incense.

> *Incense ember glowing,*
> *graceful wisps of smoke,*
> *trailing like a fragrant path,*
> *whisper of our true destination.*

HOW TO USE THIS BOOK

Because of our individual senses of smell, fragrance is unique not only to each person but also to the moment in which it is experienced. In our journey along the Fragrant Path, each experience will be unique, with different interests, needs, and tastes arising from moment to moment as we proceed. To take this evolving experience into consideration, this book has been divided into four sections that cover four distinct aspects of the Japanese art of incense: its origins, selection, use, and appreciation. Feel free to "binge read" the entire book cover to cover, or to start with the section that resonates most. The ultimate goal of this book is to deepen the enjoyment of fragrance, no matter where you find yourself along the Fragrant Path.

I: ORIGINS

The first section of this book covers the history of the Japanese art of incense. While it might seem logical for a book on Japanese incense to focus only on incense, that might encourage the misperception that the art of incense developed in isolation, which was far from the case. The Buddhist concept of interdependence known as *ji ji muge* (事事無礙) is often illustrated as a spider web covered in dew, each individual dewdrop holding the reflection of every other dewdrop on the web. Like one of those dewdrops, the Japanese art of incense developed interdependently with other art forms, reflecting the influence of poetry, literature, history, and the culture of the time, as well as the individuals who elevated these art forms to their refined states. Although I do not claim to be a trained historian, the first section of this book lends context to the 1,400 years of refinement that have shaped the Japanese art of incense and provides a glimpse into the rich culture of Japan reflected by it.

II: SELECTION

In the second section, we'll take a look at the qualities and ingredients at the root of the Japanese art of incense. With centuries of refinement behind the creation of Japanese incense, its basic ingredients have a rich history and well-documented properties and uses. The sources, characteristics, and natures of the rare fragrant woods and primary aromatic ingredients commonly found in Japanese incense are described in depth, providing a useful tool to explore the world of fragrance and to deepen the olfactory palette. Also included is information on the basic forms of incense, their qualities and uses, and practical suggestions for where to begin your journey.

III: USE

Consider the third section of this book a "quick start guide" to the use of Japanese incense. Filled with practical and actionable suggestions, this section covers the basics of safely using Japanese incense. In this section, you'll find answers to some of the questions asked most often by those new to using Japanese incense, such as how to light incense, best practices for burning, safety precautions, how to use incense holders and burners, and how to store the Japanese incense collection you are sure to amass. If you are just starting out, this section is a perfect place to begin, ensuring a safe and firm foundation for your journey.

IV: APPRECIATION

In the fourth section of this book, we'll go deeper into the philosophical underpinnings of appreciating Japanese incense, learning to listen to incense and open ourselves to the beauty of its rare and fragrant woods and natural aromatics. Filled with practical suggestions, this section describes ways to value Japanese incense for more than just its fragrance. The appreciation of Japanese incense would not be complete without an introduction to the ritual appreciation of Kōdō and its poetic and literary foundations found in the incense games of *kumikō*. Finally, a discussion of "Kō no Jittoku" ("Ten Virtues of Incense")—written over five hundred years ago yet still widely cited in the appreciation of Japanese incense today—brings our time together to a close.

I: ORIGINS

More than the color
it is the fragrance I find
a source of delight.
Whose sleeve might have brushed against
the plum tree beside my house?

KOKIN WAKASHŪ, BOOK 1: POEM 33

CHINA

YELLOW SEA

Korean
Peninsula

Tsushima •

Shimonoseki •
Iki •
Hakata Bay •

Hirado •

Nagasaki •

• Shanghai

Kyushu

• Ningbo   EAST CHINA SEA

Tanegashima •

Hakodate •

SEA OF JAPAN

Niigata•

JAPAN

• Oki Islands

Edo •

Kamakura •

Honshu

• Lake Biwa

Kyoto •

• Owari

• Nara

• Shimoda

Awaji •

• Sakai

Shikoku

PACIFIC OCEAN

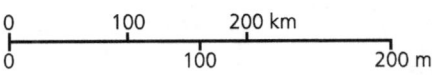

CHAPTER 1

蘭奢待

RANJATAI
Incense arrives in Japan

EVERY EPIC HAS ITS ORIGIN, AND THE STORY OF THE JAPANESE art of incense has at its beginnings the most famous piece of fragrant wood in the incense world: Ranjatai (蘭奢待). Originally known as Ōjuku-kō (黄熟香), the arrival of Ranjatai is the stuff of legend, appropriately documented in the second-oldest written record of Japanese history, the *Nihon Shoki* (日本書紀, *Chronicles of Japan*). Described as slightly more than five feet in length, sixteen inches in diameter at its greatest girth, and weighing over twenty-five pounds, Ranjatai is said to have divinely washed up upon the shores of Awaji Island in the summer of 595 CE. At first, local villagers used it for firewood. But the chronicles record that upon its heating, the villagers quickly realized the wood was extraordinarily fragrant, and it was soon thereafter presented to Empress Suiko as a luxurious tributary gift.

Like many events in history, this seemingly innocuous occurrence took place as part of larger cultural and political shifts occurring in a sixth-century Japan obsessed with emulating Chinese culture. At this time, there was no permanent Japanese capital, only a series of transient palace complexes that echoed the ornate style of the Chinese capital of Chang'an and that moved location with each successive emperor's reign. Nor was there a true written Japanese language. Instead, Chinese *kanji* (characters) were used to represent phonetic Japanese or for a close approximation of their actual Chinese meaning in Japanese—with both uses often confusingly employed in the same document. Even the *Nihon Shoki* and the *Kojiki* (古事記, *Record of Ancient Things*), the two oldest books of Japan's recorded history, were written in kanji. The ruling elite's political interest in advancing ties with China and implementing Chinese forms of government and the introduction of the Chinese form of Buddhism would serve as the foundation for Japan's art of incense.

Ranjatai was presented to Empress Suiko, who, through assassination and outright warfare, had been placed on the Chrysanthemum Throne in 593 by the Soga clan, whose influence prevailed over politics during much of Japan's Asuka period (538–710 CE). However, the Soga picked Empress Suiko's nephew, Prince Shōtoku, to rule from behind the throne as regent. The second son of Emperor Yōmei, Shōtoku was an advocate for the adoption of Chinese methods of government, cultural refinement, and Buddhism into Japanese spiritual and secular life. These beliefs meshed well with the Soga clan's desire to elevate Japanese culture in the mold of China's established dynastic ruling classes. Historically, Prince Shōtoku has been attributed with a multitude of legendary powers, such as the ability to speak from birth. In actuality, his governmental reforms, although not otherworldly, did include significant advances. Shōtoku is credited with adopting a Chinese-style calendar, introducing a type of Chinese "cap rank" system for state officials (a system that indicated rank through colored caps based upon Confucian values of merit), and directly enhancing ties with China by sending official Japanese emissaries to the Chinese court throughout his reign. Revered to this day for his achievements, Shōtoku ruled as regent of Japan from 594 until his death in 622.

It was Shōtoku who is said to have immediately identified Ranjatai as *jinkō* (沈香)—rare and fragrant aloeswood. His observation is significant because, both then and now, nearly all raw materials used in Japanese incense are not found on the islands of Japan. This is especially true of aloeswood, which is found only in the jungles of Southeast Asia, far beyond the seas surrounding Japan. With few exceptions, incense materials such as aloeswood and sandalwood would have been known only to aristocratic Japanese familiar with Chinese culture and Buddhist rites. Believed to have arrived in Japan some fifty years prior to the appearance of Ranjatai, aloeswood was brought to Japan from Baekje, one of the Three Kingdoms of Korea, as part of the introduction to Buddhism. Part of *mitsu-gusoku* (三具足), the three great offerings of incense, flowers, and light present at Buddhist rituals and altars, aloeswood would have been part of the Buddhist ceremonies imported from the continent.

Although relatively new to Japan, the use of incense in China had been painstakingly perfected over nearly a millennium by the time of Prince Shōtoku's reign. By the fifth century, the majority of today's incense ingredients were already known in China, with their various fragrant and medicinal properties well documented in compilation texts on incense use. One of the earliest of these texts was *He Xian Fang* (和香方, *Blended Incense Recipes*), written in approximately 430 by well-known Chinese politician and historian Fan Ye. Although lost to time and now known only through references in other sources, Chinese officials clearly knew about incense and were highly skilled at blending various aromatics not only for their fragrance but also for medicinal purposes. Even the Chinese word for incense, *xiāng* (香), could be used as a noun meaning "incense" or an adjective meaning "fragrant," and was used to describe fragrant Chinese medicine, *xiāng wán* (fragrant pills), that could be taken internally or burned to release their fragrance therapeutically. With its deep roots in Chinese Buddhism and Taoism, incense was believed to protect the body from illness caused by unclean or evil spirits, harmonize emotions, and assist in the pursuit of enlightenment.

The introduction of Buddhism and incense go hand in hand in Japan. Officially adopted by Emperor Yōmei in 552, Buddhism brought Buddhist thought, images of the Buddha, and sacred rites and rituals that included a central role for fragrant woods. Although Prince Shōtoku was not responsible for the introduction of Buddhism to Japan, his powerful advocacy for the integration of Chinese culture and political principles into Japanese governance is clearly evident in his creation of a Chinese-influenced constitution known as the Jūshichijō Kenpō (十七条憲法, Seventeen Injunctions). More a code of ethics than a governing document, Shōtoku's constitution emphasized reverence for the "three treasures" of Buddhism: the Buddha, the law, and the priesthood. This integration of Buddhism directly into Japanese governing precepts brought Buddhist sacred rites and ceremonies into Japanese spiritual life, exposing Japan's ruling class to the fragrances of exotic incense woods and aromatic materials imported from China and its trading network in the South Pacific. As a result, the fragrance of aloeswood and Chinese medicinal aromatics soon became well known to the Imperial Court and government aristocrats.

For use in these ceremonies, fragrant woods and aromatic materials were finely chopped into a granulated incense called *shōkō* (焼香, burning incense) that was burned *sonaekō* (供香), that is, directly upon hot coals, as an incense offering to the gods. Shōkō could be comprised of a single fragrant wood such as sandalwood or aloeswood, or it could consist of a mixture of fragrant woods and traditional aromatic ingredients such as clove, spikenard, and camphor, blended in unique recipes specific to the requirements of the ceremony at hand. Presented as an incense offering, shōkō was burned sonaekō for purification of both space and person (for the living, but especially for the deceased), or as an offering to gods and temple deities for all manner of gratitude and good tidings, such as for a good harvest season or long life for the emperor.

By a century after Shōtoku's passing, Buddhism was flourishing in the capital, so much so that Japan lacked enough fully ordained monks to formally administer the Buddhist precepts, requiring adherents to undertake dangerous and difficult travel to China to be officially ordained by a Buddhist *risshi* (律師, precepts master).

Ascending to the throne in 724, Emperor Shōmu was a deeply devout Buddhist who sought to establish Buddhism as both state religion and protector of Japan, replacing social unrest with inner peace. Shōmu undertook significant actions that created a thriving Buddhist aristocratic state government centered upon the capital. This came to be known as Tenpyō culture, named after the period of Shōmu's reign. In 733, Shōmu had two monks accompany a diplomatic emissary to China to solicit risshi willing to return with them to Japan to supervise ordinations. In preparation for their return, in 741, he issued an edict ordering the creation of a Buddhist temple system known as *kokubun-ji* (国分寺), which placed a temple in each province to form a religious connection between the capital and the countryside. Highlighting his support, each temple was supplied with a *sutra* (sacred Buddhist scripture) that Shōmu himself had copied. This was followed in 743 with the commission of an immense bronze statue of Dainichi Nyorai (大日如来, Great Sun Buddha). Completed in 751, the fifty-three-foot statue included five hundred tons of copper, tin, lead, and gold, using up all of Japan's copper reserves.

To house such a large image of the Buddha, Emperor Shōmu sponsored the construction of the correspondingly immense Daibutsu-den (大仏殿, Great Buddha Hall) at the center of a vast monastery complex known as Tōdai-ji (東大寺, Great Eastern Temple). The temple complex began construction in 745 and, when it was opened in 752, contained some two square miles within its walled and gated grounds. Tōdai-ji would serve as the chief temple in the kokubun-ji system and, as such, was the center for rituals for national peace and prosperity as well as the center for the study of Buddhist doctrine in Japan. To consecrate the Great Buddha, the Daibutsu Kaigan Kuyo-e (大仏開眼供養, Eye-Opening Ceremony), in which eyes are inserted into the image of the Buddha, was held in 752. The largest international event of its kind in East Asia, the ceremony was presided over by a Buddhist priest from Brahmin India and attended by sitting and retired Japanese emperors and empresses as well as ten thousand Buddhist priests.

Soon thereafter, Shōmu's search for a risshi from China was answered. After ten years of trying, and blinded from infection suffered during his attempts to reach Japan, a Buddhist risshi named Ganjin (鑑真)

answered Shōmu's solicitation, finally making his way to Japan by traveling with a Japanese emissary ship returning from its diplomatic mission. Despite the buffeting of heavy gales, the ship arrived safely in Japan in December 753. Ganjin would reach the capital a month later, where he was welcomed by the now-retired Emperor Shōmu and installed at Tōdai-ji. By April 754, the first *kaidan* (戒壇, ordination platform) in Japan was constructed under Ganjin's direction. There, he presided over the ordination of both Empress Kōken and her father, the retired Emperor Shōmu. Later that year, the kaidan was relocated to a permanent ordination hall constructed exclusively for its use west of Tōdai-ji's Daibutsu-den. Here Ganjin conferred the precepts upon some four hundred monks and nuns.

But Ganjin did much more for Japanese culture than just formalize the Buddhist faith among the nobility. He also served as a key source of essential knowledge of Chinese culture, his insights having a significant impact upon the Japanese art of incense.

First, Ganjin is recognized for establishing the formalized importation of Chinese medicines that were also used as raw incense materials; while common in China, they were little known in Japan at the time. As Tōdai-ji served as the chief temple in the kokubun-ji system, it assumed the role of primary consumer of incense materials imported from China. Temples throughout the kokubun-ji system served as key conduits for traders importing aloeswood and aromatic incense materials and as the chief consumers of those raw materials, offering secure trading spaces where taxes could often be avoided and the supply chain streamlined.

Secondly, Ganjin brought with him knowledge of the Chinese method of creating kneaded incense known as *nerikō* (練香). A type of fermented, blended incense, nerikō took fragrant woods and aromatic materials used in Chinese medicine, crushed them into powder, and blended them together to create unique new fragrances. Honey, sugar, or the flesh of Japanese plum was then used as a binder to make a sticky paste, and the resulting compound could be rolled into small pill-sized balls—the Chinese medicine xiāng wán. These incense balls could be stored and aged for months or even years. Unlike granulated incense burned directly upon hot coals in sonaekō, nerikō was heated indirectly on a bed of hot ash, and it emitted a long-lasting fragrance capable of scenting a large space with little smoke.

Japanese aristocrats familiar with the use of incense in Buddhist ceremonies began to appreciate its potential beyond the confines of Buddhist temples. Whereas incense at Buddhist temples was burned sonaekō as an offering for religious purposes, incense began to be burned for pleasure in a practice known as *soradaki* (空薫). Literally translated as "a pleasant smell coming from an unknown location," the "empty burning" of soradaki was divorced from religious meaning. With the new knowledge of nerikō introduced by Ganjin and the range of fragrances possible with ingredients reliably imported from China, the Japanese aristocracy began to experiment with making unique fragrances for their own personal expression. In time, soradaki came to be used as a symbol of status and identity.

Barely four years after the dedication of the Great Buddha at Tōdai-ji, Emperor Shōmu passed away in June 756. Empress Kōmyō, much like her husband, was a devout Buddhist. To honor the late emperor, on the forty-ninth day after his passing, she dedicated many of his worldly belongings to the Great Buddha of Tōdai-ji. Over six hundred items Shōmu treasured during his lifetime were offered to the Great Buddha, including the fine clothing he wore during his reign and the ritual objects and ceremonial robes worn during his ordination. But among the treasures in Kōmyō's offerings was also the emperor's incense, Ōjuku-kō. It is said that originally Ōjuku-kō was to be ceremonially renamed to the more auspicious Tōdai-ji in honor of its owner, the temple's founder. But given the nature of incense for burning, this was deemed inauspicious. Instead, the name was incorporated within the ceremonial name Ranjatai, with the kanji for Tōdai-ji hidden within Ranjatai's name, in a subtle play on words.

蘭奢待 Ranjatai　　東大寺 Tōdai-ji

Originally constructed with a footprint of nearly 49,000 square feet and 156 feet in height, and rebuilt on a smaller scale nine hundred years after its completion, the Daibutsu-den at Tōdai-ji today remains one of the largest wooden buildings in the world. Ranjatai and all the other treasures dedicated by Empress Kōmyō were stored in Tōdai-ji's treasure repository, Shōsō-in, and remain there today, having been carefully preserved for over 1,200 years. In 1998, Tōdai-ji was recognized as a United Nations Educational, Scientific and Cultural Organization (UNESCO) World Heritage site as a part of the cultural property of Ancient Nara.

CHAPTER 2

平安京

HEIAN-KYŌ
Japan's golden age of incense

EMPEROR KAMMU ASCENDED THE CHRYSANTHEMUM THRONE in 781, and his government almost immediately came under pressure from the religious leaders of the established Buddhist sects of the capital city of Heijō-kyō, today known as Nara. Since Buddhism's integration into Japanese spiritual and political life under Prince Shōtoku two hundred years prior, its influence had grown considerably. Fueled by immunity from taxation under the *shōen* system (荘園公領制, private tax-exempt landed estates) and the political aspirations of their leaders, the Buddhist sects of the capital had grown so powerful that they threatened the independence of Kammu's government. A devout Buddhist, Kammu promoted new Buddhist sects, opposing the older, established Buddhist institutions of the capital. To rein in their source of wealth, he issued edicts limiting the construction and expansion of Buddhist temple complexes and restricted the sale and donation of lands to Buddhist institutions, which rendered them exempt from taxation, practices that were starving his government of much-needed revenue.

Despite his efforts, he was unable to dislodge the influence of the entrenched Buddhist sects of Heijō-kyō. In 784, Kammu ordered the abandonment of the capital, relocating the imperial household and nobility twenty miles northwest to Nagaoka-kyō, leaving the troublesome temples of Heijō-kyō behind. After ten years of construction and a series of natural disasters and political assassinations, Kammu suddenly ordered Nagaoka-kyō abandoned in favor of a new capital farther to the north. Situated in a valley near the southern shore of Lake Biwa, Japan's largest freshwater lake, Kammu named his new capital Heian-kyō (Capital of Peace and Tranquility). The move would set the stage for the golden age of the Heian period, which would shape Japanese incense culture for the next millennium.

Freed from the influence of Heijō-kyō's established Buddhist sects, the Heian period saw new sects rise to prominence. Introduced by the Japanese priest Kūkai, the esoteric Buddhism of the Shingon sect was favored by Kammu's successors, due as much to Kūkai's poetic and calligraphic abilities as to the sect's mystic teachings and chanted mantras. An individual's calligraphy was said to be a window into their soul, and Kūkai's talent with the brush surely would have garnered credibility for Shingon's arcane teachings. Artistic abilities were highly valued by the Fujiwara clan, which came to dominate the Imperial Court and aristocratic circles of the new capital. Through arranged marriages of daughters into the lines of emperors, the Fujiwara family amassed governmental power and eventually control over Heian emperors as the children of these marriages ascended to the throne. The Fujiwara held influential roles in all areas of government and eventually controlled matters of state and the imperial treasuries.

Not only did the Fujiwara dominate the political arena of Heian-kyō, but their heightened sensitivity for beauty—expressed through the refinement of art, literature, and poetry—defined the flourishing cultural arts of the Heian period. One of the "Three Brushes," the most revered calligraphers of the ninth century, Kūkai had a profound influence on the development of Japanese calligraphy and is credited with the creation of the Japanese system of writing called *kana* (仮名), which would fuel the blooming of Heian culture.

Although Chinese kanji remained the preferred written form of the court and was viewed as the appropriate method of writing for men of status, fundamental linguistic differences limited the artistry kanji was capable of expressing in Japanese. As the Chinese and Japanese languages use different systems of grammar and as Japanese possesses fewer linguistic sounds, each Japanese word could have multiple readings in kanji. One reading approximated the original Chinese pronunciation in Japanese (the *on'yomi* reading, 音読み), and another reading used the native Japanese pronunciation (the *kun'yomi* reading, 訓読み). Additionally, kanji could be used for their meaning or for their sound, making precise expression in kanji diffi-cult; meaning was often challenging to decipher, and kanji was unable to represent subtle connotations without direct context. Kūkai's development of kana utilized a purely phonetic approach to language by simplifying kanji into unique characters that represented single syl-lables of spoken Japanese. The resulting syllabary offered the ability to fully express subtle thoughts with clear meaning more befitting of the esoteric teachings of Shingon Buddhism. This advancement enabled the development of a uniquely Japanese voice not only for Buddhism but for the expression of emotional beauty as well.

The pathos of the Heian pursuit of beauty is best defined by the term *miyabi* (雅), often understood as "courtly refinement" or "elegance." To the Heian courtier, ideal beauty was displayed through a highly trained awareness that eliminated any element of coarseness or vul-garity and instead conveyed the utmost grace through eloquence of manner, speech, and deep emotional significance in artistic expression. Closely associated with the concept of *mono no aware* (物の哀れ), the bittersweet awareness of the transience of all beauty, miyabi was integrated to such a level of refined awareness that Heian courtiers believed that only their own heightened sense of beauty was capable of appreciating it. The transient nature of the cherry blossoms of spring and the mysterious fragrance of aloeswood, famously enjoyed by imperial courtiers, serve as perfect examples of Heian miyabi.

Referred to as *onnade* (女手, woman's hand), *hiragana* (平仮名) developed as a popular kana syllabary favored by the aristocratic women of the Heian court. Better able to express the subtle feelings and artistic allusion of miyabi than kanji, hiragana was used for correspondence, diaries, and especially poetry, giving women a significant voice in the development of Heian aesthetics. As hiragana increased in popularity, its ability to express artistic vistas and complex emotions saw it become the choice of communication among the aristocratic classes. Although kanji continued to be considered more appropriate for formal use, such as in official documents, hiragana became the chosen script for poetry, and in time was adopted by men as well as women for informal communication and artistic expression.

The ability to compose—in the moment—verse about any subject at hand was highly valued by the Heian aristocracy. An essential skill for courtly life, poetry was considered an appropriate form of interaction, from expressing appreciation of the changing seasons or the beauty of a cherry blossom to deflecting or advancing romance. Poetic expression for Heian nobility was more than a superficial diversion; it reflected the cultural refinement of the writer's social status and demonstrated an individual's talent for expressing profound meaning. The quality of someone's verse could make or break their reputation at court—for example, leading to successful courtships or to being spurned as unworthy of a reply. From this point forward, Japanese poetry was judged by its ability to evoke emotional depth that captured the moment and subject at hand.

Freed from reliance upon Chinese kanji and its pronunciations found in the classical *waka* (和歌, song or verse) poetry of preceding eras, hiragana allowed for the creation of a uniquely Japanese form of waka poetry: *tanka* (短歌). Composed entirely in Japanese, tanka consisted of thirty-one *on* (音, sound units) in one line; it is familiar today in its common form of five lines with a syllable pattern of 5-7-5-7-7. While waka encompasses a variety of forms, the terms waka and tanka eventually came to be nearly synonymous. Hiragana was perfectly suited to such poetic form due to its phonetic nature. Embraced by

Heian court nobles for artistic expression and as a favored style of correspondence, tanka became the standard form of poetic speech in the Heian period, and it has remained virtually unchanged for over a millennium. One of the oldest and most well-known tanka in Japan is "Kimigayo" (君が代), the Japanese national anthem. Written by an unknown author during the Heian period, it is one of the oldest national anthems in the world:

> *May our lord endure*
> *for a thousand, eight thousand*
> *   long generations—*
> *may he live until the pebbles*
> *grow into mossy boulders.*

The *Kokin Wakashū* (古今和歌集, *Collection of Poems Ancient and Modern*) was the first anthology of poetry commissioned by imperial request. A first of its kind, published in 920 CE during the reign of Emperor Daigo, the *Kokinshū* (古今集), as it is commonly abbreviated, was composed almost exclusively of tanka poetry curated by four of the most prominent poets of the time. With over 1,100 poems, the *Kokinshū* was revolutionary in that it included the work of both classical and contemporary authors arranged in twenty thematic sections covering specific topics, such as the seasons, love, and laments. Each thematic section was arranged with poems ordered in such a way that the reader sensed the progression of time. For example, the poems of winter progress from the snows of January to the blooming of the plum blossoms in early spring. Rather than love poems in a random order, the section on love reads as the progression of a courtly affair. Even the Japanese preface, written by noted poet Ki no Tsurayuki, poetically expresses the profound meaning tanka represents to the Japanese: "The seeds of Japanese poetry lie in the human heart and grow into leaves of ten thousand words."

The influence of the *Kokinshū* upon Japanese culture is difficult to overstate. For the next millennium, it would be a part of the standard education for the refined social classes. The organization and imagery used became the model of refined poignance for Japanese poetic expression and would serve as the source for much of the work that followed it. The organization and progression of poems in the *Kokinshū* would go on to influence the linked verse of renga and the reverence for the seasons in modern haiku. Any aristocratic woman who wished to rise to service at court was expected not only to be familiar with the *Kokinshū* but to have memorized all of the poems and be able to reference them at the perfect moment with appropriate context. The poetic reverence for the seasons would influence Japanese art and literature and have a profound effect upon the Japanese incense culture of the time. Tanka of the *Kokinshū* often featured the seasons and a refined sense of miyabi, as well as allusions to fragrance that would find their way into the kneaded incense of the period and the ritual appreciation of incense of Kōdō five hundred years later. For example, through the fragrance of the flowering plum of spring, an anonymous tanka expresses the refinement of Heian sensitivity:

> *I will never plant*
> *a flowering plum near my house:*
> * it is too vexing*
> *to find myself mistaking this*
> *for the scent of one I await.*

Kūkai's kana not only allowed Japanese poetry to flower, but it also led to the proliferation of new forms of Japanese literature. Known as *nikki bungaku* (日記文学, poetic diaries) and *monogatari* (物語, narrative tales), these new forms written in hiragana would go on to create the foundations of classical Japanese literature. Nikki bungaku were personal records and musings on daily life, consisting of poetic interludes intermixed with narrative observations of events experienced from the writer's perspective. One of the most famous poetic diaries is *Makura no Sōshi* (枕草子, *The Pillow Book*), written by Lady Sei Shōnagon. *The Pillow Book* covers Lady Shōnagon's ten years serving Empress Teishi at court, and intersperses poetry, essays, and anecdotes from her experience. Compiled in 1002, *The Pillow Book* would become requisite reading for ladies aspiring to courtly duties and serves as a literary historic record of the period. The most famous and influential of the narrative tales was *Genji Monogatari* (源氏物語, *The Tale of Genji*), written by Lady Murasaki Shikibu, who served as a lady-in-waiting to Fujiwara no Shōshi, the empress consort of Emperor Ichijō. A contemporary of Lady Sei Shōnagon, Lady Murasaki is said to have written *The Tale of Genji* as entertainment for Empress Shōshi, with the work first appearing at the start of the eleventh century.

The Tale of Genji is considered a masterpiece of Japanese literature, credited with influencing a wide range of Japanese cultural arts, and it features prominently in Japan's art of incense. With fifty-four chapters and over one million words, the narrative tale of the fictional "Shining Prince" Genji is often credited as the first novel published. A brilliant example of courtly miyabi, *The Tale of Genji* is revered as a pinnacle achievement of Japanese literature for its lyrical style, expressive writing, and intricate storytelling, and serves as a historical epic that provides exquisite firsthand insight into the daily lives of Heian courtiers. Considered the first psychological novel (in which the thoughts and feelings of the characters are of key importance to the story), Lady Murasaki's epic follows the life of Prince Genji, the son of the emperor's favorite concubine, Kiritsubo. Due to the stress of a series of courtly intrigues fanned by the jealousies of her rival, Lady Kokiden, Kiritsubo becomes ill and dies an untimely death. Without his mother's backing at court, Genji is made a commoner, and Lady Kokiden's eldest son is elevated to the throne. Genji grows to be an uncommonly handsome and gifted young man, admired by all—except Lady Kokiden, who continues to see him as a threat. The story follows Genji's exploits as he matures into adulthood, and is filled with Heian courtships, romantic conquests, rivalries, and the shifting allegiances and political fortunes of the Shining Prince.

As with the *Kokinshū*, the influence of *The Tale of Genji* is difficult to overstate. Weaving the emotions and motivation of the main characters skillfully within the Heian court's worldview and its mix of Chinese and Buddhist thought, Lady Murasaki created the preeminent work of Japanese classical literature, which would serve as the model of courtly behavior for nearly one thousand years. The novel also portrays some of the best-known and most-beloved female characters in all of Japanese literature. Due to the skillful and extensive development of their thoughts, feelings, and motivations, Lady Murasaki's female characters became archetypes for the manner and conduct of refined aristocratic women. *The Tale of Genji* served as an example for nearly all Japanese literary works that followed it and influenced a wide range of cultural arts, having an especially profound influence upon the art of incense.

The Tale of Genji provides a detailed window into the Heian court's use of incense, demonstrating the importance and skill with which courtiers created nerikō. As courtiers increasingly used nerikō specifically as incense rather than as medicine, both the practice and the incense itself became popularly referred to as *takimonō* (薫物). In "Umegae" ("A Branch of Plum"), the thirty-second chapter of *The Tale of Genji*, Lady Murasaki details Lord Genji's preparation of taki-monō for the initiation ceremony of his daughter into courtly life.

Takimonō was made by blending powdered jinkō (aloeswood) with a standardized assortment of aromatic ingredients, including sandalwood, frankincense, benzoin, clove, spikenard, seashell, musk, and others, bound with honey or the flesh of Japanese plum. The resulting sticky dough was then rolled into pill-sized balls and left to ferment for a period of weeks or months prior to use. Often this was done by sealing the takimonō in a container and burying it in the earth, using the moisture of the soil to intensify the fragrance as illustrated in "Umegae":

> Certain courtiers at the palace were in the habit of burying their incense on the bank of the stream running beside the quarters of the Right Guard to allow the damp soil to intensify the aroma. Following that practice, Genji had buried his own incense next to the stream that flowed under the passageway leading off the west side of his residence.[1]

The process of creating takimonō was significant and undertaken in secrecy, as the recipes were often family secrets passed down for

---

[1] All *Genji* quotes come from *The Tale of Genji, Unabridged* by Murasaki Shikibu, translated by Dennis Washburn. W. W. Norton, 2015.

generations and required great skill in preparation. Lady Murasaki illustrates the secrecy with which these legacy recipes were prepared:

> Genji secluded himself in the main hall, where he set about diligently blending two types of incense based on a secret formula handed down from the Jōwa period by Emperor Ninmyō—how he came by the formula is anybody's guess. Murasaki had curtains put up around a space just off the main room of the east hall and withdrew there to work on creating her two incenses, which were based on formulas developed by Prince Motoyasu, a master incense maker who was a son of Emperor Ninmyō and who served as the Hichijō Minister of Ceremonials.

Takimonō began to take on a distinctive Japanese flavor, resulting in incense that expanded upon the natural fragrance palette of Japanese seasonal flowers and fruits rather than that of imported Chinese blends. An accomplished incense blender, Imperial Prince Kaya-shinnō, with the assistance of court noble Fujiwara Fuyutsuki, is credited with formalizing the Mukusa no Takimonō (六種の薫物, Six Kneaded Incenses) during the reign of Emperor Ninmyō (833–850 CE). This system organized takimonō into six seasonal themes:

Baika (梅花, Plum Blossom): The fragrance of plum blossom, representing spring.

Kayō (荷葉, Lotus Blossom): The fragrance of Indian lotus blossom, representing summer.

Rakuyō (荷葉, Fallen Leaves): An allusion to the colors of fall foliage and rustling grasses, representing autumn.

Kikka (菊花, Chrysanthemum): The chrysanthemum's ephemeral color and fragrance, representing late autumn or winter.

Jijū (侍従, Chamberlain): Evoking the bittersweet transience of autumn, representing the season of cooling love.

Kurobō (黒方, Black): Evoking retrospection for auspicious occasions of any season.

Three hundred years later, the noble-turned-traveling-poet and Buddhist priest Jakuren (Fujiwara Sadanaga) is believed to have compiled takimonō recipes of famous incense blenders of Prince Kaya's time into *Kunshū Ruishō* (薫集類抄). Based on earlier compilations no longer in existence, the two-volume *Kunshū Ruishō* served as a roadmap for the preparation of takimonō, with Volume I revealing the secret recipes of emperors and princes of acclaimed talent, and Volume II discussing best practices and blending methods. Recipes of renowned tenth-century incense artists filled its pages, including detailed recipes, such as this one attributed to Prince Kaya himself:

Plum Blossom Recipe of Imperial Prince Kaya-shinnō:

Aloeswood: eight ryō, two bu
Seashell: three ryō, two bu
Spikenard: one bu
Sandalwood: two bu, three shu
Clove: two ryō, two bu
Musk: one bu
Amber: one bu

One *ryō* was equivalent to approximately 1.7 ounces, or 49 grams; 1 *ryō* = 4 *bu* = 24 *shu*

Rather than rote formulas to be copied, the six seasonal themes of the Mukusa no Takimonō represented a metaphorical framework similar to that of the organization of the poems in the *Kokinshū*. As such, each individual was free to create their own unique fragrances inspired by their personal taste and their interpretation of the seasonal theme, much as they would write a waka poem on the subject. The amount of each ingredient used, the order in which the ingredients were blended, and the method in which they were compounded influenced the subtle variation in fragrance from creator to creator. As Lady Murasaki emphasizes in *Genji*:

> One might have assumed that the same techniques and formulas would have been passed down to all the ladies. Instead, each had blended incense according to her individual method and taste, which made for many stimulating moments in judging the depth or subtlety of the various fragrances.

This openness to interpretation allowed the creation of unique fragrances that drove Heian incense culture.

To release its fragrance over a lengthy period of time, takimonō was heated slowly by placing it on a bed of ash covering a hot coal. This was in contrast to the granulated incense of shōkō, which was burned, turning it quickly to smoke. Devoid of smoke's associated undesirable aromas, takimonō allowed for a wide range of applications, such as infusing spaces, clothing, personal items, and even women's hair with a unique fragrance. For Heian courtiers, personal fragrances were considered as important as the quality of the finery they wore, as in proper society courtiers often did not see one another, especially where members of the opposite sex were concerned. At this time, even the Japanese verb *miru* (見る), meaning "to view," possessed subtle connotations that could be interpreted to mean one was having an affair or was even secretly married. Consequently, the personal fragrance wafting from the other side of a screen or infused in a letter of courtship was one of the few windows into an individual's education, refinement, and status. As a result, the blending of takimonō was viewed as a highly valuable and skilled art form, demanding as much training and expertise as any of the other refined courtly arts, such as poetry or calligraphy.

The importance of personal fragrance is repeatedly underscored in Lady Murasaki's epic tale, as Genji's incomparable skill with incense is often noted as announcing his presence before he arrives or after he has gone, even when he wishes to go unnoticed. In "Niou miya" ("The Fragrant Prince"), the forty-second chapter of *The Tale of Genji*, personal fragrance is an important distinction between Genji's son,

Kaoru, and his rival at court, Niou. Even their names foreshadow the importance placed upon fragrance by Heian courtiers, as the words *kaoru* means "fragrance" and *niou* means "to smell," emphasizing Kaoru's association with his father's superior lineage through his unworldly, alluring natural scent:

> Miraculously, wherever he was, whatever he was doing, Kaoru had about him a fragrance unlike any scent of this world, one that wafted all around him on a following breeze, creating the impression of a perfume that truly carried a hundred paces. [...] He rarely if ever scented his robes, but he didn't have to, since the clothes in his chests absorbed his indescribable fragrance.

[...]

> Niou, who was by nature highly competitive, went out of his way to scent his clothes with the finest perfumes. He worked constantly mornings and nights mixing various formulas. [...] Niou exhibited such a passionate fondness for making perfumes that he was considered by some at the court to be rather foppish, self-absorbed and decadent.

As the blending of takimonō developed into a refined art form for the expression of individuality and status, it naturally joined the ranks of the "comparison games" favored by the aristocrats of the Heian court. In the practice known as *mono-awase* (物合せ, the comparison of things), courtiers spent their time in friendly diversion comparing virtually everything associated with courtly life. Poetry contests (*uta-awase*, 歌合わせ), picture games (*e-awase*, 絵合), flower-arranging games (*hana-awase*, 花合せ), fan games (*ogi-awase*, 荻合わせ), and chrysanthemum games (*kiku-awase*, 菊合わせ) were just a few of the popular forms of mono-awase favored by Heian-kyō's elite. Takimonō quickly became part of this tradition, with kneaded incense contests (*takimonō-awase*, 薫物合せ) becoming a favored pastime of courtiers seeking to display their blending talents.

Elevating a pleasurable pastime to something more serious, taki-monō-awase competitions were often the center of extravagant social events where music, food, and drink flowed as freely as the poetry recited under the moonlight. Incense blending was considered a highly prized social skill, and the honor of winning high-profile contests could improve the status of the winner. Teams were often sponsored by nobles, who selected skilled individuals from among their houses and those of their vassals. Even those of low birth had the opportunity to enhance their status should their work be honored at such a competition. After judges and an official recordkeeper were selected and criteria established, several rounds of comparison would take place. Eventually a winner was announced, their name recorded, and a prize sometimes offered.

The earliest recorded takimonō-awase competition was held by Imperial Prince Kaya-shinnō in the early ninth century, with the practice reaching its zenith two centuries later as the golden age of incense reached its maturity in the pantheon of Heian refined arts. The evolution of Japanese poetry and literature of the Heian period would continue to influence Japan's art of incense well beyond its golden period. And Emperor Kammu's capital of peace and tranquility, Heian-kyō, would remain the seat of the Imperial Court and epicenter of Japan's refined arts for nearly one thousand years. In time, the city would be known as Kyoto.

CHAPTER 3

征夷大将軍

SEII TAISHŌGUN
The samurai refine the art of incense

RETOLD FOR MORE THAN A THOUSAND YEARS, THE *HEIKE Monogatari* (平家物語, *The Tale of the Heike*) is an epic saga of political rivalry and bloodshed between two preeminent warrior clans fighting for control of Japan. Chronicling the clash between the Minamoto and the Taira, *The Tale of the Heike* serves as a vivid illustration of the Buddhist themes of impermanence and the inevitable decline of the powerful. Culminating in the decisive Battle of Dan-no-ura, the resounding defeat of the Taira would fundamentally realign Japan's orbit of political power for over seven hundred years. The resulting fall of the powerful would set the stage for the rise of the samurai and have a profound effect upon Japan's art of incense.

As the Heian court began to wane a century prior to the Battle of Dan-no-ura, the power of Japan's emperor had become increasingly diluted. Although still considered the divine ruler, by the late eleventh century, emperors began to abdicate their formal duties and retire from public life to free themselves from the Fujiwara regents who controlled the throne. In the practice known as *insei* (院政, cloistered rule), emperors gave up their public ceremonial duties yet continued to wield their political power under the honorary title of Daijōten-nō (太上天皇, Retired Emperor). As emperors abdicated, they were succeeded by progressively younger emperors, often children, who were easily manipulated by the Fujiwara regents. Under this practice, dual courts competed for control of the government: a court known as In no chō (院庁) formed around the retired emperor and a separate Imperial Court formed around the reigning emperor.

Progressively insulated from the countryside and unable to control the Daijōten-nō, the Fujiwara-dominated Imperial Court increasingly relied on lands in the provinces as sources of revenue and political patronage. The resulting bureaucratic corruption and poor management of the country's agriculture lands led to declining grain production and recurring famine. To protect their provincial estates, powerful land-owning clans hired *bushi* (武士, warriors) to guard their rich fields of rice and grains. Retired emperors employed *hokumen no bushi* (北面の武士), their own private armies of loyal warriors, to guard their substantial country estates as well. Although the Fujiwara looked down upon bushi as rough and unrefined, they found themselves increasingly reliant upon the martial abilities of these warrior clans for settling their disputes. As the power of the Fujiwara-controlled Imperial Court diminished, these powerful military clans became progressively independent of the centralized government and began building increasingly larger armies for the protection of the landed estates they were charged with overseeing. As their military power increased, so too did their political and economic power. The rise of the bushi, who would come to be known as the *samurai* (侍, warrior aristocracy) class, had begun.

The seeds of the bushi had been laid two centuries earlier, when the cost of providing palatial lifestyles for the offspring of emperors with dozens of children became too much for cash-strapped imperial treasuries to bear. In a process referred to as "dynastic shedding," to reduce the size of the royal family, descendants of emperors were demoted from the line of succession, given one of two surnames, and sent to oversee rich provincial countryside estates. The Minamoto (源) surname was first given to descendants of Emperor Saga, who produced forty-nine children during the opening decades of the ninth century. The Taira (平) surname was first given to the grandson of Emperor Kammu in 825. Each clan was also known by their collective name, the Genji (源氏, Minamoto Clan) or the Heike (平家, House of Taira).

Conflict over the line of succession, dual imperial courts, and the increasing power of militarized clans would light the fuse for an explosion of armed conflict in the closing decades of the twelfth century.

Hostilities first erupted when Emperor Go-Shirakawa and Retired Emperor Sutoku opposed one another's chosen successor to the throne. Known as the Hōgen Disturbance, in 1156, the Fujiwara court of the emperor and the In no chō of the retired emperor enlisted military aid from factions of both the Minamoto and the Taira to impose their respective chosen heirs by force of arms. After a week of skirmishes, the palace headquarters of Retired Emperor Sutoku were set ablaze and his forces routed by an army led by Taira Kiyomori, who supported reigning Emperor Go-Shirakawa. Retribution was swift, and little more than two weeks later, Taira and Minamoto leaders of the retired emperor's army were beheaded, in some cases by their own sons, and Retired Emperor Sutoku was banished, destined to die having never returned to the capital. Even though the Fujiwara were on the side of the victor, the use of samurai forces to resolve an internal conflict of imperial succession would fatally undermine their clan's grip on the reins of power. The warrior's world into which the Fujiwara had stepped left no doubt that the samurai were now the power to be reckoned with.

Three years later, the remaining rivalry between the Taira and the Mimamoto over the spoils of the Hōgen Disturbance would spark into flame. In what would be known as the Heiji Disturbance, Minamoto Yoshitomo attempted a coup d'état, which Taira Kiyomori quickly and brutally put down. Gaining the favor of now–Retired Emperor Go-Shirakawa for his swift actions, Kiyomori was given the title of

35

Dajō-daijin (太政大臣, Grand Minister of State). This action essentially ceded control of the government to the samurai for the first time. As the ensuing twenty-year period of Taira dominance began, Kiyomori cleaned house of Minamoto rivals, executing the traitor Yoshitomo and seizing his wealth and land holdings. However, Yoshitomo's thirteen-year-old son, Minamoto Yoritomo, was seen as nothing but a boy, so he was spared and exiled to Izu Province, southwest of modern-day Tokyo.

The act of sparing Yoritomo would come back to haunt the Taira. Seduced by the decadence of the Imperial Court, the Taira quickly fell prey to the rich trappings of the Fujiwara's approach to governing, adopting their courtly self-indulgence and ambivalence to the plight of the provinces and the warrior clans who made their bases there. Twenty years into his rule, as Kiyomori lay dying from a fever that could not be quenched, two-year-old Emperor Antoku ascended to the Chrysanthemum Throne under the control of Taira regents. Yoritomo, no longer a boy, would join the Minamoto call to arms against the Taira. Known as the Genpei War (or Genji/Taira War), the Minamoto rebellion ushered in five years of conflict between the houses of Minamoto and Taira, from 1180 until 1185.

The *Heike Monogatari* is an epic saga of the Battle of Dan-no-ura, which sealed the fate of the Taira. In the Straits of Shimonoseki off the western tip of Japan's main island of Honshu, three thousand Minamoto ships descended upon the fleeing Taira's one thousand. With the ships used more as ocean-going platforms than naval vessels, fighting at sea consisted of long-range volleys of arrows followed by the boarding of ships and fierce hand-to-hand combat between samurai. The fighting was up close and vicious.

At first, it looked like the familiarity with the straits, favorable tides, and heavenly omens foretold Taira victory. But as the arrows subsided and the bloody business of hand-to-hand combat ensued, the tide of battle shifted, and Taira general Taguchi Shigeyoshi defected to the Minamoto. In a monumental act of betrayal, Shigeyoshi identified for Minamoto commanders the disguised flagship that held Taira leaders and six-year-old Emperor Antoku. Concentrating their forces on this ship, the Minamoto soon boarded. As the Minamoto samurai were about to claim their prize, Antoku's grandmother took the child emperor in her arms and jumped into the sea, choosing to drown them both rather than be captured. Seeing the battle lost, many Taira warriors followed the child emperor's example, throwing themselves into the sea or committing suicide. The fall of the House of Taira at the hands of the Minamoto was devastatingly complete.

Dan-no-ura was not the end just for the Taira. It also marked the end of the Heian court and the dominance of the emperor over Japanese governance. In 1192, Minamoto Yoritomo became Japan's first supreme military leader with the title Seii Taishōgun (征夷大将 軍), bestowed in exchange for military protection of eleven-year-old Emperor Go-Toba. Prior to Yoritomo, the title Seii Taishōgun (more commonly known as Shōgun) had been of a temporary nature for commanders of expeditionary forces sent to subjugate the "northern barbarians," the Ainu of Hokkaido and northern Honshu. Even though shōguns were formally appointed by the emperor, Yoritomo took control of the title, making it hereditary and himself Japan's first military dictator. To outward appearances, the emperor was superior to the shōgun. But in reality, due to his control of the military, the shōgun was the de facto ruler of the economic and political leadership of Japan, with the emperor largely consigned to ceremonial function.

Learning from the Taira's fall to the seduction and decadence of the Imperial Court, and to lessen the influence of Buddhist sects of the capital, Yoritomo established his *bakufu* (幕府, tent government)—stylized after the command centers held in tents in the field of battle—in the Minamoto territory of Kamakura near the Izu Province of his banishment. Yoritomo's move of the center of government diminished the influence of courtiers, civil servants, and priests of questionable loyalty, while symbolically demonstrating that the country was now under the military control of the Kamakura shōgunate. Kamakura would now serve as the center of Japan's government with Kyoto relegated to the role of national ceremony and ritual.

The relocation of the bakufu hundreds of miles from Kyoto not only created a seismic shift in political power, but it also had a monumental effect on Japan's art of incense. The decadent practices of the Heian court, now deprived of direct influence, failed to penetrate the Kamakura shōgunate as they had the Taira. The blending of incense and the associated incense games, which were so important as the personal expression of refinement and status of Kyoto nobles, were seen as reminders of the trappings of an Imperial Court out of touch with the provinces and lacking the purity demanded of nobility.

Instead, the ruling samurai focused incense upon pure *kōboku* (香木, fragrant wood) in a practice known as *ichibokudaki* (一木薫, one-wood burning). Supreme among fragrant woods was *jinsuikōboku* (沈水香木), meaning "sinking incense wood," called such due to the density of fragrant resin that often caused it to sink rather than float in water. More commonly referred to by its shortened name, *jinkō* (沈香, aloeswood), it became the center of the samurai incense universe, around which Japan's art of incense would develop. Upon their return to the countryside, Yoritomo's loyal retainers spread the influence of the bakufu government to their home provinces, taking with them the practice of experiencing the purity of jinkō through the simplicity of ichibokudaki. Where once incense had been synonymous with the blended incense of takimonō practiced by the Imperial Court, it would now represent the purity of jinkō of the samurai bakufu. Like political power, Japan's art of incense was now firmly in the grasp of the samurai.

The samurai practice of ichibokudaki mirrored the increased importance placed upon aloeswood in the incense trade on the continent. As Yoritomo's Kamakura shōgunate matured, Tang dynasty China's aloeswood trade prospered, driven by an increasingly well-developed trade network throughout Southeast Asia and the extensive development of inland sources of domestic aloeswood. This trade network fostered the Chinese's intimate working knowledge of the fragrant wood. Through direct experience with aloeswood traders at the source of production, Chinese traders were able to classify aloeswood into five major categories, and they published trade manuals documenting the characteristics and properties of aloeswood from various points of origin, establishing consistent standards and grading. Valued on par with China's chosen currency, silver, aloeswood was a major trade and tributary item for Tang China and, at its peak, made up more than a third of China's spice trade. Trade between Tang China and the Japanese naturally brought with it increased availability of aloeswood from throughout Southeast Asia, as well as the imparting of knowledge and practices from the continent that would enrich the samurai's use of pure aloeswood.

With the increased availability of aloeswood, the samurai had a range of high-quality fragrant woods at their disposal. While the aristocrats of the Imperial Court in Kyoto continued the use of blended incense, enjoying its comparison through takimonō-awase, the Kamakura samurai adapted the practice to ichibokudaki through kō-awase (香合せ), the comparison of aloeswood. Whereas Heian courtiers compared incense to determine whose creation offered the better fragrant poetic interpretation, the samurai compared several pieces of jinkō to determine which possessed the superior fragrance.

Through this comparison of various aloeswoods, certain woods began to stand out as superior to all others. Woods that were more complex and fragrant and possessed a greater quantity of softer resins were judged to be superior; they began to be referred to as kyara (伽羅). Possibly derived from the Sanskrit word meaning "black" translated through Middle Chinese, kyara represented the highest grade of aloeswood. Just as Kurobō (黒方, Black) sat atop the takimonō of the Heian courtiers due to its high quality considered appropriate for auspicious occasions of any season, kyara was supreme among aloeswood, and prized by the samurai for its deep, rich, and complex fragrance. In the accumulation of aloeswood, kyara was the highly sought-after gem of any samurai's collection.

But just because the Kamakura samurai focused their attention on one wood at a time through ichibokudaki, this didn't limit the creativity of the kumikō (組香, incense games) enjoyed by the nobility. One of the earliest recorded kumikō was known as Jūshūkō (十種香), literally "ten types of incense." Building upon the practice of nobles being recognized by their fragrance, Jūshūkō saw participants attempt to identify randomly ordered woods by their fragrance. Games like Jūshūkō increasingly took on a social character, with gatherings featuring incense games, food, and drink. However, they often lacked the sense of miyabi and the decorum of the Heian courtiers. In true warrior fashion, the samurai were prone to turning such games into high-stakes competitions in the form of tōkō (闘香), "incense battles," where guessing the various fragrances of jinkō was undertaken for prizes. Feudal lords bet on the outcome of each tōkō and offered prizes of armor, gold, and silks for the winners. Such gatherings gained a reputation for disreputable behavior due to their often drunken, rowdy, and gambling-centered nature that highlighted competition more than the appreciation of the fragrance of aloeswood. But for the samurai, these incense games provided an outlet for relaxation through the appreciation of aloeswood, even if there happened to be a wager on the outcome.

The relocation of the center of Japanese political power to Kamakura under the control of the samurai was a sea change for the trajectory of Japan, including fundamentally altering the Japanese art of incense in ways that remain evident to this day. The focus of ichibokudaki on aloeswood imported from throughout Southeast Asia established the foundation for the art of incense that would develop over the next five hundred years.

More than eight hundred years later, the epic tale of the Battle of Dan-no-ura that launched the samurai's domination of Japan continues to hold a place in the cultural awareness of the Japanese. The Taira were so utterly decimated in the Straits of Shimonoseki that to this day Heike crabs caught in the area, named because their backs look like scowling samurai warriors, are thrown back into the sea. Crab fishermen believe them to be reincarnated spirits of dead Taira warriors who drowned themselves rather than suffer the humiliation of defeat at the hands of the Minamoto.

CHAPTER 4

ZEN
Incense transcends fragrance

A SWARM THAT BLOTTED OUT THE HORIZON, NINE HUNDRED ships carrying Kublai Khan's massive Yuan invasion force dropped anchor off Komoda Beach on the Japanese isle of Tsushima. Located in the Korea Strait midway between Japan and Korea, Tsushima had been protected by the Sō clan for generations. Said to be descended from Emperor Antoku, Sō Sukekuni, Tsushima's governor, prepared for the Mongol invasion with trepidation. With only eighty samurai and few troops, Sukekuni's forces were outnumbered at least one hundred to one. With no chance of survival, their heroic end at the Battle of Tsushima Island would become legend.

The Mongol onslaught would shake the samurai of the Kamakura bakufu, setting the stage for a new form of Buddhism to rise—one that would awaken the spirit of the warrior and infuse Japan's art of incense with a spirituality that would transcend fragrance.

As the Kamakura period neared the end of its first century, Shōgun Minamoto Yoritomo's time had long since ended, seventy-five years having passed by the time of the Mongol invasion at Tsushima. Although the shōgunate remained in Kamakura after Yoritomo's sudden death in 1199, his heir would be marginalized by his mother and grandfather, both of the Hōjō clan, who decided to usurp the power of the shōgun for themselves. Just as the Fujiwara had controlled Heian emperors through powerful regents behind the throne, the Hōjō installed shōgunal regents known as *shikken* (執権), reducing the shōgun to a figurehead. Japan's real political power rested in the hands of Hōjō regents, and by the time of the first Mongol invasion in 1274, Hōjō Tokimune had become the eighth shikken of the Kamakura shōgunate to lead Japan. Groomed from birth to assume power, upon his ascension, Tokimune was immediately confronted by Kublai Khan's not-so-thinly veiled threat that Japan must become a Chinese vassal state and pay tribute to the Great Khan, or else face invasion. Having ignored and defied these threats, Tokimune now heard the first reports of the troops bearing down on the Japanese mainland and was filled with dread.

The Yuan's enormous invasion force overwhelmed and slaughtered Sukekuni's heroic samurai at Tsushima. As the Mongols continued their crossing of the Korean Strait, the inhabitants of Iki Island met the same fate. Striking terror into the local villagers, Kublai Khan's warriors lashed the naked, bloody bodies of slaughtered Iki to the prows of their ships as a warning to all who would oppose them. They made landing at Hakata Bay on the Japanese mainland six days later. After several days of fierce fighting, the Japanese defenders were pursued inland to Mizuki Castle (水城), an ancient, rarely used earthen fortress built by Emperor Tenchi over six hundred years earlier. But during the samurai's retreat, an arrow launched in desperation at the Yuan pursuers found its mark, striking one of the three commanding Yuan generals, mortally wounding him and halting the Mongol pursuit. As night fell, the invaders returned to the safety of their ships while the Japanese defenders at Mizuki prepared for an attack that would never come.

During the night, a great storm arose, and the hastily constructed ships of the Mongol invaders, which had been lashed together for battle at sea, were consumed by the waves, taking nearly half of the invasion force to their deaths. The fabled *kamikaze* (神風, divine wind) had saved Japan.

But the great Kublai Khan would not be deterred, and in 1281, he launched an even larger invasion of Japan. Despite Japan's many preparations for such an attack, Tokimune was overwhelmed with fear. In the face of the second Mongol invasion, he turned to his advisor Mugaku Sogen for guidance on how to alleviate his own cowardliness and that of his men. Sogen recommended Tokimune sit in meditation and look within for the source of his cowardice.

Tokimune had invited Sogen to Japan in 1279 after hearing the legendary story of Sogen overcoming a Yuan warrior, sword in hand ready to kill him, with nothing but a poem. Sogen was said to have composed the following four-line poem in the moment, which so awed the warrior that he praised Sogen and walked away, leaving him unharmed:

> *Throughout heaven and earth there is not a piece of ground*
> *   where a single stick could be inserted;*
> *I am glad that all things are void, myself and the world:*
> *Honored be the sword, three feet long, wielded by the great*
> *   Yüan swordsmen;*
> *For it is like cutting a spring breeze in a flash of lightning.*

An accomplished painter, poet, calligrapher, and Zen master, Sogen had a reputation for self-discipline and courage that meshed well with the samurai spirit. However, by Sogen's time, Zen was not new to the samurai. Myōan Eisai, a Japanese monk who studied in China, had originally introduced Chinese Ch'an (Zen) Buddhism to Japan in 1191. Without the influence of Kyoto's Imperial Court or its Buddhist sect politics, Kamakura Shin Bukkyō (鎌倉新仏教, Kamakura New Buddhism) flourished in the bakufu's capital. Among these new forms of Buddhism, key for the samurai was the Rinzai Zen school founded by Eisai. A second school, the Sōtō Zen school, introduced by Eihei Dōgen in 1227, flourished as well.

Unlike the aristocratic Buddhism of Kyoto, which focused esoterically on escaping the cycle of death and rebirth in this world through study or ritual recitation of Buddhist scripture in preparation for the next, Zen focused on *satori* (悟り), an awakened state of enlightenment and intuitive understanding achieved through self-discipline and meditation in the everyday world. The importance Zen placed on the intuitive transmission of enlightenment has its roots in the Flower Sermon of the Buddha, the earliest written record of which, by Chinese Ch'an monks, dates to 1036 CE. Unlike many other sermons in which the Buddha taught with words, during the Flower Sermon, the Buddha remained silent and only held up a lotus flower. None present understood this teaching except one disciple who smiled in response, intuitively understanding the Buddha's appreciation for the fleeting nature of all things. Seeing his smile, the Buddha taught that enlightenment did not reside in words or letters, but instead involved a special transmission outside the scriptures.

To Zen masters like Eisai, satori was not something expressed in words or found in the study of scripture but directly encountered through intuitive experiences known as *kenshō* (見性), glimpses of the true nature of reality often referred to as "Buddha nature." Kenshō could occur during both profound and mundane experiences—during meditation, through admiration of a cherry blossom, or while sweeping the floor. Temporary, fleeting, and powerful, like a flash of lightning, kenshō provided a glimpse of the very essence of everything and hinted at the total enlightenment of satori. Zen prioritized the sacredness in all experiences to the point where there was no separation between being and doing. The two became one as a natural expression of Buddha nature, where there is no duality, only the moment. The calligrapher becomes the brush, the warrior becomes his sword. Dōgen instructed simply: Practice Zen in daily life; be fully aware of every moment and every action.

To increase awareness and aid in meditation, Eisai brought with him tea seeds from China. Having learned how to propagate tea plants during his journey to the continent, Eisai is said to have sowed the first tea seeds in Japan in the gardens of Ishigamibō on Mount Sefuri located in northern Kyūshū. Tea was viewed as a medicinal plant, and Eisai promoted the Chinese cultural practice of drinking tea for good health in his influential book, *Kissa Yōjō-ki* (喫茶養生記, *Record of Drinking Tea for Health*), written in 1214. In it, Eisai alluded to the spiritual nature of tea, noting, "The gods have a taste for tea, so when making an offering to them, one should present it; if one does not present tea, the offering will be wanting." In time, prior to meditation, Zen monks participated in a simple ritual tea service that used prescribed utensils and maintained austere decorum. Tea was also cultivated for its qualities as an alertness aide for meditation and monastic study, and its benefits can be found in copies of medieval sutras in postscripts such as this: "After seven cups of tea I have conquered the devil of sleep and burned nine wicks in my lamp to accomplish the copying [of this sutra]."

Even though Zen viewed the study of sutras and especially the description of its precepts in writing as equivalent to grasping at smoke, waka (Japanese song) was able to create subtle and intuitive understandings in ways that mirrored the flashes of insight of kenshō, making it an appealing form of expression for Zen priests like Sogen. The use of waka to express Buddhist ideals was already well established by the time Eisai returned from China with Zen, occupying its own genre of waka called *shakkyōka* (釈教歌, Buddhist poetry). Derived from Sakyamuni, the Chinese name for the Buddha, shakkyōka expressed the spiritual teachings of the Buddha through waka's everyday themes of the four seasons, love, and lament.

Shakkyōka was known to the samurai and their Zen advisors, with examples included in some of the most famous waka anthologies of the period, such as the *Shin Kokin Wakashū* (新古今和歌集, *New Collection of Poems Ancient and Modern*), which was commissioned in 1201 by Emperor Go-Toba and contained a sixty-poem section dedicated to shakkyōka. Written by the Tendai priest Jakuzen in the twelfth century, the *Hōmon hyakushū* (法門百首, *One Hundred Poems of the Dharma Gate*) is a collection of waka inspired by Buddhist scripture and written within traditional waka poetic themes. Dozens of Jakuzen's poems would be selected for publication in imperial anthologies, adding to the value placed upon his work. Jakuzen's "Thoughts of Enlightenment Alone, No Other Thoughts" beautifully demonstrates how shakkyōka blended the common waka theme of love with the Buddhist practice of meditation on the natural world:

where shall I rest my heart?
adrift on waves of thoughts (in, out)

then sunk, wondering—

is there something?
is there nothing?[2]

Compiled in the thirteenth century, the *Hyakunin Isshu* (百人一首, *One Hundred Poets, One Poem*) is one of the best-known and most-admired waka anthologies by famous poets, and spans the Nara (710–794) and Heian (794–1185) periods. Even today, Japanese children study the *Hyakunin Isshu* using a type of playing-card matching game that is centuries old. The book includes shakkyōka by many leading Buddhist priests, including Sōtō Zen founder, Eihei Dōgen. Well known for the prolific use of poetry in his teachings, Dōgen animated the core precepts of Zen with sweeping poetic language that breathed life into Zen's spiritual teachings. For example, in his poem "Furyu monji wo yomu" (詠不立文字, "Not Depending on Words and Letters"), Dōgen vividly illustrates the mind-to-mind understanding of the famous Zen axiom after which the poem is named, elegantly contrasting the limitations of the written word with the infinite nature of universal truth:

Because [the Dharma] is
outside the words
I spoke,
it does not leave any traces
in [my words written using] a brush.[3]

---

[2] Poems from Jakuzen, translated from Japanese by Patrick Donnelly and Stephen D. Miller, Four Way Books. Accessed June 28, 2024. https://fourwaybooks.com/site/poems-by-jakuzen-translated-by-patrick-donnelly-and-stephen-d-miller/.

[3] Translation by the Sanshin Zen Community. "Not depending" page on the Dōgen Institute website, accessed June 28, 2024. https://dogeninstitute.wordpress.com/2015/02/05/not-depending/.

Poetry expressed the poignant, transient nature of the moment, illustrating the Buddha's teachings as found in the natural world. Zen monks composed poems in the moment, much as Sogen had done with a Yuan sword above his head. Through allusions to complex concepts, shakkyōka evoked intuitive understanding of the Zen spirit in ways traditional discourse could not. Although waka poetry originated in the rarefied environs of the imperial nobility, it was the samurai and Zen masters who cultivated it throughout the provinces, sharing the spirit of Zen with commoners and nobles alike.

Eisai promoted Zen through a national defense appeal, present-ing the Kamakura nobility with *Kōzen gokokuron* (興禅護国論, *The Promotion of Zen for the Protection of the Country*) in 1198. Arguing through extensive use of the Prajnaparamita Scripture for Humane Kings Who Wish to Protect Their States, Eisai sought to not only justify his status as a Buddhist master but also to demonstrate con-clusively that Zen was superior to all other forms of Buddhism for protecting Japan. According to Eisai, it was Zen's monastic and ethical discipline, combined with its simplicity and purity, that made it the most potent form of Buddhism and the one from which prayers and offerings for the protection and prosperity of Japan were best made.

Eisai's appeals to the samurai's military instincts were well received. Zen's highlighting of monastic discipline resonated with the samurai, for whom military discipline was an intimate companion. Zen's lack of moral abstraction appealed to the samurai's sense of duty, honor, and loyalty. Zen's simplicity and mindfulness during daily activity resonated with a warrior's practicality. The ability to achieve satori through meditation and self-discipline mirrored their martial training. The inexplicable nature of kenshō meshed well with the life of a samurai, in which any battle could be their last and an intuitive reaction could turn a battle in their favor. As Zen assumed a new importance in samurai spirituality, the warrior elite of the Kamakura bakufu began to practice meditation under the guidance of Zen masters like Sogen. Zen medi-tation brought to the samurai a way to still the mind, increase focus, and overcome the fear of death—all powerful attributes that would enhance a warrior's martial abilities and provide an advantage in battle.

Zen also promoted the use of incense as a direct companion of spiritual practice. The difficulty of putting into words Zen's intuitive teachings was similar to the mysterious way fragrance was perceived, creating a closely interwoven relationship between Zen and incense. Just as fragrance often eluded description in words, so too did kenshō often defy description. Just as no two people experienced fragrance the same way, Zen's teachings were also understood in unique and personal ways. And just as fragrance rose and fell in awareness, a gradual and evolving process of understanding occurred through Zen practice.

This connection between fragrance and Zen's intuitive understanding is illustrated in the story of a young devotee who went to a temple asking for an understanding of Zen. He had been taught the scriptures but did not understand their teachings and was discouraged. That day, plum trees were in bloom in the temple courtyard, and the fragrance of their fruit hung in the air throughout the temple. Seeing the young monk's discouragement, the master asked if he had perceived the sweet fragrance of the unseen blooming trees. The young monk nodded and at that moment experienced kenshō, realizing that there was no fast way to learn Zen: understanding would come through small intuitive insights that led to deeper wisdom. Much as the fragrance of plum blossoms had led to a spontaneous understanding of Zen awareness, the fragrance of incense was believed to stimulate the flow of energy and enhance the meditative experience, strengthening one's intuitive perception, priming the consciousness for deeper insight.

Due to the connection between Zen and incense, jinkō assumed a significant place in the spiritual life of the samurai. Used for its calming and purifying effect, aloeswood was employed as an aid in meditation and served to sharpen awareness, refine the personality, and purify both mind and body for battle. Armor scented with aloeswood was believed to be spiritually pure as well as impenetrable. Given Zen's focus on *kanso* (簡素, simplicity and purity), the one-wood burning of ichibokudaki solidified its position of importance in the samurai's spiritual training. Unveiling an even deeper purity of fragrance was a technique imported from Song China that used small silver-leaf plates known as *gin'yō* (銀葉, silver leaves) to protect jinkō from burning yet still release its fragrance. Small pieces of aloeswood were placed on the squares of thin silver, and then positioned over hot ash or coals. In time, silver was replaced with mica, a silicate mineral whose crystalline structure allowed easy splitting into exceptionally thin sheets that possessed thermal properties superior to raw silver. The use of gin'yō allowed for better control of the heat applied to fragrant wood, freeing the aromatic molecules of jinkō's fragrant resins to evaporate without creating smoke or burning the wood fibers. This technique enabled the appreciation of the intricate, sublime, and pure fragrance of jinkō that was not possible when it was burned directly, and opened a new depth to the multitude of fragrances jinkō offered.

With Zen's emphasis on kenshō and the purity of fragrance available using gin'yō, the meditative use of incense expanded beyond smell to include all the senses, opening the samurai to even more profound insights through aloeswood's mysterious spiritual nature. Harkening back to the teaching that the words of the Buddha were like incense and therefore incense was "listened" to, the Chinese term *wénxiāng* (聞香) was translated into Japanese as *kō-o-kiku* (香お聞, hearing incense), and eventually as *monkō* (聞香, listening to incense). The meaning of the Chinese character *wén* (聞), which translates as "to smell," was expanded in Japanese to mean "to pay attention to with one's whole being." The practice of monkō was quickly adopted by the samurai, and through the subtle and enigmatic fragrance of aloeswood, the highest form of natural beauty opened them to the insights that only Buddha nature could provide. As Dōgen taught, "The whole moon and the entire sky are reflected in one dewdrop on the grass." By opening their whole being to jinkō's Buddha nature, the samurai could know themselves as well, stilling their minds in the face of an uncertain future steeped in war and death.

Prior to Kublai Khan's assault, Tokimune followed the discipline of Ritsu Buddhism, but under Sogen's guidance he had converted to Rinzai Zen Buddhism. Sitting in meditation as Sogen suggested, Tokimune would have employed the use of jinkō for its fragrance and as a spiritual aid to discover his Buddha nature and the origin of his fear. Through meditation, Tokimune famously achieved kenshō regarding the Mongol invasion: "Finally there is a great happening in my life!" When asked by Sogen how he would face this great happening,

Tokimune shouted *"Katsu!"* ("Victory!"). Sensing Tokimune's enlightenment, Sogen replied with satisfaction, "It is true the son of a lion roars as a lion!" With this encouragement, Tokimune would face the Mongol invaders with newfound confidence and clarity.

The second Mongol invasion of 1281 met stiff resistance thanks to Tokimune's preparations for its arrival. Yet after several weeks of intense fighting, the second Yuan invasion would end as miraculously as the first. As the battle raged, a fierce storm roiled the Sea of Japan into a tempest that pummeled the Mongol ships. Legend has it that the storm drowned one hundred thousand of Kublai Khan's men, ending the second invasion and souring the Great Khan's taste for subjugating Japan. The divine wind of the kamikaze had once again come to Japan's defense. Having displayed its divine backing in protecting the nation, Zen's popularity increased significantly among the Kamakura samurai. Tokimune increasingly linked Zen teachings directly with elements of Shintō and Confucianism to form an unwritten moral code for the samurai—one that stressed simplicity, loyalty, and honor, and that in time would be referred to as Bushidō (武士道, the Way of the Warrior). With official state backing, Zen flourished and enjoyed a wave of popularity that exposed new followers to its teachings and its use of incense.

To serve as a memorial and provide eternal rest to the Japanese and Yuan warriors who perished during the invasion, in 1282, Tokimune commissioned the building of a great Zen temple. He reportedly named it Engaku-ji (円覚寺), in honor of Engaku-kyo (円覚経), the Sutra of Perfect Enlightenment, after a stone chest containing a copy of the sutra was unearthed during construction. Intending the temple to serve as a center from which Zen teachings could be spread throughout Japan, Tokimune installed Sogen as the founding priest. It is said that during the opening ceremony, a white deer entered the temple grounds and listened to Sogen as he spoke. Considered an auspicious omen, Engaku-ji was also given the name Zuiroku-san (瑞鹿山, Auspicious Deer Mountain) and was considered one of the Five Great Mountains in the Kamakura Zen temple system. Tokimune would not live to see Engaku-ji spread Zen throughout Japan, as he would succumb to tuberculosis shortly after its completion in 1284.

However, he was so dedicated to Rinzai Zen that he took his vows and became a Buddhist monk on the day he died. After his death, many of his loyal samurai vassals honored him by adopting Zen, spreading its teachings and emphasizing jinkō's preeminent role in the spiritual life of the samurai.

The seemingly divine intervention of the kamikaze during the Yuan invasions led to a belief in the invincibility of Japan that would endure until the Second World War. Kamakura New Buddhism would go on to form the basis of Japanese Buddhism, with most modern-day Japanese affiliated with forms of Buddhism that originated in Kamakura. Engaku-ji became one of the most influential and important Rinzai Zen Buddhist temples in Japan. Zen's adoption as the state religion by the Kamakura bakufu had a profound influence on nearly all aspects of Japanese culture and continues to this day to influence the Japanese art of incense.

CHAPTER 5

婆裟羅

BASARA

Incense as an expression of wealth and status

ELD IN OPULENT SETTINGS FIT FOR KINGS, WHERE LUXURIES of all natures were consumed with abandon, all-night gambling sessions filled the social calendars of the samurai elite in the capital of Kyoto. As dueling imperial courts fought over supremacy, an aristocratic warrior class was forged, imposing its unique flavor on the culture of the imperial capital through sheer force of excess. Flush with cash from the spoils of war, the newly enriched samurai derided the culture of the Imperial Court with gleeful disdain—the lower supplanting the higher through ever-more-spectacular events filled with conspicuous consumption and displays of riches. Amid this potent brew of excess, cultural competitions involving warriors would forever intertwine the Japanese art of incense with poetry, tea, and courtly refinement.

By the time twelve-year-old Hōjō Takatoki became the final Hōjō regent of the Kamakura shōgunate in 1316, more than three decades had passed since Hōjō Tokimune had repelled the attempted Yuan invasions of Japan. Despite Japan's victory, the significant cost of war with the Mongol invaders had severely strained the resources of the Kamakura bakufu, and the Hōjō-controlled shōgunate in Kamakura was in steep decline. Control of Japan's political power was increasingly fractured between the weakened samurai government controlled by Hōjō regents and the divided Imperial Court in Kyoto, which was fighting over succession. The shōgunate had muted courtly hostilities for decades by imposing *ryōtō tetsuritsu* (両統迭立), an alternating pattern of succession between senior and junior branches of the imperial family. By eliminating bloodline heredity, the dynastic reign of emperors was eliminated; the bakufu imposed succession, creating an uneasy peace by frustrating both branches of the imperial family equally. As he grew into a leader of dubious intelligence who favored gambling over governing, Hōjō Takatoki delegated important affairs of state to political appointees who owed their positions to favoritism or nepotism rather than to any qualification or skill. Under Takatoki's lackadaisical leadership, the continued feud over succession between rival branches of the imperial family boiled over—with disastrous results for the Kamakura shōgunate.

Two years into Takatoki's regency, Go-Daigo of the junior imperial branch ascended to the Chrysanthemum Throne. With little more than ten years until ryōtō tetsuritsu would force him to abdicate (once a successor from the senior branch came of age), Go-Daigo immediately began fomenting plans to overthrow the Kamakura shōgunate and restore the superiority of the Imperial Court. After years of intrigue, his plot was exposed, and Go-Daigo fled the Imperial Palace in Kyoto to a monastery on Mount Kasagi, taking with him the Three Sacred Treasures of Japan, imperial regalia symbolizing the emperor's ruling authority. After a brief standoff with Kamakura forces, Go-Daigo was arrested by the bakufu and exiled to the Oki Islands in the Sea of Japan.

With Go-Daigo removed and despite his refusal to abdicate, Takatoki appointed Kōgon of the senior imperial line as emperor. In response, Go-Daigo escaped exile and waged brutal civil war upon the Kamakura shōgunate and Emperor Kōgon, whom he branded as an illegitimate usurper. Fighting would culminate two years later in 1333 with two stunning defeats for the Hōjō. Ashikaga Takauji, the general in charge of Kamakura forces sent to secure Kyoto for the bakufu, defected and seized the capital for Go-Daigo. In Kamakura, *daimyō* (大名, feudal lords) sympathetic to Go-Daigo then rose in revolt, sacking Kamakura. The swiftness of these betrayals so surprised Takatoki and his family that they chose ritual suicide rather than being captured. After 150 years of rule, the Kamakura bakufu had come to a swift and bloody end.

Returning triumphantly to Kyoto, Go-Daigo began to restore the ruling practices of imperial supremacy in what would later be known as the Kenmu Restoration. However, the governmental protocols reinstated by Go-Daigo proved more suited to a bygone era and were not well received by the samurai. This dissatisfaction was magnified when Go-Daigo was unable to retain the backing of landowning daimyō, who felt they were not rewarded sufficiently for their support in overthrowing the Kamakura bakufu. Compounding this lack of support, Go-Daigo also quickly alienated General Takauji, who expected to be rewarded by being named shōgun for his great victory in seizing Kyoto. Instead Go-Daigo named his own son as shōgun, insulting Takauji and losing the support of many samurai in the process. With dissatisfaction among the samurai reaching its peak in 1335, Ashikaga Takauji again switched allegiances, proclaimed himself shōgun, and drove Go-Daigo from Kyoto. With Go-Daigo forced from the throne, Imperial Prince Kōmyō of the senior imperial line was elevated as emperor in exchange for his recognition of Takauji's claim as shōgun, and he formed the new Ashikaga-backed Northern Imperial Court. Go-Diago fled Kyoto to the mountains of Yoshino south of Nara, establishing the Southern Imperial Court. The Northern and Southern Courts would fight for supremacy for the next fifty years during what became known as the Nanboku-chō jidai (南北朝時代, Northern and Southern Courts period).

With the Ashikaga shōgunate established, Takauji moved the bakufu from Kamakura to Kyoto, returning to the imperial capital with a renewed affinity for the Imperial Court. Named for the Muromachi street location of the Ashikaga military headquarters, the Hana no Gosho (花の御所, Flower Palace), the Muromachi period saw a gradual refinement of the provincial samurai. Takauji himself was known as a man of cultural refinement, his fondness for composing poetry displayed even in his armor, with its extravagant multi-colored lacing poetically representing a rainbow's fleeting beauty as well as its good fortune. However, as the samurai nobility and their retainers made their way from the provinces to the capital of Kyoto, the clash of cultures was stark. Where the aristocrats of the capital had always looked down upon the provincial samurai as rough and uncultured, the warriors of the Ashikaga bakufu looked upon the aristocratic tastes of the capital as outdated, overly conservative, and conformist. The disdain between the two classes, fueled by the turbulence of dueling imperial courts, sowed the seeds of what would come to be known as *gekokujō* (下克上), "the low overturning the high," which would unsettle Japanese society for the next 250 years.

Flush with cash from the overthrow of the Kamakura bakufu, the Ashikaga samurai set about creating their own standards of culture by highlighting their newfound riches. The term *basara* (婆娑羅) originally denoted a flamboyant and garish style of clothing worn by affluent military men who eschewed traditional fashion, but it became an all-encompassing term for the extravagance of this new class of monied warriors during the turmoil of the Northern and Southern Courts period. Made wealthy from the spoils of war, money lending, and especially gambling, basara lords displayed their virtues through amassing collections of rare and valuable treasures and the nouveau riche practice of ostentatious exhibition.

Examples of basara excess are well documented in Japanese literature, most notably in the *Taiheiki* (太平記, *Chronicles of the Great Peace*). An epic example of *gunki monogatari* (軍記物語, war tales) with over forty volumes, the *Taiheiki* recounts the political, military, and social events of the Northern and Southern Courts period. The authors were often openly critical of basara activities, detailing the extravagant and unconventional behavior of several specific basara lords. One of the most highlighted exemplars of basara was the magistrate of Sado Province and Buddhist lay priest Sasaki Dōyō. A wealthy and politically influential member of the samurai elite, Dōyō cultivated connections within the Imperial Court and served as a military advisor to the Ashikaga shōgunate. Highly educated and with a well-developed cultural awareness, Dōyō exemplified the evolution of the samurai from military dictators to aristocratic administrators, equally at home in military affairs as with imperial courtiers. A patron of the cultural arts, Dōyō was virtually unrivaled in his display of wealth and opulence, hosting events ranging from marathon poetry sessions to extravagant flower-viewing parties to sumptuous tea gatherings to ostentatious incense displays.

In amassing collections of fine art and rare valuables, basara lords like Dōyō displayed a great affinity for the accumulation of *karamono* (唐物), imported works of rare and elegant Chinese art and culture. Karamono were sought as symbols of wealth and power as much as for their cultural significance. Sophisticated monochrome sumi ink paintings, fine porcelain, elegant calligraphic works, tea and its associated ornate utensils, and imported fragrant woods were highly sought after by basara lords desirous of filling their villas with riches. Exotic, rare items like tiger and leopard skins from China's extensive trading network throughout the Southwest Pacific epitomized the virility and flamboyant tastes of the basara and were displayed prominently during social gatherings.

The accumulation of pieces of jinkō was a popular basara pastime, due to jinkō's collectability as well as its potential for flaunting a lord's wealth, its extraordinary fragrance a commodity to be possessed. Basara lords accumulated significant collections of jinkō like modern connoisseurs collect bottles of fine wine or rare cigars, using them to impress their peers. Dōyō is said to have amassed one of the largest and most impressive collections, with more than 170 pieces of the rarest jinkō in Japan.

Known as *meikō* (名香), exquisite pieces of aloeswood were distinguished from average quality woods by giving them names from poetic and literary classics, especially the *Kokin Wakashū* and *The Tale of Genji*. When their names were not taken directly from classical sources, meikō were named using *gago* (雅語), elegant words grounded in the speech that formed the accepted basis for courtly poetry, typically confined to "polite" topics such as nature, the four seasons, and the weather. Names alluded to the meikō's fragrance, were inspired by their shape, or came from the season represented, and added significantly to the prestige, exclusivity, and value of the piece. Meikō might have been given names like Hanashōbu (Iris), a harbinger of the start of summer as well as a representation of the spirit of the samurai due to its sword-like leaves; Kumorizora (Cloudy Sky), representing the chill of winter and melancholy of mono no aware; Yoshino, the mountain region known for its natural beauty and famous spring cherry blossoms; or Fujitsubo, the empress and secret love obsession of Prince Genji in Lady Kokiden's literary classic. A meikō's pedigree added to its value, especially if it had once been part of a famous collection, as pieces were often passed down through generations or given as political gifts.

Meikō was often used in basara displays of conspicuous consumption to highlight the rare and exclusive nature of its fragrance. An example recounted in the *Taiheiki* describes Dōyō at one event ordering the burning of an entire piece of precious meikō. The extravagant act was said to have produced such a redolence that the guests were left feeling "as if they were in the Buddhist Paradise of Floating Fragrance."

Basara was a social phenomenon, as an effective demonstration of wealth required an audience to be awed by it. As such, basara lords went to great lengths to outdo their peers, hosting larger and more extravagant social events in which they could flaunt their riches and exhibit their collections of karamono. The grander the event, the rarer and more exquisite the karamono, and the more likely the event was to attract powerful and highly influential individuals, increasing the prestige of the host as well as his potential for political influence. Poetry gatherings were common events for such displays, showing off the host's linguistic abilities and quick wit in a setting surrounded by his collection of karamono.

By Dōyō's time, a social form of poetry known as *renga* (連歌) had become popular among basara samurai and imperial courtiers alike. A type of linked verse that was constructed by a group rather than composed by an individual, renga contrasted the courtly sense of miyabi found in waka with a poetic competition that followed rules the samurai were at home with. Like many waka, renga utilized the poetic meter of five lines of 5-7-5-7-7 syllables (more technically, morae, or sound units) as well as the thematic and poetic vocabulary established by the *Kokin Wakashū*. Unlike courtly waka, however, renga divided a poem's composition between two individuals: one taking the first three-line *chōku* (長句, long verse) and the other taking the following two-line *tanku* (短句, short verse). Early forms of renga were a type of competitive dialogue between two poets, demonstrating the linguistic skill and quick wit of each in a lively social setting as a sort of call-and-response performance. As renga's popularity increased, so too did its length and the number of authors, growing from a single linked verse composed by two poets to dozens, hundreds, or even thousands of verses composed by groups of contestants.

Composition was not left entirely to the whims of the individual poets, however, as strict rules for the linking of verses, known as *fushimono* (賦物), were imposed upon the poets. Functioning as a sort of thematic device, fushimono challenged each poet's ability to respond to the *maeku* (前句, preceding verse) with their *tsukeku* (付句, the responding verse) and to do so with wordplay, puns, and literary juxtapositions that met the rules of the renga and also challenged the following poet to respond appropriately. Competing poets could respond to a preceding verse by integrating the theme of the originating poet, or by contrasting it through wordplay or other poetic devices that conformed to the objective rules set forth in the fushimono. Over time, fushimono began to appear in the title of the renga poem, written larger than the verse to emphasize the subtext of the poem's creation, and more holistic rules of composition known as *shikimoku* (式目) were imposed to ensure a cohesive literary structure to the entire work.

While *hyakuin* (百韻, one hundred rhymes) became the eventual standard length, it was not unusual for basara lords to hold competitions where renga sessions would run until dawn and total one thousand verses or more. As a game, renga stood in contrast to the courtly individual expression of waka, with fushimono providing objective standards from which players competed. Gambling on the outcome of renga competitions was common, and basara lords wagered significant sums of money and valuables on their chosen representatives. For over a decade in the mid-1300s, Dōyō held monthly poetry gatherings at his villa, and his much-sought-after social invitations helped develop and maintain his political influence.

As renga grew in popularity, its verses joined the compilations of imperial anthologies. Initially compiled in 1356, the *Tsukubashū* (菟玖波集, *The Tsukuba Anthology*) was the first imperial collection of renga. Containing twenty volumes with over 2,100 poems, renga were grouped into topics such as the four seasons, love, and travel, following the structure of the *Kokin Wakashū*. Most of the poems presented were single pairs of verses (sometimes extracted from a longer linked work) with only the name of the poet of the responding verse recorded, emphasizing the deliberate way in which each poet linked his verse to the preceding one. The *Tsukubashū* was also notable for its inclusion of *haikai no renga* (俳諧の連歌, comic linked verse), a shortened form of linked verse featuring the vulgarity and risqué comedic wit familiar at basara events. The *Tsukubashū* was not originally created as an imperial anthology; Dōyō played an instrumental role in lobbying for its elevation to that status by marshaling his network of political connections with both daimyō and the Imperial Court. Imperial status ensured his own contribution—he was one of the most cited poets with the inclusion of eighty-one poems—and enhanced his reputation. For example, here is renga 562 from the *Tsukubashū*:

> *pheasants in the hunting grounds*
> *each of their calls distinctive*
> *snow-capped mountain beyond the field,*
> *a white falcon*
> *set on my hand—*[4]

In this hunting-themed poem, Dōyō responds to the plurality of pheasants found in the maeku with a single falcon poised for action

---

[4] Selden, Kyoko and Lili Selden. "Renga by Sasaki Dōyō: Selected from the *Tsukubashū* (*Tsukuba Anthology*)." *Asia-Pacific Journal: Japan Focus* 14, issue 14, no. 6 (2016). Accessed July 8, 2024. https://apjjf.org/2016/14/selden-3.

in the tsukeku, and unifies the two parts by comparing the falcon in the latter to the snowy mountain in the former.

Renga sessions of basara lords like Dōyō were often marathon affairs filled with all manner of extravagance, including the finest incense. The combination of renga with incense would lead to another basara pastime: a type of kumikō (incense game) called *takigumikō* (たき組香, linked incense). As basara lords like Dōyō amassed ever-growing collections of exceptional pieces of aloeswood, incense games like takigumikō gave them a method to display these collections in the same way renga allowed them to display their quick wit and cultural knowledge. Participants of takigumikō sessions brought with them prized meikō from their collections for use in the game. Contestants then used the name of each piece to link them together, much like the linking of maeku and tsukeku in renga sessions. The host or honored guest contributed the first meikō to start the takigumikō. The name of the first piece was then used as a type of fragrant preceding verse for the responding piece of jinkō offered by the next participant. For example, a piece of jinkō named Fuji (藤, Wisteria) might be linked with a following piece of jinkō named Asatsuyu (朝露, Morning Dew), highlighting the link between the wisteria and the morning dew of springtime in which it blooms. The next incense linked in the game had to relate in some way with an aspect of morning dew, either through contrast or likeness, such as its cool freshness or fleeting nature. The takigumikō continued in this way, with each subsequent piece of rare incense linked to the preceding piece through a relevant poetic allusion to its name. Often a prize—gold, silk, or a piece of meikō—would be awarded to the team judged to have contributed the superior links of the session. Basara lords often gambled on the outcome, spicing up the game but over-shadowing the fragrances of the rare meikō being linked.

Incense games gave rise to the practice of *tōkō* (闘香), the "incense battle" upon which money and prizes were wagered as teams of warriors symbolically battled one another through their skill with incense. The game Jūshūkō offered a popular format for waging such battles, with ten rounds of incense in which the players sought to discern the "fragrant stranger" among the "known guests" while correctly naming all the fragrances in order. In time, the format of Jūshūkō was applied to tea-tasting competitions, creating "tea battles" known as *tōcha* (闘茶). In Shishu Jippukucha (四種十服茶, Four Kinds of Tea in Ten Cups), over ten rounds of tea, contestants battled to discern the difference between *honcha* (本茶, real or true tea) and *hicha* (非茶, non-tea or lesser tea). The "true tea" of honcha referred to tea from the plantations of Kōzan-ji in Toganoo, said to be grown from original seeds provided by Eisai himself on his return from China. Tea from plantations in Toganoo not only had a superior pedigree due to its supposed link to the founder of Rinzai Zen but also was considered of superior quality to that of teas grown in other plantations throughout Japan. Over time, Toganoo's reputation would be surpassed by tea from Uji, which would assume the label of honcha as well. As the popularity of tōcha increased, tea battles grew from ten rounds to a hundred rounds in epic campaigns of tea tasting to determine where the Zen-inspired drink had been produced. As a lay priest, Dōyō was familiar with the tea ceremonies of Zen temples and replicated these ceremonies in his own tōcha events. But although he styled his extravagant tea gatherings on Zen's tea ceremony, the *Taiheiki* describes them as being held in opulent settings where he could display his collection of karamono:

> Assembling priceless treasures from both Japan and abroad, he adorned a great hall. He spread the skins of leopards and tigers over all the chairs, lavished damask and brocade to his liking and formed four files of seats. When one saw how they were all lined up like glorious manifestations of the Buddha, it looked no different from the haloes of a thousand deities emanating from the lines of seats.

In time, tōkō and tōcha were joined together in exorbitant social gatherings centered around games of ten types of tea and incense, where teams of participants squared off in both kinds of battle. The opulence of events held by basara like Dōyō set the social standard, and they grew to include renga, incense, and tea competitions that often ran through the night, with luxurious prizes for the victors and significant wagers placed upon the outcomes. Such events were attended not only by the samurai but also by courtiers, Buddhist priests, and nobles, creating an environment rich in diversity of classes and in which political influence and patronage could be developed. The *Taiheiki* records the stakes of such events. In one example, Dōyō held a flower-viewing party, the purpose of which was to undermine a rival's renga gathering for the new shōgun. Combining flower arrangement, renga, incense, and tea competitions, and featuring seven halls, seven types of food, seven hundred prizes, and seventy rounds of honcha and hicha, as well as the burning of an entire piece of rare aloeswood at one time, Dōyō spared no expense. Given such a spectacle, the new shōgun decided to attend Dōyō's extravaganza despite having previously accepted his rival's invitation.

Ever the military men, daimyō carefully assembled their teams for cultural battles with military precision, selecting the most talented "warriors" to represent their houses in the skirmishes of incense, tea, and renga. With the battle joined, basara lords placed large wagers of gold, silk, swords, and incense on the outcome, only to give the prizes away to lucky attendees at the events in grand displays of the disposability of their riches. The outlandish exhibitions of wealth and consumption by basara lords were so prevalent that the Muromachi bakufu officially banned them under the Kenmu-Shikimoku (建武式目, the Kenmu Code). More a statement of governing principles than actual laws, the Kenmu Code specifically addressed basara practices, noting that frugality was to be universally practiced, and gambling, drinking, and "wild frolicking in groups" must be suppressed. In practice, the code was unenforced and mostly ignored, in large part due to basara lords like Dōyō having significant roles in drafting it.

As the basara cultural battles increased in size and displays of affluence, and the gambling on their outcomes offered larger prizes, bragging rights, and prestige, the samurai sought an advantage in preparing for "battle." As the provincial samurai had not been educated in the literary classics or the elegance of speech and manner of imperial courtiers, interest in courtly etiquette and Heian period literary classics saw a marked increase. As highlighted in the *Taiheiki*, the contrast in fortune of the imperial courtiers and the samurai could not have been starker during the Northern and Southern Courts period:

The civilian aristocrats were thus impoverished, passing through a dark vale, unable to find their way. The military houses, by contrast, daily increased their affluence a hundredfold.

This presented an opportunity for samurai and aristocrat alike. Courtiers out of favor fell upon hard times, yet still retained their expertise in the cultural arts; samurai in need of tutelage in these arts had become wealthy and were willing to pay for expertise. So just as a warrior would seek out a swordmaster to improve his ability with a blade, the Ashikaga samurai sought out aristocratic experts in renga, tea, incense, karamono, and the literary classics as cultural advisors. As the prestige required to attract the rich and powerful to basara events surpassed the prizes wagered on their outcomes, a new class of aristocratic cultural connoisseurs joined the ranks of the samurai in support of their refinement. Through the blending of bureaucratic, feudal, and aristocratic influences, the refinement and eloquence of miyabi applied to the discipline of the warrior honed the Ashikaga shōgunate into a cultural force greater than the mere military dictatorship of its predecessor.

By the time Ashikaga Takauji's grandson Ashikaga Yoshimitsu rose to shōgun in 1368, the private villas of Ashikaga shōguns in the eastern hills of Kyoto had become elegant salons where social gatherings centered around the collection of art and culture as well as the display of the wealth and power associated with them. The third shōgun of the Ashikaga shōgunate, Yoshimitsu would prove the most successful, tempering the spirit of the warrior with the miyabi of the Imperial Court, coming to represent the paragon of the aristocratic warrior. He would marry into a noble court family, taking Hino Nariko, whom he adored for her poetic and calligraphic skill, as his principal wife in 1375. In 1381, he was the first bakufu leader to host the visit of a sitting emperor at his residence, featuring six days of royal pageantry and the remarkable act of Emperor Go-Eńyū pouring a cup of sake for him. As an astute politician, Yoshimitsu eliminated most of his rivals, making many of the daimyō supporting the Southern Court his vassals, and eventually brokered a resolution that unified the Northern and Southern Courts in 1392. For his efforts, Yoshimitsu was awarded the title of Dajō-daijin (太政大臣, Grand Minister of State), the highest rank of the Imperial Court. Two years later he would retire as shōgun, ceding the title to his son yet retaining much of his political authority.

Seeing the insatiable desire for collection of karamono and the riches a monopoly on supplying these items would bring, after several attempts, Yoshimitsu was able to reestablish direct trade with Ming China. To do so, however, he capitulated to the demand that he accept a vassal state role for Japan and the subservient title Nihonkokuō (日本国王, King of Japan). Although this submission would later tarnish his legacy, his diplomatic acquiescence opened the door for tribute trade with China to resume. A treasure trove of sophisticated sumi ink paintings, fine porcelain, elegant calligraphic works, ornate tea utensils, and fragrant woods and aromatic materials flooded into Japan, brought by Zen monks returning from study in China.

To display the wealth and power he amassed, Yoshimitsu commissioned the building of the retirement villa of Kitayama-dono (北山殿) in the eastern hills of Kyoto. He acquired the property from the Saioninji clan, influential supporters of the Kamakura bakufu whose fortunes had waned significantly under the Ashikaga shōgunate. In place of the estate in disrepair, he constructed a sprawling complex filled with impressive architecture, a Zen-inspired strolling garden, and a large reflecting pond. It was so grand that it was said to evoke paradise on earth. The central focus of Kitayama-dono's design was its famed Golden Pavilion, Kinkaku shari-den (金閣舎利殿). Built overlooking the tranquil reflecting pond, the Golden Pavilion was three stories in height, with each floor representing a different architectural style. The first story was designed in the style of Heian palaces, with natural wood pillars and white plaster walls. The second story was designed in the style of a samurai residence with its exterior covered completely in brilliant gold leaf. The uppermost story was designed in the style of a Chinese Zen temple and was gilded completely, inside and out, in pure gold. The entire structure was capped with a golden phoenix, an auspicious symbol of new beginnings and immortality.

From within its golden walls, Kitayama culture flourished among Yoshimitsu's close circle of samurai elite, cultural advisors, aristocrats, and influential Zen priests. His collection of karamono conspicuously displayed, Yoshimitsu astonished dignitaries including emperors, influential Zen priests, and official emissaries from China with a level of wealth rarely seen. Yoshimitsu's promotion of tribute trade with Ming China especially enriched his holdings of priceless karamono, leading to one of the largest and most impressive collections ever— one that would have astounded even the basara lords of Dōyō's day. From within the Golden Pavilion, Yoshimitsu awed daimyō with a level of cultural refinement so enthralling that their desire to emulate the refined opulence of the capital was insatiable. Returning to their home provinces, they would take with them the cultural games made popular by the basara lords of Kyoto, indelibly linking poetry and tea with the art of incense.

After Yoshimitsu's death in 1408, Kitayama-dono became the Rinzai Zen temple Rokuon-ji (鹿苑寺, Deer Garden Temple), named for Yoshimitsu's posthumous name, Rokuon-in. Yoshimitsu's glorious Golden Pavilion was then used as a *shariden* (舎利殿, Buddhist relics hall) and named Kinkaku-ji (金閣寺, Temple of the Golden Pavilion). The entire complex is now commonly referred to as Kinkaku-ji and, one of the most photographed sites in Japan, was designated as a UNESCO World Heritage site in 1994.

CHAPTER 6

HIGASHIYAMA
The foundation of uniquely Japanese arts

ASHIKAGA YOSHIMASA WAS BARELY A TEENAGER WHEN PROCLAIMED the eighth Ashikaga shōgun in 1449. Yoshimasa's ascension would take place at a time when famine was rampant outside the capital and control of Japan's countryside by the bakufu government of the Ashikaga shōgunate was becoming increasingly untenable. Yoshimasa was a military leader with few military skills. Having never commanded an army or brokered an alliance, in only a few short years, he saw the power of the shōgun severely diminished. As tens of thousands died from famine, civil war raged over his ill-chosen heir, and Kyoto burned to the ground around him, Yoshimasa retreated into the cultural arts, seeding a garden from which blossomed Japan's quintessential arts of refinement and shaping the art of incense to this day.

Nearly fifty years after the passing of Ashikaga Yoshimitsu, his grandson Ashikaga Yoshimasa inherited a countryside largely divorced from the shōgunate's control. Unlike his grandfather, Yoshimasa had neither the inclination to rule nor the disposition of a warrior. In the power vacuum his ineffectual leadership created, the political influence of the provincial landowning daimyō expanded. As Yoshimasa progressively lost their respect, his frequent requests for financial assistance to remodel, move, and build lavish new palaces went increasingly unanswered. Consequently, taxes were raised and quickly passed on to the peasantry, who, in turn, rose up in revolt with growing frequency. As famine and unrest spread across the countryside, Yoshimasa's frustration grew unbearable. Embittered, at twenty-nine, he decided to retire from public life and immerse himself in his true passion: the cultural arts.

However, retirement presented Yoshimasa with a problem. His marriage to Hino Tomiko, a noblewoman of bold ambition and well-known desire for wealth and power, had not produced an heir. To address this, in 1464, Yoshimasa approached his brother Ashikaga Yoshimi, who had taken vows as a Buddhist monk, and requested that he return to public life to assume the role of successor. Yoshimi agreed to do so only after securing his brother's solemn vow of continued support should Tomiko ever produce an heir. Shortly thereafter, Yoshimi's fears were realized. In 1465, Tomiko gave birth to a son, whom she demanded be named heir instead of Yoshimi. Caught between his brother and his wife, Yoshimasa retreated into the arts as an escape from his dilemma. His paralysis in choosing a successor presented samurai clans the opportunity to take up arms behind either Tomiko or Yoshimi as an excuse to wage war against their rivals.

In what became known as the Ōnin War, fighting began with each force attacking the palatial Kyoto villas of their rivals with volleys of arrows and fire, leaving nothing but charred ruins for bands of looters to scavenge. As the fighting spread throughout Kyoto, Yoshimasa remained ambivalently removed from it. From its start in 1467, the Ōnin War raged for ten years, devastating Kyoto and reducing the once-beautiful capital of peace and tranquility to ruins and ashes. As the fighting reached a costly stalemate, the leaders of warring factions succumbed to age and disease, and any reason to continue fighting evaporated, as control of a powerless shōgunate was pointless.

While fighting raged in the streets of Kyoto, Yoshimasa's attention remained on the cultural arts and the planning of his retirement villa in the Higashiyama hills east of Kyoto. In what would come to be known as Higashiyama culture, Yoshimasa's significant patronage and direct involvement with a wide range of arts placed him in the leading role for Japan's cultural development. During the Ōnin War and the decades that followed it, he filled his orbit with icons of art, architecture, poetry, literature, drama, flower arrangement, tea, incense, and Zen.

Known as *dōbōshū* (同朋衆), a quasi-priestly artist class made up of professional connoisseurs and talented experts with extensive knowledge of the arts, the leading figures of Higashiyama culture read like a list of historical luminaries. These talented individuals not only helped Yoshimasa refine and elevate their respective arts, but they also cataloged his many collections of rare objects, including detailed teachings on their appreciation, display, use, and philosophy. With extensive writing on the finer points of the refined arts, many of these manuscripts would go on to be referenced as cultural manuals for centuries.

In 1482, delayed by war and perpetually short of money, Yoshimasa was finally able to begin construction of the long-planned palatial hermitage where he would realize the ultimate expression of his aesthetic vision. Jisho-ji (慈照寺, Temple of Shining Mercy) would serve as the retirement villa for Yoshimasa to retreat from the world and immerse himself fully in the arts. Although Jisho-ji is a complex of multiple buildings, it is most often referred to as Ginkaku-ji (銀閣寺, Temple of the Silver Pavilion) for its Kannon Hall constructed in 1489. The two-story building stands as a visual representation of the break from emulation of Chinese culture, with its top floor designed in the style of a Chinese Zen meditation hall and its ground floor displaying Japanese Shoin-zukuri (書院造) architecture, a style that emerged at Higashiyama.

The name Ginkaku-ji was first recorded more than a century after the temple's completion, most likely adopted to differentiate it from the Kinkaku-ji, the Temple of the Golden Pavilion, of Yoshimasa's grandfather. Despite its name, the Silver Pavilion is not gilded in silver as the Golden Pavilion is in gold. Its name is likely derived from the hue that the once-black lacquered exterior presented in the moon-light. Gazing at the moon was a symbol of Buddhist enlightenment, and events centering on moon viewing were filled with cultural significance. Ginkaku-ji was oriented to moonrise, and the later addition of the unique Kogetsudai (Moon-Viewing Mound) in Ginkaku-ji's dry garden known as the "Sea of Silver Sand" reflects Yoshimasa's lifelong devotion to Buddhism. The inclusion of Buddhist elements at Ginkaku-ji was intentional, and many of the dōbōshū Yoshimasa associated with were Zen monks or lay priests. It was at Ginkaku-ji that these cultural luminaries created the foundation for Japan's refined arts, elevating them from the gambling-filled gatherings of basara lords by infusing them with courtly miyabi and the sober, spiritual simplicity of Zen.

Zen had brought flowers, tea, and incense together, and Zen would be at the forefront of elevating each to a refined art form. Yoshimasa was a devotee of *chanoyu* (茶の湯, hot water with tea), and his esteemed dōbōshū Nōami, himself a Zen monk, was instrumental in harmonizing the Buddhist ritual service of tea with the entertainment of basara tea-tasting contests. Nōami removed the ostentatious basara displays, simplifying the ornamentation of the *shoin* (書院, a type of Zen study used as a reception hall) and creating the *shoin kazari* (書院飾, reception hall ornamentation) layout for tea service. Although it contrasted with the extravagance of basara tea battles, shoin kazari did not fully replicate the sober simplicity of the Buddhist temple tea rites. Rather, Nōami created a Zen-inspired style of simplistic ornamentation known as *daisu kazari* (臺子飾, utensil stand decoration). The *daisu* (臺子) was a simple two-tiered portable shelf the narrow width of a tatami mat. The lower shelf rested directly upon the tatami mat floor and was connected to the upper shelf by posts at each of its four corners. Upon the daisu were placed the most exquisite Chinese karamono tea utensils, displayed formally in a precise layout. Nōami's shoin-style tea still employed much of the formal ritual of Buddhist temple tea service, but removed the gaming and gambling elements of basara tea contests, and had the host be the one to serve tea to his guests. Nōami's chanoyu blended a refined display of wealth with the Zen spiritual simplicity of Buddhist tea rites, creating a tranquil atmosphere reminiscent of a Zen meditation hall in which to gather and enjoy tea.

Nōami also cataloged Yoshimasa's extensive collection of Chinese karamono and artwork, creating an instruction manual for their proper display known as the *Kundaikan-sōchōki* (君台観左右帳記). His grandson Sōami continued his work, writing a companion volume for later acquisitions titled *O-kazari-sho* (御飾書). Each volume consisted of two primary sections, one covering paintings and one covering utensils, with each section giving specific instruction on the display and use of all manner of tea accoutrements: the daisu, incense containers, incense censers, candle stands, flower vases, tea bowls, and tea caddies. The two volumes became some of the most influential references on the tea ceremony and the display of Chinese artwork, and were used as manuals for the ornamentation of shōgunal palaces for the next three hundred years.

It was Nōami who introduced Yoshimasa to the Zen priest Murata Jukō, credited as the founder of the Japanese tea ceremony. Having dedicated himself to the mastery of tea since the age of thirty, Jukō had delved more deeply than anyone of the era into perfecting the art of tea. The Zen-inspired tea of Jukō was simpler than that of Nōami, highlighting the Zen inherent in chanoyu's origins, moving away from a Chinese-inspired tea to something much more authentically Japanese. Rather than tea being used for medicinal, entertainment, or religious purposes, Jūko channeled Zen's simplicity and directness into the ritual service of tea as a form of meditation capable of revealing one's Buddha nature on the path to enlightenment. Jukō took the teachings of his mentor, the eccentric Zen monk Sōjun Ikkyū, and wove them into a simple ritual tea service hosted in a *yojohan chashitsu* (四畳半茶室), a four-and-a-half-tatami-mat tearoom. It was Ikkyū's suggestion that rather than multiple works of art, Jukō hang a single *kakejiku* (掛軸, hanging scroll) of Zen calligraphy in the tearoom *tokonoma* (床の間, alcove) to hasten enlightenment. This suggestion led to Jukō's famous inspiration *"Chazen Ichimi"* (茶 禅 一味), or "Zen and tea have one taste," where tea is viewed as a form of spiritual activity akin to meditation. Jukō was the first to use the daisu not only to display tea implements but also to hold the utensils used to prepare tea, utilizing simple rustic Japanese ceramics alongside Chinese karamono, laying the foundation for the *wabi-cha* of preeminent tea master Takeno Jōō half a century later. Jūko's Zen-inspired tea, his use of the daisu, and the elevation of Japanese ceramics to be on par with Chinese utensils transformed the tea ceremony into a uniquely Japanese art form.

The "Kokoro no fumi" (心の文, "Letter of the Heart") is the earliest known document describing the tea ceremony as a spiritual art. In it, Jūko succinctly summarizes his guiding principles of chanoyu and encourages the use of the sober renga concepts of *hie* (冷え, chill) and *kare* (枯れ, withered) in its decorum. The "Kokoro no fumi" served as a guide to the practice of chanoyu and would be referenced in the teachings of Japan's most famous tea master, Sen Rikyū, a century later.

The nascent tea ceremony that emerged from Higashiyama culture transcended the bounds of the ritual service of tea by encompassing a wide variety of art forms. The sophistication and refinement of the host was displayed across the natural beauty of the tea garden, the architecture of the *kaisho* (会所, reception hall) and chashitsu, and the choice of Zen calligraphy scroll, flower arrangement, and incense container in the tokonoma. Of the karamono displayed, an arrangement of a celadon, bronze, or silver incense burner between a filled flower vase and candleholder often featured prominently. Known as *mitsu-gusoku* (三具足), the offering of flowers, incense, and light was commonly displayed in front of a painting of the Buddha or scroll of Zen calligraphy, creating an atmosphere for tea reminiscent of a Zen meditation hall.

Yoshimasa's fondness for the display of flowers brought the art of flower arrangement from the Buddhist temple to the shoin reception hall and tearoom tokonoma. The origins of the art of flower arrangement are unknown, but have roots in the mitsu-gusoku flower offerings created for Buddhist temple altars, as well as in the Shintō practices of using new greens from pines and cypress to ceremonially invoke the *kami* (神, gods, deities). Yoshimasa was a significant patron of early ornamentation using flowers, employing Ryūami as his dōbōshū in charge of creating flower arrangements for his palatial estates. Once, Yoshimasa received a gift of especially exquisite chrysanthemums and requested Ryūami to arrange them. Ryūami declined to appear, claiming illness, but it is believed his failure to respond was due to his concern that his arrangement of such regal flowers might not please his patron. Displeased, Yoshimasa then summoned him to appear and ordered him to arrange the flowers. Ryūami is said to have created a "standing flower" arrangement in the *rikka* (立花) style of Ikenobō Senkei, a Zen monk renowned for his skills with flower arrangement. Yoshimasa was pleased with Ryūami's work, praising the arrangement glowingly, leading to both Ryūami and the rikka style gaining renown.

As part of mitsu-gusoku, incense was never far from Zen thought or practice. Incense assumed an important role in the tea ceremony for purifying the space for the service of tea and welcoming of guests in the kaisho. The display of Chinese lacquerware incense containers and celadon incense burners in the tokonoma was seen as a sign of high culture and wealth. The unique Higashiyama three-tier shelving was used to display collections of exquisite incense burners alongside ornate Chinese karamono teaware. The art of incense at Higashiyama naturally transitioned from the basara incense battles to a uniquely Japanese cultural art form, developing in tandem with the refinement of chanoyu.

Yoshimasa was considered highly accomplished in the art of incense, having such an appetite for fragrant woods that he amassed a significant collection of meikō, many of which he obtained from Dōyō's extensive collections. It was due to the destruction of temples, shrines, and palaces during the Ōnin War that Yoshimasa would be given a piece of the rarest jinkō in existence. As a result of the financial collapse of the Imperial Palace brought on by the destruction of Kyoto, Emperor Go-Tsuchimikado was forced to flee to avoid the fighting. Taking up residence in Yoshimasa's Muromachi palaces, the emperor would remain a guest of the shōgun for many years during the conflict. As thanks for his protection, Yoshimasa was the first to be granted a small piece of the famed Ranjatai, crowning Yoshimasa's collection of rare jinkō with the exquisite gift of the emperor's incense and displaying the symbolic power such rare incense represented.

It is believed that Yoshimasa was initiated into the ritual appreciation of incense by Sanjōnishi Sanetaka. Rising through the ranks of the courtly literati at an early age, Sanetaka was a distinguished literary scholar, poet, and calligrapher, and was in charge of all incense matters of Yoshimasa's court. He was charged with copying classical literary manuscripts for both Emperor Go-Tsuchimikado and Shōgun Ashikaga Yoshimasa, as the elegance of his calligraphy was said to be unparalleled. Yoshimasa had Sanetaka document the incense games of the time, including listing the proper etiquette, rules, and woods that should be utilized during their play. Sanetaka rejected the rowdy, drunken gambling practices associated with basara incense battles, and instead substituted references to literary classics such as the *Kokin Wakashū* and *The Tale of Genji* into the gaming aspect of incense appreciation, elevating the practice to a cultured art form in which the appreciation of fragrance within a literary framework superseded competition.

To bring order to his collection of jinkō, Yoshimasa enlisted Shino Sōshin, a trusted vassal and a chief military strategist for the shōgunate. As a samurai, Sōshin brought to bear his military expertise in organizing Yoshimasa's collection of kōboku. Much as Jūko had done with tea, Sōshin elevated the ritual appreciation of incense to a Zen-inspired art form by infusing it with spiritual elements through the practice of monkō, "listening" to incense. Sōshin created order from the chaos of basara incense games, forgoing the emphasis on competition by adopting Sanetaka's literary framework for kumikō incense games. Held within a tranquil environment with Zen meditative decorum and centered on monkō, the ritual appreciation of incense was returned to a focus upon fragrance rather than competition.

Together, Sanjōnishi Sanetaka and Shino Sōshin organized Yoshimasa's extensive holdings of meikō into cohesive collections such as the "Ashikaga Shōgun's Collection of 120," "Incense Selected by Emperors," and "Shino Family Collection." However, the process of cataloging Yoshimasa's collection of exquisite fragrant woods resulted in more than just a detailed record. Sōshin and Sanetaka are credited with leading roles in creating the Rikkoku (六国), the "Six Nations" framework used extensively to classify aloeswood. Most likely building on the cataloged knowledge of aloeswood traders in the spice routes from China and the South Pacific, Sanetaka and Sōshin classified aloeswood based upon the characteristics typically associated with its country of origin, much the same way wine is categorized by its region of origin today. However, as origin alone fails to adequately describe the unique and complex character of fragrant woods, Sōshin and Sanetaka further illustrated each nation by combining it with archetypal personalities of the time. Descriptions such as "aristocrat," "warrior," "bitter woman," "peasant," "a servant disguised as a noble," and "monk" were used to portray the ineffable fragrance of the various types of aloeswood, creating living, breathing archetypes from which to describe the sublime fragrance of aloeswood.

To enhance the status of the ritual appreciation of incense as a refined art form, the influential Zen monk Sōjun Ikkyū transcribed a poem extolling the virtues of incense and distributed it among literati, merchants, nobles, and samurai alike. Originally written in the eleventh century by Song Dynasty master poet and calligrapher Huang Tingjian, "Kō no Jittoku" (香の十徳, "Ten Virtues of Incense"), lists the qualities and benefits of exceptional incense, lauding the virtue of its use. Several of the virtues Ikkyū included closely mirror an earlier poem, "Ten Virtues of Tea," written by Tang Dynasty poet Liu Zhenliang, hinting at the inspiration for Tingjian's work that served as the basis for Ikkyu's iteration. This was no doubt intentional in the cause of elevating the appreciation of incense as a truly virtuous practice, giving it noble origins and a lineage associated with Tang Dynasty China's high culture.

In the hills of Higashiyama, the cultural salons Yoshimasa held created a feeling of unity among those who enjoyed the cultural arts known as *ichiza konryū* (一座建立), and they were attended by luminaries from all social classes—daimyō, monks, courtiers, merchants, and even the emperor. In a paradox of tranquility and excitement, never-to-be-repeated gatherings for the ritual appreciation of incense, tea, flower viewing, art, poetry, and drama were held at Ginkaku-ji. At these events the foundation of uniquely Japanese arts began to take shape. However, Yoshimasa would not see the fruition of his artistic vision or the completion of the Ginkaku-ji complex. Following the death of his son in 1489, Yoshimasa was paralyzed on his left side by the onset of palsy. His condition worsened rapidly, and he fell into a coma and died in January 1490.

Yoshimasa's ambivalent leadership during the Ōnin War and the resulting destruction of Kyoto severely weakened the Ashikaga shōgunate—to such an extent that it would never recover. Over the following decades, Ashikaga shōguns were powerless to resist the various samurai clans that violently seized control of the shōgunate from their rivals. No longer restrained by a strong shōgunate, clan rivalries extended their reach far outside the smoking ruins of the capital as daimyō felt free to act on their desires for power and conquest. During the constant fighting, many of the aristocracy and priestly class left the capital for the relative safety of the provinces and wealthy port cities like Sakai, spreading Higashiyama culture and the nascent refined arts to their daimyō hosts throughout central Japan.

Despite his failings as a military leader, Yoshimasa's elevation of the refined arts would create a legacy that forms the cultural aesthetic Japan is known for today. Yoshimasa's retirement villa, Ginkaku-ji, is considered a National Treasure of Japan and was designated a UNESCO World Heritage site in 1994. The Rikkoku of Sanjōnishi Sanetaka and Shino Sōshin continues to be used to classify aloeswood more than five hundred years after its creation. And Ikkyū's interpretation of the "Ten Virtues of Incense" continues to be widely cited today.

CHAPTER 7

三芸道

THREE GEIDŌ
Flowers, tea, and incense

THIRTY YEARS AFTER ASHIKAGA YOSHIMASA'S DEATH, LARGE portions of Japan were embroiled in civil war. Known as Sengoku Jidai (戦国時代), the Warring States period of Japan saw widespread bloody military conflict between rival daimyō intent upon expanding their domains and the power associated with them. The gekokujō begun by the basara who upended the social order of the capital now turned to the "low overturning the high" through military intimidation or pure force of arms, engulfing generations of Japanese in nearly 150 years of civil war. Yet, paradoxically, it was the patronage of these warlords that continued Yoshimasa's cultural legacy, elevating the nascent refined arts born of Higashiyama culture into uniquely Japanese cultural traditions that shape the art of incense to this day.

After Yoshimasa's death, his dōbōshū, their descendants, and their disciples continued to teach the ritual appreciation of incense alongside the ritual service of tea and the formal arrangement of flowers—all three enjoyed by their warring daimyō patrons. Over successive generations of experts, the arrangement of flowers was formalized into the art of Kadō (華道, the Way of Flowers), the ritual service of tea was refined into the art of Chadō (茶道, the Way of Tea), and the ritual appreciation of incense was perfected into the art of Kōdō (香道, the Way of Fragrance). As the warfare of the Sengoku Jidai intensified, the schools of Kadō, Chadō, and Kōdō elevated these practices to their highest artistic expressions known as *geidō* (芸道, art of refinement).

At the heart of the geidō is *dō* (道), often translated as "the way." Appended to many forms—for example, Bushidō (武士道, the Way of the Warrior)—at one level, dō can represent the way a specific art form is performed, in which prescribed forms known as *kata* (型) create a detailed, choreographed practice used to learn and perfect the art, be it the use of a sword or the ritual appreciation of incense. These kata often formed the fundamental teachings of the schools of any given art form.

On a deeper level, dō represents the indefinable Tao, the way of life itself described in the *Tao Te Ching* that animates Zen's Taoist roots. More than just a collection of kata, dō in this understanding represents an indescribable blending of subtle, spontaneous, natural, spiritual, and skillful action in harmony with life itself. Just as Zen taught that sitting in meditation was, paradoxically, also a form a vigorous activity, through the self-discipline of mastering the geidō, an individual could transcend the art form into the refinement of the body, mind, and spirit, reaching a place where there was no separation between the art and the practitioner.

The Way, or dō, and the geidō are inseparable. Although Zen includes the study of Buddhist texts, awareness in each moment of experience is more highly valued. Because satori (enlightenment) could arrive as a flash of insight during the practice of any task undertaken with one's whole being, walking, sweeping, practicing martial arts, and practicing the geidō were all spiritual disciplines that could lead to potential enlightenment. As Miyamoto Musashi, the famous swordsman and author of the legendary *Go Rin no Sho* (五輪書, *Book of Five Rings*), noted, "Getting up, sleeping, and eating your meals are all the practice of swordsmanship." The ability to keenly focus the mind to the point of achieving a state known as *mushin* (無心, "no-mind"), where there is no thought or form, only the spontaneous action required in the moment, appealed greatly to the samurai. In the martial arts, mushin was illustrated by the sword as an extension of one's whole being, the wielder acting intuitively, without thought or form to delay action, or the rider whose mind was so quiet and calm that there was no horse beneath the rider and no rider upon the horse, but only the mind of horse and rider working as one. Disciplining the mind to the point of mushin was highly prized by the samurai, for whom a fear of death might delay their reaction and hasten a glorious demise. Through discipline and practice, the geidō offered a path for samurai, noble, merchant, and commoner alike to refine not only the art but their body, mind, and spirit. All could seek the point of no separation between the transience of the flower arrangement and the transience of the observer, between the service of tea and the one serving tea, or between the fragrance of jinkō and the one listening to jinkō.

The formal arrangement of flowers created a way to appreciate the fleeting beauty of the world in both the arrangement and the observer. When the dōbōshū Ryūami arranged flowers for Yoshimasa, his standing flower design was inspired by the rikka style of Ikenobō Senkei. Senkei was a Zen priest of the Rokkaku-dō, the eight-sided Kyoto temple said to have been founded by Prince Shōtoku over a thousand years earlier. Priests in charge of making the *tatehana* (立花, standing flower) arrangements for the altar of the temple are said to have lived by a pond (*ike*) in small huts (*bō*) and were thus known as "ike-no-bō." Over time, *Ikenobō* (池坊) became the honorific given to the *iemoto* (家元), the head of those in charge of flower arrangement for the temple.

As the twelfth ikenobō, Senkei took the tatehana style of standing flowers beyond its mitsu-gusoku roots as a religious offering to the Buddha and developed it into an art form for the laity. His standing flower arrangements were popular in the *zashiki kazari* (座敷飾) style of interior decoration used in the villas of samurai and court nobles, and they were favored for the shoin reception room. Written shortly before the death of Ashikaga Yoshimasa, the *Kao irai no Kadensho*

(花王以来の花伝書) is the oldest known manuscript of Kadō. Used as a reference for flower arrangement for centuries, the *Kao irai no Kadensho* illustrated the Ikenobō tradition of flower arrangement and is one of the earliest examples of this uniquely Japanese art form.

Building upon the work of Senkei, Ikenobō Sen'ō, the thirteenth ikenobō, systematically formalized flower arrangement into an art form. He founded Ikenobō Kadō and defined the philosophy of the Ikenobō school, which remains the oldest school of Kadō today. The Ikenobō school's approach looked beyond the mere arrangement of flowers to see the flowers as representing the timeless moment that simultaneously holds past, present, and future. The oral teachings of Ikenobō were compiled in the book *Sen'ō Kuden* (専応口伝), which provided the guiding principles for Kadō for centuries. In it, Sen'ō taught, "Not only beautiful flowers but also buds and withered flowers have life, and each has its own beauty. By arranging flowers with reverence, one refines oneself."

Kadō's standing flower arrangements were highly admired display pieces in the tokonoma of the tearoom. Displayed next to a featured hanging scroll, a tatehana arrangement was used to highlight the season or theme of a specific tea ceremony. Just as Ikenobō Sen'ō defined the philosophy of Kadō, Takeno Jōō would define the art of tea, creating a uniquely Japanese refined art. A member of a prosperous merchant family from Sakai made wealthy by the patronage of the Miyoshi clan for whom they supplied leather armor, Jōō was born in 1502 and spent his first thirty years immersing himself in renga poetry. At the age of twenty-three, his thirst for a deeper understanding of the classics led him to seek out Yoshimasa's former dōbōshū Sanjōnishi Sanetaka for his secret knowledge of classical poetry. As a member of the merchant class, the lowest social class of feudal Japanese society, Jōō had little hope of being received by such a lofty teacher, who was nearing his seventieth year and at the height of his reputation. But Sanetaka had fallen on hard times and relied on patrons of means like Jōō to support his household. After initially turning him away, Sanetaka relented and received into his home Jōō and his gifts of food and patronage. After years of requests, Sanetaka gave Jōō a copy of the *Kokinshū*, eventually initiating him into the secret knowledge of the classics.

It was this foundation of classical poetry that would inform Jōō's vision for Chadō. Returning to Sakai at age thirty-one to become a Zen priest, he studied chanoyu from students of renowned tea master Murata Jukō, learning his early "grass hut" style of tea that had been shared with Yoshimasa. Jōō combined his deep knowledge of renga poetry with the simplicity of the "grass hut" style, blending the spirituality of Zen, the simplicity of Japanese utensils, and the sober decorum of the renga concepts "chill" and "withered" to define *wabi-cha* (侘茶), the tea of quiet taste. A concept with few direct translations, *wabi* could represent the beauty found in simplicity, quiet contentment, humility, or a combination of these. Just as Zen used poetry to illustrate concepts that were difficult to express in words, Jōō often quoted poetry by Fujiwara no Teika, using one of his poems to assert that the tenth month (November in the modern calendar) best represented wabi:

> *The Month without Gods tells no lies.*
> *What more sincere than the first drops of an autumn shower?*
> *Whose are the honest tears that fall?*

By citing the tenth month as the season of wabi, a month prone to a cloudy sky and light rain and devoid of the beauty of cherry blossoms or vibrant autumn foliage, Jōō drew upon the poetic framework of renga's chill and withered aesthetic as the ideal for the ritual service of tea. To Jōō, just as the study of poetry led to personal refinement, so too could the mastery of tea lead to personal refinement. Wabi-cha sought quiet, subtle beauty in the everyday world, using simple, imperfect Japanese utensils to create a form of tea that was as far from the ostentatious basara tea contests of Dōyō as possible, and in complete contrast to the Chinese karamono-filled shoin tea service of Nōami. Wabi-cha drew upon renga's sensitivity to subtle natural beauty, even in the worn and broken. In fact, Jōō encouraged the use of ordinary, worn, and even discarded utensils in wabi-cha, emphasizing the ability of these items to capture a deeper, natural inner beauty that contrasted with the polished and pristine surface beauty of Chinese karamono.

The wabi-cha of Jōō was not to be practiced in isolation or seclusion. Just as renga was created through an exchange between poets, the spiritual exchange of wabi-cha could only occur between host and guests. Gathering for tea was an act of hospitality even when those in attendance were not of like mind, introducing into wabi-cha the spirit of group unity and harmony known as ichiza konryū. As though linked verse had come to life, Jōō taught that this unity was cultivated by a renga-inspired decorum and sober aesthetic.

Jōō emphasized that every gathering for tea was an event that could never be duplicated; as such, both host and guests should rise above worldly matters and devote their full concentration to the occasion at hand, as always at the heart of Chadō was Zen and its focus upon the moment. There was to be no separation between the preparation of tea and the one preparing it, nor between the host and guests. Jōō taught, "Let there not be a single act divided from heart and mind." Sen Rikyū, Jōō's student who became the preeminent tea master of Japan and elevated wabi-cha to its highest artistic expression, built upon the unity and spiritual exchange Jōō highlighted, emphasizing the once-in-a-lifetime nature of each gathering and the qualities of harmony, respect, purity, and tranquility.

Incense was never far removed from the ritual service of tea. Used in the shoin reception hall to welcome guests and on the tearoom hearth to set the atmosphere during the preparation of tea, incense was an ever-present part of Chadō. But incense also occupied its own place within the refined arts, with the ritual appreciation of incense evolving from basara incense battles just as tea had evolved from its tea-tasting competitions. In fact, many of the earliest schools of tea taught the ritual appreciation of incense concurrently, viewing the two arts as complementary with overlapping elements. Just as Kadō and Chadō had transcended their base forms, Kōdō transcended fragrance, inviting participants to not merely use their sense of smell but, through monkō, to listen to incense deeply using all the senses. By emptying the mind, the senses were free to expand from what was accessible in the physical world to the infinite possibilities available in the emptiness of the void, thus allowing "the ears to see and the eyes to hear," as the renowned Rinzai Zen master Daitō Kokushi described it. Through Sanetaka's literary framework, the ineffable nature of fragrance was expressed through classical poetry and literature, creating a comprehensive art form that was uniquely Japanese.

Although many different schools of Kadō and Chadō arose from Higashiyama's influence, only a handful of schools of Kōdō came into being. This may have been due to the availability of native flora and tea in Japan, whereas at the heart of Kōdō was jinkō, a rare commodity imported from abroad at significant cost. Additionally, Kōdō was the most comprehensive of the three geidō, taking decades to master, as it required a wide range of knowledge and talents that extended beyond the auspices of jinkō itself. Besides thorough knowledge of aloeswood, mastery of the art of incense required fluency in classical poetry, such as the *Kokinshū*, and thorough knowledge of monogatari, including narrative prose such as *The Tale of Genji* and war tales such as the *Taiheiki*. To this knowledge, a sensitivity to the four seasons was added, carried forward from the blended incense games of the Heian courtiers, in order to skillfully combine a seasonal theme with a literary reference and an appropriate selection of jinkō. Together, these elements formed the kumikō (incense game) selected for the *kōseki* (香席, incense gathering) chosen by the *kōmoto* (香元, ceremony host). In time, hundreds of different kumikō developed that a skilled incense master must commit to his repertoire, from basic games like Jūshūkō with ten paper-wrapped packets of jinkō, to more advanced games like Genji-kō with twenty-five packets to choose from. The elegant choreography of the ceremony itself and the proper use of a wide array of *kōdōgu* (香道具, incense utensils) also required extensive practice, as did the preparation of bamboo charcoal and ash in a special three-footed incense burner known as a *kikigōro* (聞香炉). Additionally, although competition was not emphasized, a record of scores was created at the conclusion of the kōseki and was given by the kōmoto to the guest who had achieved the most correct answers. Skill with the brush was emphasized for years during Kōdō training, as these records were written in elegant calligraphy and considered important mementos of the unique moment that each kōseki represented. Overarching all the skills required to master the art of incense was the influence of Zen's meditative focus on aloeswood, where, during monkō, incense was listened to with all the senses until no separation existed between jinkō and listener.

The appreciation of incense was thus elevated from the rowdy basara incense battles, where competition was paramount, to an event in which literary references and cultural sophistication were central to the Zen-inspired meditative appreciation of jinkō. The perfect blend of Heian miyabi and samurai culture, the kōseki became a refuge of peace and harmony; participants were able to step outside the turbulent daily world and into a tranquil environment where their troubles were left behind.

With Kōdō's comprehensive nature, high cost, and period of study measured in decades rather than years, there was a barrier of entry to mastering it. As a result, it was practiced primarily by the nobility, samurai, and affluent merchant classes. The schools of Kōdō knowledgeable enough in the art to teach such upper-class patrons were directly linked to the Higashiyama dōbōshū Sanjōnishi Sanetaka and Shino Sōshin, the two charged by Yoshimasa with cataloging his extensive collection of jinkō and credited with establishing the Rikkoku classification of aloeswood. Over several generations, these men's descendants established the two preeminent schools of Kōdō and refined their teachings into the highest artistic expression of the ritual appreciation of incense.

Sanjōnishi Sanetaka is considered the founder of Oie-ryu (御家流, Oie School of Kōdō), which was the style originally favored by members of the imperial household and nobility. (Note that *ryu*, 流, can mean both "school" and "style"). Oie-ryu emphasizes the game-playing aspects of Kōdō and is, in a way, the heir to the incense games passed down since the takimono-awase of Heian aristocrats. However, Oie-ryu elevated these incense guessing games by placing them within references to classical literature and poetry, especially works for which Sanetaka held the secret teachings, such as the *Kokinshū* and *The Tale of Genji*. Oie-ryu was originally intended for the imperial household and its courtiers, as they had knowledge of the literary references utilized in its kumikō, but over time, the samurai and wealthy merchant class, seeking refinement and greater status at the Imperial Court, studied Oie-ryu as well. Blending the Zen-inspired elegant choreography of the tea ceremony with literary kumikō, the goal of Oie-ryu was to create an enjoyable diversion, the essence of which was to enjoy fragrance in an enlightened atmosphere.

Shino Sōshin is considered the founder of Shino-ryu (志野流, Shino School of Kōdō), the form that originally spread through the samurai and affluent merchant classes and, like Oie-ryu, was eventually studied by courtiers and commoners alike. A loyal samurai vassal to the Ashikaga shōgunate, Sōshin served three successive Ashikaga shōguns and studied jinkō with Ashikaga Yoshimasa. Shino-ryu was founded upon a Zen-inspired ritual appreciation of incense and the insight achieved through monkō. Focusing upon listening to incense and the exclusive use of jinkō, Shino-ryu combined the ritual and formality of the Zen tea service with specific rules of decorum. Uniting the meditative contemplation of aloeswood through monkō with the gaming aspects of kumikō based on Sanetaka's framework of classical poetry and literature, Shino-ryu replaced the competition of incense guessing games with that of cultural sophistication and refinement and an emphasis on enjoying fragrance.

Over three generations, from Shino Sōshin to his grandson Shino Shoha, the ritual appreciation of aloeswood and the choreography of its kata were refined into Shino-ryu's highest expression. The overlapping kata of incense and tea were emphasized, and Shino-ryu taught Kōdō and Chadō as a unit all the way until the Meiji Restoration in the late 1800s. The third-generation iemoto, Shino Shoha, even counted among his students future renowned tea master Sen Rikyū. Upon Shoha's retirement, the Shino-ryu tradition passed to the Hachiya family, whose descendants still serve as iemoto of the school today.

After the death of Ashikaga Yoshimasa, the three geidō of Kadō, Chadō, and Kōdō continued to grow in esteem, practiced by the warlords who rose above all other hegemons in their quest to rule Japan. Still taught today throughout Japan and beyond its shores, the three remain the quintessential Japanese arts of refinement, now more commonly referred to as ikebana, the tea ceremony, and the incense ceremony. The Oie School of Kōdō and the Shino School of Kōdō survive as well, the refined art of incense still taught by the descendants and heirs of Sanjōnishi Sanetaka and Shino Sōshin more than five hundred years later.

CHAPTER 8

南蛮

SOUTHERN BARBARIANS
Guns, Catholicism, and the incense trade

ON JULY 24, 1511, THE EVE OF THE FEAST OF ST. JAMES THE Apostle, the forces of Afonso de Albuquerque stormed the city of Malacca, the richest port on the Malay Peninsula, at the center of the South Pacific spice trade. With fifteen ships, three heavily armed galleons, and 1,400 soldiers, Albuquerque intended to conquer the strategic trading port for King Manuel I of Portugal just as he had taken Goa on the western coast of India the previous year. As Albuquerque's forces battled their way to the bridge entering the city, they came under attack by the ruler of Malacca, Sultan Mahmud Shah, who entered battle upon the back of a terrifyingly large war elephant, with two more elephants at his flank. The Sultan's three giant beasts wreaked havoc upon the melee while, from the turrets on the elephant's backs, his men rained poisoned darts on Albuquerque's forces. But poison darts were no match for the superior firearms of the

Portuguese, who soon wounded the beasts severely with a barrage of musket and cannon fire. When the terrified animals turned and fled, trampling the Sultan's forces in their path, the battle turned decisively in Albuquerque's favor. The Portuguese forces set the surrounding buildings to the torch, and by nightfall they had taken the mosque at the center of the city. Nine days later, every one of the Moorish inhabitants of Malacca had either fled or been slain.

As Kōdō rose to take its place as one of Japan's three preeminent geidō, the appetite of the Sengoku-period daimyō for aloeswood was as insatiable as their appetite for conquest. Yet aloeswood was not native to Japan, and trade in fragrant woods and aromatic spices was subject to embargoes by the Ming and the whims of pirate smuggling networks. The arrival of the black ships of the Portuguese circumvented these obstacles and provided direct access to goods not only from the South Pacific trading hub of Malacca but also from China's wider trading network. These "southern barbarians" brought large quantities of aloeswood, sandalwood, and aromatic riches from far-off shores, anchoring Japan and its art of incense at the furthest end of the Maritime Silk Road connecting East and West. They also brought European guns and Catholicism, which would alter the course of Japanese history.

At the heart of Kōdō is the ritual appreciation of rare and fragrant aloeswood. Like most raw materials used in the Japanese art of incense, aloeswood was imported at great cost, as it was sourced from the far-off shores of the six countries of the Rikkoku in the South Pacific. Trade in aloeswood from points south of Japan had existed informally for centuries. However, formal trade in fragrant woods, aromatic spices, and other items highly desired by the Japanese elite, such as Chinese silks, porcelain, and artwork, was restricted by a tribute system imposed by the Ming Empire through a series of *haijin* (海禁, sea bans). When the Ming overthrew the Yuan Dynasty in 1368, one of their first acts of foreign policy was to impose haijin along China's coast as a national security measure geared toward rooting out the remnants of Yuan loyalists seeking refuge in coastal islands and waterways. Foreign trade was limited to formal tribute missions between Ming officials and licensed foreign nationals from countries that had accepted vassal status, as Ashikaga Yoshimitsu had done in 1402. Haijin restricted the number of foreign persons and ships and the frequency of trade missions, and private foreign trade was outlawed. Violations of haijin were met with draconian punishment, including the death sentence for those conducting illegal trade and exile for their families and neighbors.

Regardless of the intended effect, Ming haijin were difficult to enforce, and the reduction of foreign trade to official tribute missions, spread years apart, created a hardship for Chinese traders, sowing the seeds for illegal trade to flourish. Tribute missions were fabulously profitable for both Chinese traders and Japanese daimyō, as demonstrated by the substantial wealth accumulated from the Ashikaga shōgunate's tribute missions. Struggling economically under the sea bans, and often in an attempt to fill a shortage in highly sought-after aromatics, local officials frequently ignored restrictions, opening Chinese ports to ships that arrived from overseas, regardless of their number or appointed schedule.

Although highly ineffective and poorly enforced, haijin restricted the flow of official Japanese trade with China to a limited number of licensed trade exchanges at the port of Ningbo. Located in the plain of the Yong River on the eastern coast of China, Ningbo is one of China's oldest cities. Situated at the eastern end of the Silk Road, even by the time of the Ashikaga shōgunate, Ningbo had been a well-known port for foreign trade for over two thousand years. Chinese sailors would pray at Ningbo's temples for safe journeys at sea, giving the port its name, which meant "peaceful waves." Unfortunately, Chinese prayers for peaceful waves did not make for peaceful trade relations, as a byproduct of the Ming haijin was a boom in dispossessed traders resorting to illegal trading. By the time Albuquerque sacked Malacca, illegal smuggling was widespread along China's coast.

The Ming branded any type of trading in violation of the haijin as "piracy," blaming the practice on *wokou* (倭寇)—a combination of the Chinese expression *wō*, meaning "dwarf," used as an ethnic slur referring to the Japanese, and *kou*, meaning bandit. In the aftermath of the Yuan invasions of Japan over two centuries earlier, the survivors of Tsushima Island and Iki Island had resorted to raiding the Korean and Chinese coasts as a means of survival. However, according to the *Ming Shi* (明史), the official history of the Ming, by the time Albuquerque conquered Malacca, fewer than a third of wokou were Japanese, with the overwhelming majority being Chinese traders eking out a subsistence living after their livelihood had been curtailed by haijin.

Although the Ming branded them as pirates, the primary activity of wokou was a continuation of trade practices, albeit now deemed illegal. Some raiding did occur, but much of their activity involved smuggling along China's poorly defended coast. As trade was restricted, wokou smuggling networks filled the void and became integrated with Korean and Japanese trading networks, which helped them smuggle highly desirable goods in and out of Chinese ports. Illegal trading was profitable, which led to corruption of Chinese officials, who benefitted financially from a direct involvement with wokou, adding another layer of difficulty in enforcing the Ming sea bans. The fruits of illegal trade created significant unofficial trading channels with Japan, further angering the Ming, who wished to monopolize lucrative foreign trade through the tribute system.

Because Ningbo lay at the farthest end of the Silk Road, tribute missions to it were fabulously profitable endeavors. The immense potential for riches spurred daimyō to undertake trade missions to Ningbo with increasing frequency. Turmoil at the start of Shōgun Ashikaga Yoshiharu's reign led to a dispute over which Japanese clan had been awarded the official Ningbo trade license—with disastrous results for Chinese-Japanese trade relations. In 1523, competing daimyō from the Hosokawa and Ōuchi clans claimed the license to the official tribute mission. They each sent trading fleets with hundreds of armed men to Ningbo, the two fleets arriving within days of each other. Shortly thereafter, hostilities broke out between the rival clans, with the Ōuchi killing the head of the Hosokawa contingent and setting the Hosokawa ships ablaze. The fighting and destruction spilled over into the surrounding town and turned into a melee with the port authorities, destroying merchant shops and homes in the process. The resulting naval battle between the fleeing Ōuchi and Chinese authorities left Ningbo in flames and its Ming commander dead. The

Ningbo Incident, as it would later be called, resulted in a significant deterioration of diplomatic relations between China and Japan, ultimately leading to the closing of Ningbo to the Japanese and, by the end of the 1540s, elimination of tribute trade with Japan entirely.

The closing of Ningbo made sought-after Chinese luxuries and fragrant woods and aromatics more difficult to obtain, but the divine wind of the kamikaze again intervened. In 1543, a typhoon blew a Chinese junk en route to Ningbo out to sea. The ship eventually made landfall, battered and broken, on the Japanese island of Tanegashima off the southern tip of Kyūshū. In addition to the Chinese crew, onboard were Portuguese traders Antonio Mota and Francisco Zeimoto. The Portuguese had now been in China for nearly three decades, arriving shortly after Albuquerque took control of Malacca. By establishing permanent settlements with garrisoned fortresses at key ports, such as Goa in India and Malacca in the South Pacific, Albuquerque had sought to monopolize the lucrative maritime spice trade for Portugal. Malacca was ideal for this purpose. Strategically located, the port city controlled the Strait of Malacca that connected sea routes between the Indian Ocean to the west and the South China Sea to the east, through which all trade between East and West sailed.

Serving as the key point of distribution, Malacca welcomed North African, Arab, and Indian traders from Ormuz on the Red Sea, Aden on the Arabian Peninsula, and Calcutta in India, as well as traders arriving from points east—China, Borneo, Timor, and the Spice Islands of modern-day Indonesia. Prior to the discovery of the sea route around the Cape of Good Hope at the southernmost tip of Africa, spices were laboriously transported overland from India to European markets at a premium cost, leading to the Malay Peninsula being known by the ancient Greeks as the "Golden Peninsula." All manner of aromatics found only in the South Pacific were concentrated in Malacca's port: clove, nutmeg, mace, camphor, cinnamon, pepper, saffron, anise, cumin, and ginger as well as sandalwood from India and aloeswood from the six nations of the Rikkoku. Used in spiced wine, sweets, medicines, and incense, these aromatics were often exchanged by Malacca's merchants for simple, low-cost commodities such as rice, cotton, and copper. The aromatics were then shipped to points far and wide, and exchanged for gold, silver, gems, and silks, enriching those who traded them.

After Albuquerque garrisoned Malacca, fortifying it against counter-attack, he sent emissaries to Burma, Siam, Sumatra, and the Spice Islands to establish trade outposts. In November 1511, Albuquerque loaded the *Flor do Mar* (Flower of the Sea), a 400-ton Portuguese treasure ship armed with fifty guns, with his Malaccan spoils and sailed for Goa. However, the ship had experienced many repairs over its long service life and was difficult to maneuver when fully loaded. Shortly after setting sail, holds full of riches, the *Flor do Mar* was caught in a storm in the Strait of Malacca. It ran aground upon a shoal, split in two, and sank off the coast of Sumatra, taking down almost four hundred men with it. Albuquerque barely escaped with his life.

After Albuquerque's departure, the Portuguese continued to send envoys east from Malacca, and by 1517, had established a trading site at the Chinese city of Guangzhou, named Canton by the Portuguese. At Canton, the Portuguese faced stiff opposition by the Ming, who were not impressed by Portuguese cannon or pleased by the establishment of fortifications on Chinese soil. Branding the Portuguese as pirates, Ming forces sank two Portuguese ships and executed Portuguese envoys. Not until the 1540s were positive relations established between the Ming and the Portuguese, when the Portuguese aided the Ming in the suppression of wokou pirates along their southern coast. The Chinese allowed the Portuguese to establish a permanent settlement at Macau as long as no fortifications were constructed, and granted them the lucrative opportunity of spending several weeks a year at the silk trade fairs held in Canton each January and June. Trading for Chinese silks, porcelain, and gold, the Portuguese provided China with silver, spices, and aromatic woods from India and Southeast Asia. Thus establishing a maritime trading route, Portuguese ships made a two-year round-trip journey from Lisbon, Portugal, around the Cape of Good Hope off the southern tip of Africa, on to Goa on the western coast of India, then to Malacca and the Spice Islands in Indonesia, and finally ending in Macau at the end of the Silk Road in southern China.

But when Mota and Zeimoto accidentally landed on Tanegashima, it wasn't the opportunity for trade the Japanese saw. Beside the novelty of strangely dressed foreigners, what caught the attention of the Japanese were the Portuguese weapons. Demonstrating their matchlock arquebuses for the lords of Tanegashima, Mota and Zeimoto fascinated the Japanese with a weapon that could accurately fire lead shot farther than the reach of the samurai's bow and arrow. Gunpowder and iron weapons were familiar to the Japanese by the time of Mota and Zeimoto's demonstrations, as Chinese *teppō* (鉄砲, iron cannon) had been utilized in Japan for two centuries by warring daimyō, but the Portuguese matchlock was much lighter and easier to aim. When their ship was eventually repaired and able to set sail for China, before they departed, Mota and Zeimoto presented two muskets as gifts to extremely happy Tanegashima lords.

The Japanese on Tanegashima immediately set their local ironsmiths to replicating the weapons. Within a year, Japanese ironsmiths had learned how to reproduce the Portuguese weapons and had begun making improvements to them. The Portuguese teppō would come to be known as *tanegashima* (種子島) for the Japanese island where they were first demonstrated. Within fifty years, batteries of *teppō ashigaru* (鉄砲足軽), foot soldiers armed with tanegashima, would be well established in samurai armies in numbers that far exceeded their European contemporaries, serving as devastating additions to the forces of daimyō vying for control of Japan.

After their accidental landing at Tanegashima, the Portuguese quickly returned to Japan to set up trade operations and Jesuit missionaries at the port of Hirado on Hirado Island in the northwest of Kyūshū. Hirado had become the port of call for wokou pirates and was a center for goods smuggled from Chinese ports. Serving as intermediaries between the Portuguese traders and their eager Japanese hosts, the Jesuits used the allure of lucrative Portuguese trade as a conduit to introduce Christianity throughout Japan. By 1548, the venerated Jesuit missionary Francis Xavier traveled to Japan, writing in a letter to Rome, "All the Portuguese merchants coming from Japan tell me that if I go there I shall do great service for God our Lord, more than with the pagans of India, for they are a very reasonable people." Regarding science and religion, Xavier noted, "They listened to us most eagerly, and appeared delighted to hear us, regarding us with profound respect as extremely learned persons. This idea of our great knowledge opened the way to us for sowing the seed of religion in their mind."

At first, due to translation issues and Christianity being explained through the lens of Buddhism, many early Japanese converts viewed Christianity as just another sect of Buddhism. In time and with "great labor," as Xavier put it, the central teachings of Christianity were translated into Japanese and read aloud in the streets as well as in audiences with the missionaries' host daimyō. The first daimyō to convert to Christianity was Ōmura Sumitada, who after his baptism took the Christian name Dom Bartolomeu. Sumitada was a minor daimyō who ruled a portion of Hizen Province overlooking Ōmura Bay, which was located to the south of Hirado Island. The Ōmura were increasingly under threat from the more powerful Ryūzōji, who were intent on expanding their domain. In 1561, as sharing the port city of Hirado with wokou pirates had become too dangerous, the Portuguese began to look for a safer harbor from which to base their Japanese trading operations. Seeing a chance to make powerful allies and lure a profitable trading partner to his domain, Sumitada assured the Portuguese safety in the domain of the Ōmura, first offering the port of Yokoseura and then, after Yokoseura was destroyed by anti-Christian forces, opening Nagasaki as a trading hub. Additionally, Sumitada vowed not only to convert to Christianity but to require all his retainers and subjects to do so as well. Favorably impressed, the Portuguese moved their trading operations to Nagasaki. There the Jesuits worked with Sumitada to transform the quiet fishing village into a thriving hub of European trade and a base for their Jesuit mission in Japan. The Ryūzōji attacked Nagasaki in 1578, but the Portuguese, with their superior weapons, aided the Ōmura in driving them back, thus cementing the relationship. As a reward, Nagasaki was declared sovereign soil under a grant giving control to the Jesuits. That control would last until 1586.

The Portuguese saw a lucrative opportunity in the Chinese trade embargo of Japan, and actively sought to capitalize on it. Nagasaki quickly became the Portuguese's primary port of call at the end of the sea route between Lisbon and the Far East. From Nagasaki, the Portuguese served as a go-between for trade with China, increasing the flow of much-desired Chinese goods through annual voyages rather than the official ten-year increments of Chinese tribute missions. The Portuguese also brought with them riches in the form of fragrant aromatics and large quantities of aloeswood and sandalwood from the six nations of the Rikkoku. Portuguese ships with their massive holds dwarfed Chinese and Japanese trading vessels. And rather than the small amounts typically imported by Japanese and Chinese traders, Portuguese manifests of that time detail cargoes that included hundreds of pounds of rare fragrant woods and significant quantities of aromatic spices. In Nagasaki, the Portuguese traded aromatic spices and fragrant woods from Malacca and silks and porcelains from China for painted screens, kimonos, lacquerware, and swords, but it was Japanese silver they sought most. On their return voyage to Lisbon, the Portuguese traded Japanese silver, highly desired by the Ming, for Chinese silks, tea, porcelain, gold, and gems, which were then shipped to Portugal. From Nagasaki, Chinese goods, aromatic spices, and fragrant woods were distributed to Japanese ports like Sakai, where merchants became wealthy selling them to samurai lords eager to possess such precious items.

However, not all cargo carried by the Portuguese was so welcome. On their return journey to Goa, Portuguese ships also carried slaves, including Japanese and Chinese women and children sold by kidnappers. Although the Jesuits in charge of Nagasaki turned a blind eye to the practice, it did not go unnoticed by the Japanese or the Ming. Originally, the Japanese had referred to traders arriving by sea from southern China as *nanban* (南蛮, southern barbarians). Soon the Portuguese would assume this label, and trade with all Westerners would come to be known as nanban trade. The Portuguese practice of transporting slaves would also earn them the label *gaijin* (外人), meaning "foreigner not of Asian descent" but with the overtone of "outsider not to be trusted."

Seeking to monopolize the trading opportunity Japan represented, once a year Portugal's King John III awarded a single nobleman the rights to trade with Japan. The Portuguese trading ships used for these annual voyages were a combination of cargo ship and war vessel. Known as carracks, these immense ships featured much heavier armaments and greater ocean-going capabilities than Chinese or Japanese trade vessels, which were a fraction of the size. The Japanese referred to the Portuguese carracks as *kurofune* (黒船, black ships) because of their blackened exteriors, treated with pitch to deter the growth of the marine worms that would feast on the wooden hulls. Capable of carrying hundreds of tons of cargo over vast distances upon the open seas, Portuguese carracks were able to deliver an immense amount of treasure and defend it from any pirate vessel that might threaten them.

As Japan assumed a lucrative and important role at the eastern end of the Maritime Silk Road, aromatic spices and fragrant woods from the holds of Portuguese black ships increasingly found their way into the tearooms and Kōdō ceremonies of the Imperial Court and the daimyō fighting for control of Japan. The nanban trade with the Portuguese provided Japan significant quantities of fragrant woods and aromatic spices for nearly a century, satiating the samurai's increasing desire for these items and enriching the merchant classes of Nagasaki and Sakai.

Over the following centuries, Malacca would change hands between successive European colonizers, from the Portuguese to the Dutch to the British. Malacca eventually became a backwater port, its harbor silted to the point it could no longer accommodate large vessels, and the British relocated trade to Singapore, which would go on to become one of the busiest ports in the world. Now a burgeoning tourist destination, Malacca was designated a UNESCO World Heritage site in 2008 for its important role in maritime trade. Linking the Indian Ocean and South China Sea, the Strait of Malacca remains the shortest shipping route between East and West and is one of the most important shipping lanes in the world—on par with the Suez and Panama Canals—with over fifty thousand ships a year passing through its waters. It is believed that when Afonso de Albuquerque's *Flor do Mar* broke up and sank, it was carrying, among its Malaccan riches, eighty tons of gold, two hundred chests of gems, and four life-sized gold lions. Treasure hunters and historians value the treasure, none of which has ever been found, at more than $3 billion.

CHAPTER 9

織田 信長

ODA NOBUNAGA
Tea, incense, and power

UNDER THE COVER OF THUNDERCLAPS AND DRIVING RAIN, ODA
Nobunaga's troops stealthily worked their way down the rain-
soaked slopes of the forested hills surrounding the camp of
the Imagawa. The invasion of Owari Province in 1560 by Imagawa
Yoshimoto was yet another example of larger, more powerful clans
seeking to seize the lands of their smaller neighbors during the civil war
of the Sengoku period. Given that the Imagawa were a larger and far
superior force to the Oda, with the strength of twenty-five thousand
soldiers under Yoshimoto to fewer than two thousand ashigaru and
a handful of samurai under Nobunaga, the eventual outcome was all
but assured. After the success of the morning's initial battle, Yoshimoto
pitched camp to ride out the storm, passing the time with a victory
feast and *kubi-jikken* (首実検), a viewing ceremony of the severed
heads of the vanquished samurai taken earlier that day.

Yet after more than a hundred years of civil war, the practice of gekokujō saw "the low topple the high" with increasing frequency and ferocity. As the rain poured down and Yoshimoto sat with his commanders viewing the severed heads of his enemies, Oda Nobunaga unleashed a surprise attack. In what is known as the Battle of Okehazama, Oda Nobunaga's men cut down Yoshimoto and routed the Imagawa army in a stunning victory, elevating Nobunaga from a minor lord of a small farming province to a major regional daimyō of legendary status. The stunning defeat of the Imagawa at Okehazama set in motion the eventual unification of Japan by Oda Nobunaga, Toyotomi Hideyoshi, and Tokugawa Ieyasu. The pursuit of one Japan took place not only on the battlefield, however, but also within the tatami rooms where Chadō and Kōdō were performed. In his march to dominance, Nobunaga seized on tea and incense not only as expressions of art but also as statements of his authority and power.

Born in 1534 as the second son of Oda Nobuhide, a minor daimyō of Owari Province near present-day Nagoya, Oda Nobunaga was not his father's favorite. Those in the Oda clan knew that Nobuhide had a clear preference for his first-born son, Oda Nobuhiro, but due to the boy's illegitimacy, he was required to name Nobunaga as his heir. The tension this created between father and son forged in Nobunaga a disdain for tradition that was matched only by his contempt for his father.

Seen as impetuous, reckless, rude, and disgraceful, Nobunaga cemented his moniker as the "Fool of Owari" at his father's funeral by acting dishonorably, attending dressed in his daily clothes—dirty from travel and with only a simple rope sash and unkempt hair—rather than formal dress. During the funeral, he disrespectfully threw incense at the altar, shocking those in attendance. His outlandish behavior drove his mentor and senior retainer, Hirate Masahide, to perform a special type of ritual suicide meant to shame Nobunaga into reform. But even Masahide's *seppuku* (切腹) would not alter Nobunaga's unconventional nature.

Nobunaga's lack of faithful obedience to tradition influenced his rise to power and provided an edge in overcoming his rivals. Like many daimyō of the time, Nobunaga was ambitious, but he augmented his ambition with innovation on a scale rarely employed by his contemporaries. He had a keen interest in nanban trade, Western ideas, and Portuguese weapons, which he put to novel use in his conquest of Japan. For example, he employed teppō ashigaru, foot soldiers armed with Portuguese-derived matchlock arquebuses, in ranked "firing squads" three squads deep. As one squad fired, the other two reloaded, resulting in a devastating rate of fire, unrivaled not only in Japan but by European armies of the time as well. Applying the powerful effects of Portuguese weapons to those who stood in his way, Nobunaga was also known to wear Portuguese nanban armor capable of stopping the arquebus bullets employed in his own tactics. Unconventionally, he surrounded himself with a retinue of junior retainers who had proved themselves in his service, some even from the lower classes, and encouraged his generals to provide their honest opinions rather than sycophantic obeisance. He also courted Christianity to his own advantage, believing that the nanban religion taught passivity, nonviolence, and obedience to authority—qualities in stark contrast to the militant beliefs of the Ikkō-ikki (一向一揆), the warrior monks who stood defiantly in his path.

But the Fool of Owari had an even darker side. European missionaries described Nobunaga as short-tempered and cruel, rarely showing mercy to his enemies, especially those of his own family. When his younger brother Noboyuki plotted against him, Nobunaga feigned his own death to lure his brother to his bedside. Once there, Nobunaga sat up abruptly, thus signaling one of his retainers to assassinate the horrified Nobuyuki right in front of him. In another example, after convincing his brother-in-law to safely return his sister to him during the Siege of Odani Castle, Nobunaga forced him to commit seppuku, then removed his head from his neck and had it pickled, displaying it during future New Year celebrations as a warning to those who might harbor thoughts about betraying him. Before returning, his sister had hidden the couple's infant son to protect him from Nobunaga's retribution, and after regaining her trust, Nobunaga coaxed the location of the boy from her. Much to his sister's horror, he then immediately had the child executed and the child's head displayed on a stake.

Nobunaga's personal seal from 1567 onward was inscribed with the words *"tenka fubu"* (天下布武)—"rule by military force"— which was brutally illustrated by his march to unify the nation. To the Jesuits, he seemed driven to merciless cruelty toward Buddhist monks. He underscored this reputation in 1574 with his destruction of the Nagashima compound on Mount Hiei, which was held by the militant monks of the Ikkō-ikki, who had opposed him for years. Unable to take the compound through force of arms, as the Ikkō-ikki employed nanban firearms from well-fortified positions, Nobunaga surrounded the compound and on a windy day ordered it set ablaze, incinerating over ten thousand men, women, and children. Any who escaped the flames were shot down by Nobunaga's teppō ashigaru.

Along with nanban firearms, tea and incense found their way to the center of Nobunaga's political strategy. In 1568, Nobunaga entered Kyoto, defeating the Miyoshi clan, who were in control of a puppet shōgun they had installed through assassination. Nobunaga replaced the Miyoshi puppet with his own, the fifteenth Ashikaga shōgun, Ashikaga Yoshiaki. Yoshiaki immediately set about seeking retribution for the assassination of his brother, demanding the head of Matsunaga Hisahide. Seeking to avoid Yoshiaki's wrath, Hisahide sought Nobunaga's lenience not only by pledging his armed forces and knowledge of the Miyoshi clan in service to Nobunaga, but also by giving him an exceptional, square-shouldered, dark reddish-brown glazed ceramic tea caddy.

Named Hatsuhana (初花), meaning "first flower of the season," by Shōgun Ashikaga Yoshimasa, this tea caddy was a type of *tsukumo-gami* (付喪神), an object over one hundred years old, believed to be given a soul for its service, thus becoming an almost supernatural object. Exquisitely made by skilled Chinese artisans, Hatsuhana was extremely delicate, with construction so accomplished that its sides were only millimeters thick, exceptional even by modern standards. Hatsuhana was one of the *katatsuki* (肩衝, square-shouldered tea caddies) considered the three great tea caddies of the world, Narashiba and Nitta being the other two. These three tea caddies were *meibutsu* (名物, famous, highly prized objects) considered more valuable than an entire fiefdom. It was believed that anyone who possessed all three tea caddies would possess enough wealth to rule the whole of Japan. Not only did this gift cause Nobunaga to spare Hisahide's life, it lit in him a spark that would grow into a full passion for tea culture and the collection of exquisite meibutsu.

By the time Nobunaga took Kyoto, the trading port of Sakai had become the center of the Chadō universe. Although the merchants who prospered in Sakai were considered the lowest of social classes, they were also one of the wealthiest, affording them considerable influence as well as access to meibutsu tea implements through their direct connection with nanban trade from Nagasaki. Considered "parasites" under the Confucian worldview because they produced nothing yet made their fortunes off the efforts of others, merchants were restricted by law from flaunting their wealth. But as meibutsu and fragrant woods were valuable imports, it was in the trading port of Sakai that they were concentrated. Nobunaga coveted not only the rich imports of the Sakai merchants, but also their wealth and trade connections—the ones he needed to keep his army supplied with gunpowder and military wares.

In 1569, Nobunaga imposed a military tax levy of 20,000 *kan* on the wealthy port city, including a thinly veiled threat of consequences for not meeting his demand. This was a significant sum, as 20,000 kan was the equivalent of 5,000 *koku* (斛), enough rice to feed five thousand people for one year. A feudal lord was considered a daimyō when he had an annual income of 10,000 koku. To resist Nobunaga's demand, members of Sakai's town council initially sought an alliance with the Myoshi clan. But knowing that Sakai stood no chance against Nobunaga's armies, the wealthy merchant Imai Sōkyū quickly offered to serve as liaison between the council and Nobunaga. Sōkyū was known as one of the great tea masters of Sakai, having served as an attendant to Shōgun Ashikaga Yoshiaki in performance of the tea ceremony. He had built his wealth as a supplier of military leather goods, which established relationships for him with daimyō of the period, adding another layer of value for Nobunaga's interest. Acting as intermediary, Sōkyū held a tea gathering for Nobunaga and his retinue, using the tranquil setting to avoid conflict. The event culminated with Sōkyū gifting Nobunaga a rare and valuable meibutsu tea kettle and a collection of tea implements from Ming China. Deeply impressed by Sōkyū's grace and elegance in performance of the tea ceremony, not to mention the value of Sōkyū's meibutsu gift, Nobunaga spared Sakai, awarded Sōkyū a fief with an annual 2,200 koku rice yield, and dedicated himself to employing chanoyu strategically in his march to unify Japan under one sword.

Nobunaga appreciated the aesthetic value of chanoyu, but he also realized the strategic opportunity presented by tea gatherings. At tea gatherings the social classes could more freely mix, allowing strategic alliances both clandestine and overt to be forged. As it required significant wealth to acquire the fine tea utensils and rare fragrant woods employed at such events, these gatherings often attracted wealthy merchants and influential individuals who could afford such luxuries. Such individuals often possessed access to lucrative trading networks or other strategic assets that could be advantageous to Nobunaga's military goals. In what would come to be known as *o-chanoyu-goseido* (御茶湯御政道, tea ceremony government), in a strategic masterstroke, Nobunaga brought together renowned tea masters, influential merchants, and rare meibutsu, placing chanoyu at the center of a powerful system capable of uniting Japan under his rule.

Rare and exquisite tea utensils and the knowledge of how to skillfully perform chanoyu were prerequisites for tea gatherings that would attract and impress those most influential. To address utensils, Nobunaga ordered a "hunt" for rare and famous meibutsu, amassing an impressive collection through payment, coercion, and military force. Known as *meibutsu-gari* (名物狩り), the compulsory collection of meibutsu served multiple purposes in advancing Nobunaga's rise. First, it illustrated Nobunaga's wealth and power, as the greater his collection of meibutsu, the greater his ability to impress and woo influential guests. Second, Nobunaga's order of meibutsu-gari increased the demand for rare tea paraphernalia, causing the value of such items to increase dramatically. This, in turn, enhanced the value of Nobunaga's collection, further increasing his wealth, status, and power. Meibutsu displayed at Nobunaga's tea gatherings were objects of incredible wealth and status, often reaching values greater than that of entire fiefdoms. Nobunaga used this opulence to inspire loyalty by gifting retainers, merchants, and generals with meibutsu, further cementing his influence as supreme in all of Japan. Finally, by exhausting the supply of available meibutsu, Nobunaga deprived his rivals of the wealth and power meibutsu offered—power that went beyond monetary value. The relationships developed through collecting meibutsu from individuals with rich trade networks and other strategic advantages limited rival clans' access to those networks—which they, too, needed to supply their armies—while at the same time depriving them of the ability to reward those in their service with meibutsu of significant value or pedigree.

To address the knowledge required to skillfully perform the tea ceremony, Nobunaga sought out the preeminent tea masters of his time, learning how to perform the tea ceremony himself in an effort to persuade them to ally themselves with him. Through his efforts and, no doubt, the allure of his unprecedented collection of meibutsu, by 1573, Nobunaga employed the three greatest tea masters of Sakai: Imai Sōkyū, Tsuda Sōgyū, and Sen Rikyū. Nobunaga leveraged their knowledge and reputation in performance of Chadō to attract wealthy and influential individuals to his tea gatherings, impressing them with his display of wealth and power, and enticing them to ally themselves to his cause and cease their support of his rivals.

Of the three tea masters, Rikyū would go on to become the most revered in Japan, influencing all aspects of the tea ceremony and shaping chanoyu into what it remains today. Rikyū defined chanoyu's aesthetic, returning it to Murata Jukō's embrace of wabi-cha's deliberate simplicity, appreciation for aged and imperfect patinas, use of Japanese ceramics, and direct ties to nature. He redesigned the architecture of the tea house, surrounding it with a tea garden filled with a lush natural landscape through which participants would pass, and shrinking the chashitsu to as little as two tatami mats in size, with a small, low door that required participants to bow down or crawl through, humbling all who entered. Rikyū wrote extensively about all aspects of environment, etiquette, and technique associated with the tea ceremony, from how the garden path led to the tea house, to how meibutsu was displayed in the tokonoma in the shoin, to the spirit of the tea master in preparing tea. These writings still form the basis for the tea ceremony and continue to be taught in schools of chanoyu today.

Rikyū built upon Takeno Jōō's ichiza konryū, that spirit of group unity and harmony, and emphasized the ephemeral nature of an event that would never be repeated. The uniqueness of the items displayed in the tokonoma, the quality of the tea and incense chosen, the rarity of the meibutsu employed, and the skill of the tea master's performance all were intended to elevate these events. Yamanoue Sōji, a student of Rikyū, wrote in his notes on the tea ceremony, "Treat your host as if the meeting were going to occur only once in your life." Later referred to as *ichigo ichie* (一期一会), the popular saying can now be found displayed in tea shops and tearooms throughout Japan.

During these extraordinary occasions, which lasted many hours and sometimes even days, guests worked their way through a choreographed dance between reception hall, tea garden, and chashitsu. They enjoyed savoring multi-course meals, imbibing exceptional sake, and listening to rare jinkō, and they were ritually served both thin and thick tea with *wagashi* (和菓子), sweets specially prepared to balance the bitterness of powdered matcha tea. The greater the reputation of the tea master, the rarer the meibutsu on display, the more extravagant the various stages of the event, the higher the quality of tea and incense employed, the greater the significance the event would achieve. Nobunaga viewed these tea gatherings as so important that he granted permission to host such events to only a small number of his most trusted subordinates, and gaining permission was considered a great honor.

Incense, *kō* (香), was indispensable to the tea ceremony, and Rikyū was exacting about its use and display. Incense was burned in the shoin for purification and to set the tone for the event as guests arrived. The tea master carefully selected the incense to highlight the season in which the tea gathering was held, and it was lit within a *kōro* (香炉, incense burner) chosen to emphasize the theme of the event. In the chashitsu tokonoma, a scroll featuring calligraphy or a sumi painting of nature that emphasized the event theme was typically displayed with a seasonal flower arrangement to its left and a specially chosen *kōgō* (香合, small incense container) to its right.

Considered an important tea implement, the kōgō held three pieces of incense carefully chosen by the tea master. Made of ceramic, wood, bamboo, or other material, kōgō came in all styles, from simple design to highly ornate patterned lacquerware, and used motifs that included everything from animals to flowers to figurines. Carefully chosen to reflect the season and event theme, the kōgō was a symbol of great importance presented for the guests to admire. The specific placement of kōgō was described in detail by Rikyū, who noted exact measurements for its placement in relation to the hanging scroll in the tokonoma.

During the ceremonial arrangement of charcoal used to boil water for tea, one piece of incense from the kōgō was placed in the center of the coals to create an immediate release of fragrance. A second piece was placed on the periphery of the coals to create a gradual, long-lasting fragrance as it warmed while the tea was prepared. The third piece of incense remained in the kōgō for the possibility of appreciating the incense after the tea ceremony had ended. As an alternative to the pieces of incense placed in the coals, a specially selected kōro would be displayed in the tokonoma; for this practice, Rikyū emphasized the need for the kōro to always be filled with burning incense, as that was the kōro's nature.

The seasons guided the tea master's choice of fragrance, with lighter, sweeter floral fragrances used for spring and summer, and heavier, woody tones chosen for fall and winter. The form of incense would often change with the season as well, with nerikō (kneaded incense) selected for the warmer months and kōboku (fragrant wood), usually jinkō or kyara, in the cooler months. Incense was burned in the coals while preparing water for tea, in a *kikigōro* (聞香炉, listening incense burner), or more commonly in an ornate kōro meant for display on a tray specifically designed for presentation, with the kōro often being meibutsu. One of the most famous meibutsu kōro was the Chidori-kōro (千鳥香炉), a kikigōro passed down to Rikyū from Takeno Jōō. Featuring three symbolic feet and a low palm rest for more comfortable support while listening to incense, the Chidori-kōro was a celadon-glazed ceramic kōro with a flat, dark lid, created in thirteenth-century Song Dynasty China. The lid concealed special monkō ash and was adorned with a *chidori* (千鳥, plover, a type of coastal bird) figurine that served as a handle and from which its name was derived.

Much like meibutsu, meikō, those rare pieces of aloeswood that had been given names, were desired for both their fragrance and their exceptional value. Meikō were highly sought-after collectables and often some of the most prized spoils of battle. A gathering in which one of these rare pieces of jinkō or kyara might be listened to was a highly anticipated, once-in-a-lifetime event that presented a coveted opportunity to significantly enhance the status of the host. No greater or more prestigious piece of meikō existed than Ranjatai, the legendary piece of jinkō that drifted ashore on Awaji Island in 595. Nearly one thousand years later, Ranjatai remained safely under imperial seal, locked within the Shōsō-in Repository.

As Nobunaga was not of Minamoto descent, he could not be named shōgun. Instead, he had Ashikaga Yoshiaki named to the position, planning to rule from behind the scenes of his puppet's bakufu government. Before long, though, Yoshiaki chafed at the arrangement and sought to free himself from Nobunaga's control, repeatedly plotting rebellion against him with rival daimyō and the Ikkō-ikki. After a series of betrayals, in 1573, Nobunaga removed Yoshiaki from the office of shōgun, exiling him from the capital; never allowed to return, Yoshiaki would eventually die in obscurity. By effectively ending the 237-year Ashikaga shōgunate, Nobunaga had seized the power of the shōgunate even without the desired title. He then sought to have this power acknowledged by making a shocking request of Emperor Ōgimachi: Nobunaga demanded the doors of the Shōsō-in be unsealed to allow a piece of the legendary Ranjatai to be cut for him, thereby forcing the emperor to acknowledge his status as supreme in Japan, with or without the title of shōgun.

The request is said to have outraged Emperor Ōgimachi. Ranjatai was an imperial treasure under the direct purview of the emperor. Only once, one hundred years prior, had such a gift been given—when Emperor Go-Tsuchimikado presented a piece of Ranjatai to Shōgun Ashikaga Yoshimasa. Since then, no emperor had broken Shōsō-in's imperial seal. To this point, Ōgimachi had been seen as having Nobunaga's favor, and his Imperial Court had benefitted from Nobunaga's support, as it helped reverse the court's failing fortunes. But by 1573, Nobunaga's military grip on Japan had tightened and the relationship had become more antagonistic. Nobunaga began to call for Ōgimachi's abdication. Unable to risk a confrontation with

Nobunaga's military might, Ōgimachi reluctantly consented to his request for a piece of Ranjatai.

In March 1574, surrounded by a guard of three thousand soldiers, Nobunaga traveled to Tamonyama Castle to await the presentation of Ranjatai. Shōsō-in was unsealed, and the emperor's incense was retrieved and carefully transported to Tamonyama, where it was displayed in the castle's reception hall. Capitalizing on the rare experience, Nobunaga encouraged his entourage to view the famous fragrant log, gifting them with a memory they would tell their descendants. Dressed in priestly ceremonial white robes, Todai-ji's sculptor of Buddhist images ritually cut two small pieces from the treasured fragrant log, directly to the left of where the piece had been cut for Ashikaga Yoshimasa. Nobunaga kept one piece and, following the precedent set by Ashikaga Yoshimasa, told Ranjatai's attendants that the other was to be given to Emperor Ōgimachi.

Symbolically, this was a coup for Nobunaga, as it forced the emperor to acknowledge that he was shōgun in all but name, and it demonstrated to all that his power was so absolute that the emperor himself could not resist him. However, Nobunaga would keep only a small amount of Ranjatai for himself. Shortly after collecting the prized aloeswood, he held a tea gathering at Shokoku-ji Temple in Kyoto to show off the new crown jewel in his collection. During the extravagant event, from atop his fan, he presented Tsuda Sōgyū, who had first introduced him to Chadō, and Sen Rikyū, his preeminent tea master, with pieces of Ranjatai for their loyal service, astonishing the two men with such a priceless gift. Regardless of how much wealth or status they had achieved, for two men from the lowest social class to receive a piece of Ranjatai from the imperial treasury was unthinkable. But with his gift, Nobunaga had again demonstrated to all present that he alone was the supreme authority in Japan and that allying with him had benefits none other could equal.

In 1579, the construction of Oda Nobunaga's retirement castle, Azuchi-jo, was completed on the eastern shore of Lake Biwa. Azuchi Castle was an impressive military stronghold strategically located on the northeastern approach to Kyoto, yet outside the political and sometimes literal fires that raged within the capital's borders. Having subdued his rivals in the east and solidified his control over Kyoto, the only significant resistance to Nobunaga's complete domination of Japan rested with the Mori clan in the west. To subdue this remaining threat, in 1582, Nobunaga dispatched two armies under the control of Toyotomi Hideyoshi and Akechi Mitsuhide. Hideyoshi was the first to decisively engage the Mori and, quickly gaining the upper hand, sent word to Nobunaga that if he sent reinforcements, the Mori could be crushed once and for all.

Sensing a final victory in his quest to unite Japan, Nobunaga chose to leave the safety of Azuchi to personally lead his army to triumph. Lagging his army and protected by only a handful of guardsmen on his march west, Nobunaga stopped for the night in Kyoto, his affinity for chanoyu drawing him to a tea ceremony at Honnō-ji temple. Learning this, Mitsuhide turned east and marched his troops through the night to Kyoto. Upon crossing the Katsura River on Kyoto's western boundary, Mitsuhide announced, "The enemy awaits at Honnō-ji!" and unleashed his troops on the exposed Nobunaga. On the morning of June 21, 1582, the few guards with Nobunaga were overwhelmed and Honnō-ji encircled. Knowing his end was at hand, Nobunaga ordered the temple set ablaze, denying his betrayer not only his head but also the precious collection of tea implements and incense woods that had traveled with him from Azuchi. As the temple burned to the ground, Nobunaga and his attendants committed seppuku and were consumed by the flames, their bodies never to be recovered. Throughout Kyoto, assassinations of Nobunaga's son and heir as well as other leading retainers were carried out, and the tumultuous morning quickly ended in victory for Mitsuhide.

Learning of Mitsuhide's treachery and recognizing the power vacuum Nobunaga's death created, Hideyoshi quickly negotiated peace with the Mori and turned his men east in an all-night march back to Kyoto, joining forces with Nobunaga's third son, Oda Nobutada. Five days after Nobunaga's assassination, Hideyoshi's forces quickly routed Mitsuhide's at the Battle of Yamazaki. Mitsuhide escaped the battle, only to be killed by local bandits a short time later as he fled.

With Nobunaga's death avenged, Hideyoshi was poised to fill the void left by the death of his greatest benefactor. In life, Nobunaga had used aloeswood to demonstrate his authority and power and, in a display of his dominance, had forced the emperor himself to allow Nobunaga to cut a piece of the legendary Ranjatai. Since Nobunaga's body had been consumed by the flames of Honnō-ji, for ceremonial cremation, Hideyoshi substituted two life-sized statues of Nobunaga carved from rare aloeswood. The ethereal fragrance of jinkō is said to have filled the entire capital on the day of the ceremony, emphasizing Nobunaga's power even in death.

Oda Nobunaga's place in history as the first of Japan's unifiers continues to resonate deeply in Japanese culture to this day. At Kenkun-jinja (Kenkun Shintō Shrine) in Kyoto, every year on October 19, the anniversary of the day Nobunaga first entered the city in 1568, the Funaoka Matsuri (Funaoka Grand Festival) celebrates the contributions of Nobunaga in unifying Japan. Constructed in the Shintō *nagare-zukuri* (流造, streamlined roof) architectural style, the shrine features a large stone that marks the entrance to its sacred space. The stone is engraved with a passage from the Noh drama *Atsumori* (敦盛), a story from the *Heike Monogatari* that became a favored play of the time, with famous lines that Nobunaga is said to have quoted on the morning of the Battle of Okehazama:

> *A man's life of fifty years under the sky is nothing compared to the age of this world.*
> *Life is but a fleeting dream, an illusion—*
> *Is there anything that lasts forever?*

CHAPTER 10

鎖国令

SAKOKU-REI

A new golden age of incense

AS THE FRAGRANCE OF JINKŌ FILLED KYOTO IN TRIBUTE TO Oda Nobunaga, the question of who would fill the power vacuum created by his death left the political landscape of Kyoto unstable. Nobunaga's two most trusted generals, Toyotomi Hideyoshi and Tokugawa Ieyasu, evenly matched yet polar opposites, occupied the strongest positions for filling the void. After generations of civil war, patience as much as bloodshed would unite Japan under one banner, ushering in a great peace and a new political center that even the emperor was powerless to resist. As Japan closed its borders to Western influence, a cultural revival modeled on the Heian court reinvigorated the geidō, propelling the refined art of Kōdō to its zenith and creating a new golden age of incense that reverberates to this day.

In the wake of Oda Nobunaga's assassination, the fragile unification of Japan he had begun was thrown into doubt, placing his two most powerful generals at odds for control of his legacy. Toyotomi Hideyoshi and Tokugawa Ieyasu had completely contrasting backgrounds. Hideyoshi was believed to be the son of a peasant ashigaru, and at a young age, he ran away from his father's farm to seek his fortune with up-and-coming daimyō like Nobunaga. The quintessential example of gekokujō, through raw talent, ambition, and a well-connected marriage, Hideyoshi raised himself from holding the lowest position as Nobunaga's sandal bearer to holding one of the highest as his senior military advisor.

Tokugawa Ieyasu's background could not have been more different. Born the son of prominent daimyō Matsudaira Hirotada of the bountiful rice-farming Mikawa Province, at the age of six, Ieyasu was offered as a hostage to the Imagawa clan to support a military alliance. Raised by Imagawa Yoshimoto, Ieyasu was educated in the ways of the refined arts and learned the literary and military arts under the training of Rinzai Zen warrior-monks, as was befitting of a samurai lord-in-waiting. Seeing the impressive rise of Oda Nobunaga, Ieyasu became an early ally, protecting Nobunaga's eastern flank while parlaying his support into the steady expansion of his own domain.

After a tense period that saw the two men lead armies into battle against one another, Hideyoshi and Ieyasu made peace, neither wanting to waste the strength required to overcome the other. As a gift, Ieyasu presented Hideyoshi with Nobunaga's famous meibutsu tea caddie, Hatsuhana. Miraculously, Hatsuhana had been recovered from the ashes at Honnō-ji and acquired by Ieyasu. By gifting Hideyoshi with Nobunaga's most prized possession, the political symbolism of Ieyasu's submission was clear, and in 1585, Hideyoshi assumed Nobunaga's mantle as de facto ruler of Japan.

With the fighting for domination largely concluded, Hideyoshi set about strengthening his control of Japan through a series of shuin-jō (朱印状, red-seal edicts) that enacted sweeping societal reforms. In 1588, one of the red-seal edicts, the Taiko no katana-gari (太閤の刀狩り, Taiko Sword Hunt), strictly forbade the possession of "long swords, short swords, bows, spears, muskets, or any form of weapon" by any class other than the samurai, thereby disarming the lower classes. In 1591, the Mibun Tōsei Rei (身分統制令, Social Status Control Order), known as the Separation Edict, ended the social upheaval of gekokujō by permanently freezing the social classes of all Japanese, establishing a rigid class order based on the Confucian *shi-nō-kō-shō* (士農工商) system. The four social classes of warrior (*shi*), farmer (*nō*), artisan (*kō*), and merchant (*shō*) were made permanent, restricting a person born to a samurai family to being a samurai, and one born to a peasant farmer to being a farmer. There was to be no changing of profession, no dual roles in society, no movement between the classes. The resulting fixed social status meant the samurai, often farmers when not fighting, were now divorced from their lands and made solely dependent for their existence upon the annual koku stipends of the lords they served. As the prime example of gekokujō, having risen from the lowest of social classes to become the ruler of Japan, Hideyoshi with his red-seal edicts paradoxically closed the door to anyone who might follow in his footsteps and rise to power.

Although they may have made peace, Hideyoshi was not about to have his eastern flank under the control of a powerful daimyō who had expressed his own thoughts of ruling Japan. Reallocating the Tokugawa holdings to his own loyal supporters, Hideyoshi removed Ieyasu and his retainers from their ancestral homelands in the Mikawa Province, which was strategically and economically important due to its lands and key castles that controlled the eastern approach to Kyoto. The entire Tokugawa household was uprooted, and Ieyasu's domain was relocated to Edo, a small backwater fishing village on the Kantō Plain far to the east, where any threat from Ieyasu would be minimized.

Constructed in 1457, Edo Castle kept watch over the sleepy village. Well past its glory days, the dilapidated castle was worn from siege, its roof leaking and its main gates fashioned from cast-off timbers from an old ship. Nicknamed "the Badger" for his legendary patience, Ieyasu moved to Edo on August 1, 1590, and biding his time, set about rebuilding Edo Castle and developing the surrounding town. Capitalizing on Hideyoshi's red-seal edicts that separated samurai from the land, Ieyasu stationed living quarters of retainers and guardsmen in close proximity to the castle rather than in their own fiefs, eliminating having to mobilize them from the countryside in time of need. This innovative approach not only increased the military readiness of his army but also made his retainers even more dependent upon the annual koku stipends Ieyasu paid, further ensuring their loyalty.

Ieyasu's forced relocation to Edo was a blessing in disguise. Despite its humble condition, Ieyasu's new domain included the rich farmland of the Kantō Plain, worth over two million koku annually, making him one of the richest daimyō in Japan. Edo's location far from the capital also saved Ieyasu from having to contribute men and resources to Hideyoshi's two disastrous invasions of Korea in his vain attempt to conquer China, which allowed Ieyasu to grow stronger as potential rivals were weakened. By Hideyoshi's death in 1598, Ieyasu's patience was rewarded: he was now in the strongest position to take control of Japan.

On the foggy morning of October 21, 1600, the Battle of Sekigahara saw the massive armies of the west, led by Ishida Mitsunari, face off against Ieyasu's army of the east. The scale of the battle was of epic proportions, with Mitsunari's coalition of eighty-two thousand men loyal to Hideyoshi's heir against Ieyasu's force of eighty-nine thousand men loyal to the Tokugawa, all converging at the intersection of two main roadways in a mountainous valley at Sekigahara. The battle was over in a mere six hours after two of the western generals defected to the east, placing Ieyasu decisively in control of all Japan. In the aftermath, Mitsunari was beheaded and the lands of the western daimyō, with a combined worth of more than five million koku, were seized and redistributed. Daimyō who were hereditary Tokugawa vassals prior to the Battle of Sekigahara were classified as *fudai daimyō* (譜代大名, insider daimyō), and those who became Tokugawa vassals after the battle were classified as *tozama daimyō* (外様大名, outsider daimyō). Daimyō were subsequently relocated, much as Hideyoshi had done with Ieyasu, with fudai daimyō placed at key strategic and economic locations near Edo and Kyoto, and tozama daimyō situated on the periphery and the coasts.

Three years following Sekigahara, Emperor Go-Yōzei appointed Ieyasu as shōgun. Establishing the Tokugawa shōgunate in Edo, Ieyasu followed the model of the Kamakura shōgunate by removing his military government from the political influence of the Imperial Court and Buddhist sects of Kyoto. With its fifty-foot-tall outer stone walls and five-story *tensu* (天守, main keep) rising more than 190 feet in height, Edo Castle was transformed from the dilapidated ramshackle of Ieyasu's relocation to a monumental military and palatial structure befitting a shōgun of his status. Daimyō from the provinces bore the brunt of the massive construction project, keeping Ieyasu's potential adversaries busy while also depleting their resources by requiring them to send stone and labor.

Unlike Hideyoshi, who sought legitimization with the Imperial Court through intense devotion to the tea ceremony, Ieyasu was not enamored with the art of tea. Although the Tokugawa employed tea masters of their own, by 1650, the golden age of Chadō had come to an end. The innovation of the art seen under Sen Rikyū ended after Hideyoshi ordered him to commit seppuku for reasons that remain unclear to history, and the art of tea became largely fixed in form under Rikyū's descendants and disciples, who taught the nobility of both samurai and imperial households. Instead, Ieyasu's passion was jinkō. He even acquired a piece of the Ranjatai cut by Nobunaga for his growing collection, and under the Tokugawa, the art of incense flourished. But, as had always been the case, jinkō was a rare, imported commodity sourced through maritime trade.

One of Ieyasu's earliest actions as shōgun was to send Japanese ships throughout the South Pacific, trading Japanese silver for luxuries like Ming silk, aromatic spices, and fragrant woods. He rewarded favored daimyō and merchants with lucrative three-year trading licenses, granting their ships trading rights under the official protection of the shōgunate. The brilliant vermillion seal on the license led to the moniker *shuinsen* (朱印船), or "red-seal ships." Red-seal trading routes were established running from Nagasaki to Portuguese Canton in China, Manila in the Philippines, Jakarta in Java, the Malay peninsula near Malacca, and Bangkok in Siam. Over time, Japanese settlements were established in jinkō-producing Rikkoku nations: at Ayutthaya in Siam, Pinhalu and Phnom Penh in Cambodia, and Hue and Hoi-an in Vietnam. Many Japanese Christian converts moved to these settlements to escape persecution at home.

Of the 350 red-seal ships, more than one-third travelled to the port of Hoi-an in Vietnam, a center for Southeast Pacific trade and an area rich in kyara. Frequent letters exchanged between the Tokugawa shōgunate and the Nguyen lords who ruled central Vietnam showed a close trading relationship and Ieyasu's keen interest in high quality aloeswood. Aloeswood from Vietnam was considered a precious gift and was listed first among gifts exchanged in diplomatic relations. On multiple occasions, Nguyen lords gifted Ieyasu with pieces of the finest aloeswood, weighing several pounds each. Over the thirty-five-year span of the red-seal ships' existence, an average of ten voyages were undertaken annually. This surpassed the volume of the larger yet less frequent Portuguese black ships of the nanban trade, increasing the supply of fragrant woods and aromatic spices used for incense and Kōdō ceremonies throughout the imperial and shōgunal courts.

As trade under the Tokugawa expanded, so too did the growth of Edo. Maeda Toshinaga, lord of the Kaga Domain on Japan's northern coast, sent his mother to reside as a voluntary hostage in Edo as a gesture of fealty to Ieyasu. For this, he was rewarded with a prime building site for his palatial mansion directly outside the main gate of Edo Castle. As daimyō often traveled to Edo for their official duties in service to the shōgun, having a second residence in the Tokugawa capital was a practical way to avoid the time-consuming process of arranging room and board at local temples, which offered comfort far beneath what they were accustomed to. Following Toshinaga's example, other daimyō voluntarily relocated family members to Edo and applied to build luxurious mansions in the shadow of Edo Castle. To address the influx of daimyō households, Ieyasu assigned land to the southeast of the castle's main gate for their residences, and this area eventually came to be known as Daimyō-kōji (大名小路, Daimyō Alley). Filled at first with residences of fudai daimyō and enclosed by an outer moat for defense, in time, tozama daimyō were granted residential lots there as well.

By the time of his death in 1616, Ieyasu had an advantage Hideyoshi had not had: children. Unlike Hideyoshi, who had a single infant heir at the time of his death, Ieyasu had sired at least eleven sons and five daughters. To ensure there would be no conflict over succession, Ieyasu's son Tokugawa Hidetada had been installed as the second Tokugawa shōgun a decade prior to Ieyasu's death, and his grandson Tokugawa Iemitsu became the third Tokugawa shōgun in 1623 only a few years after Ieyasu's death. Ieyasu, in his fondness for fragrant woods, had amassed a treasure trove said to contain hundreds of pounds of exquisite kyara and jinkō. In addition to his collection of fragrant woods, countless treasures were passed on to Ieyasu's heirs, including the famous incense burner Chidori-kōro, once owned by luminaries Ashikaga Yoshimasa, Sen Rikyū, and Toyotomi Hideyoshi.

With Malacca falling to the Dutch in 1639, the Portuguese monopoly on trade with Japan ended. Making contact with the shōgunate, the Dutch informed the Japanese about the religious wars taking place between European Protestants and Catholics. The Dutch emphasized the political instability caused by the Catholic proselytizing that was part and parcel of Portuguese trade, and they intimated that the Jesuits aimed to turn Japan into a Catholic nation more loyal to the pope than the shōgun, thus making it ripe for Iberian colonization. In contrast, the Dutch offered commerce without religion, emphasizing their intentions with gifts of gunpowder and lead shot more in line with the warrior nature of the samurai than the gospels of the Jesuits. The Dutch warnings of the Jesuit threat were vividly brought to life in 1638 during the Shimabara no ran (島原の乱, Shimabara Rebellion), as Japanese Christian converts, with the aid of displaced *rōnin* (浪人, masterless samurai), rose in a revolt against the taxation of the shōgunate. When the Tokugawa army of one hundred thousand troops was unable to put down the rebellion, a costly siege of the rebel stronghold at Hara Castle ensued. The Dutch provided gunpowder and cannon to the shōgun's troops, and ultimately the Tokugawa called on their gunboats to level Hara Castle, ending the rebellion once and for all.

In response to Shimabara, Iemitsu increasingly treated Christianity as a virus threatening Japan and Tokugawa rule. What started as anti-Christian policies under Ieyasu reached their peak under Iemitsu in a series of edicts known as Sakoku-rei (鎖国令, the Closed Country Edicts). Through the Sakoku Edicts, the Tokugawa shōgunate quarantined Japan from the influence of the West and its nanban religion, banning Japanese ships from sailing for foreign ports and making leaving the country punishable by death. It closed Japan to the return of Japanese nationals living overseas, many of whom were Christian converts, and mandated that any who returned were to be put to death. It further required all domestic Japanese to register with local Buddhist temples to ensure the eradication of Christianity from Japan entirely. Finally, in 1639, the Portuguese were expelled from Japan, all ports closed to the black ships of the West, and all trade with the Portuguese outlawed.

The only Westerners allowed to continue trade in Japan were the Dutch; however, they were ordered to leave Hirado and were restricted to the port of Nagasaki. There they were all but quarantined on the small fan-shaped island of Deshima in Nagasaki's harbor. Measuring approximately 600 feet by 240 feet, the artificial island was originally constructed to house the Portuguese, but by 1641, it served to isolate the Dutch and their trading operations from the curious Japanese who watched Deshima like it was a human zoo. With the island surrounded by a high wooden fence and connected to the mainland by only a stone bridge, interaction between the Dutch and Japanese was strictly minimized, and the number of Dutch ships diminished in the decades that followed to only one or two per year. The most important Dutch import became intelligence about the wider world, with each arriving captain required to provide to the shōgunate an official account of world affairs since their last visit. In time, Japanese scholars learned to read Dutch, and through *rangaku* (蘭学, Dutch studies) studied Western technology, medicine, and military science using imported Dutch books.

The Sakoku Edicts halted all Tokugawa red-seal ships, thereby cutting off the supply of fragrant woods and aromatic spices from South Pacific ports like Hoi-An. Turmoil on the mainland provided a solution when the Qing overthrew the Ming Dynasty in 1644, lifting the Ming-imposed embargoes and allowing trade to resume with Japan. Without official relations between the Tokugawa and the Qing, Chinese ships were restricted by the shōgunate to only the port of Nagasaki. In 1640, seventy-four Chinese ships landed in Nagasaki; by 1688, that number swelled to nearly two hundred ships. While the Dutch were restricted to small numbers and confined to Deshima, almost five thousand Chinese were housed at Nagasaki's *tōjin yashiki* (唐人屋敷, Chinese quarter) on more than seven acres of Japanese soil. Chinese ships brought large quantities of silk and other luxury items from Canton, as well as substantial quantities of fragrant woods and aromatic spices from China's trading network that included the kyara-rich port of Hoi-an. With aromatic spices and fragrant woods concentrated in Nagasaki, merchants and daimyō alike thronged to its markets to secure the valuable commodities, shipping them through Japan's inland sea route to Sakai and then on to the Imperial Court in Kyoto and the thriving Tokugawa capital in Edo.

As unofficial trade resumed with China, relations between Kyoto and Edo were strained at best. The Tokugawa had sought to limit the emperor's power beginning in 1615 with Ieyasu's passage of Kinchū Narabi ni Kuge Shohatto (禁中並公家諸法度, Laws for the Imperial Court and Court Nobles), which relegated the role of the Imperial Court to ceremony, scholarship, and the arts. In an unprecedented action, it also stripped the emperor of the right to award the purple robes that elevated Buddhist monks to abbots. This was a significant action by the shōgunate, as never before had anyone placed such limits upon the emperor. Then in 1620, Emperor Go-Mizunoo was forced by the shōgunate to take as his wife Tokugawa Masako—the grand-daughter of Tokugawa Ieyasu, the daughter of Tokugawa Hidetada (the second Tokugawa shōgun), and the sister of Tokugawa Iemitsu (the third Tokugawa shōgun). The political symbolism was clear: the Tokugawa were in control. In 1624, Masako was named Empress Consort of Japan, creating a direct link between the imperial throne and the Tokugawa.

Chafing at bakufu restrictions on his power, in 1627, Go-Mizunoo ignored shōgunal prohibitions and awarded purple robes to fifteen priests, leading to a showdown with Iemitsu. In what was known as the Purple Robe Incident, Iemitsu used the violation as pretext not only to rescind the fifteen appointments but also to confiscate the purple robes awarded in prior years, stripping nearly 150 sitting abbots of their titles. This action was too much for Go-Mizunoo to take, and in 1629, he abdicated in favor of his five-year-old daughter, Meishō, who became the first empress to rule Japan since the eighth century.

While Go-Mizunoo continued to rule from his position as retired emperor because his young daughter had not yet come of age, having a direct Tokugawa descendent on the Chrysanthemum Throne further strengthened the ties between the Tokugawa and the Imperial Court.

The friction between Kyoto and Edo was soothed somewhat by the generous financial support provided to the Imperial Court by the shōgunate, sent each year ostensibly for Masako's personal needs. She worked to smooth the tensions between the shōgunate and the retired emperor, using her wealth to reinvigorate the Imperial Court, rebuilding court villas and shrines and serving as a patron of the arts. Together, Masako and Retired Emperor Go-Mizunoo revitalized the flagging fortunes of the Imperial Court, promoting traditional Japanese arts and the geidō with a vigor that had been muted during the constant warfare of the previous 150 years.

Go-Mizunoo took inspiration from the classical Heian court, sparking an artistic movement that highlighted the elegance of courtly miyabi through a revival of traditional arts and literature. A resurgence in the classical arts followed, creating a growing interest in poetry, literature, and the refined arts of Chadō and Kōdō. This movement became known as Kan'ei culture (寛永) for the era in which it originated.

Thriving in their roles as keepers of *yūsoku kojitsu* (有職故実), knowledge of ancient wisdom and refined practices of the Imperial Court, Kyoto aristocrats served as experts to the growing number of samurai households in Edo that sought to enhance their rank and status through proper displays of courtly refinement. Through these cultural exchanges, the Imperial Court reestablished its place within the Tokugawa-dominated nation and breathed renewed life into the traditional culture of Kyoto.

As Kan'ei culture spread from Kyoto to Edo, reverence grew for classical literature and the traditional rituals that were embodied in the geidō. The art of incense saw an increase in the popularity of Kōdō as well as a revival of the blended incense of the Heian court. Unlike in previous eras, now the blending of Heian takimonō was practiced alongside ichibokudaki's singular focus on jinkō. As high-quality fragrant woods made their way from Nagasaki to Kyoto and Edo, the practice of naming the highest quality jinkō also saw a resurgence, with meikō named by the emperor assuming astronomic fame and value. Housed in elegant lacquer boxes—finely engraved, gilded with gold, and inlaid with tortoise shell—made by master craftsmen, collections of meikō were curated like fine wines and passed down as treasured family heirlooms.

As Kōdō reached the heights of its popularity, hundreds of new and unique kumikō were created, often based upon classical poetry, literature, and the war tales of gunki monogatari. The most famous kumikō of all, Genji-kō (源氏香), illustrated Lady Murasaki's Heian classic *Genji Monogatari* through fragrance, with its score kept in five-line motifs, known as *Genji-mon* (源氏紋), that represented specific chapters in *The Tale of Genji*. So powerful was the resurging reverence for *The Tale of Genji* that the Tokugawa acquired the *Genji Monogatari Emaki* (源氏物語絵巻), the famous twelfth-century scroll in the Yamato-e (大和絵) style of classical Chinese narrative illustration. Exquisitely painted and gilded with gold, the *Genji Monogatari Emaki* had a significant influence upon Japanese artwork, and Japan's art of incense continues to reference its motifs to this day.

Tokugawa policy and Kan'ei culture merged through the education of women. Under Tokugawa policy, all women were to be educated to a level appropriate for their station. For the women of the Imperial Court and the wives and daughters of daimyō and their retainers, that meant the study of classical literature and the geidō. Masako herself was said to be particularly adept at calligraphy, poetry, and the tea ceremony, serving as an example of beauty through her courtly refinement. Unlike past eras in which only men were tea and incense masters, women now displayed their sophistication, elegance, and beauty through the performance of the ritualized appreciation of tea and incense. In the pursuit of the elevation of family rank and status, husbands could display the refinement of their households by having their wives host incense gatherings and tea ceremonies to impress influential guests. When daughters of Daimyō Alley were wed, a key item in their dowry was an opulent Kōdō incense set. Highly ornate incense utensils, gilded incense boxes, and lavish travel cases were often covered in rich *maki-e* (蒔絵), a decorative technique in which powdered gold or silver was sprinkled onto wet lacquer to create landscapes, patterns, or symbols. The rich elegance of such a Kōdō set, an exquisite work of art in and of itself, represented the lord's worthiness of the status he strived to attain.

Today the cultural artifacts amassed by Tokugawa Ieyasu are considered National Treasures of Japan, and the Chidori-kōro and the *Genji Monogatari Emaki* are preserved by the Tokugawa Art Museum in Nagoya. In May 2022, the Shino School of Kōdō held an incense ceremony to honor the spirit of Tokugawa Ieyasu, still revered in Japan today, using the most precious jinkō in existence: a piece of Ranjatai.

CHAPTER 11

THE FLOATING WORLD
Commerce, popular culture, and incense

KNOWN FOR HIS CORRUPTION, GREED, AND ARROGANT, disdainful nature, Kira Yoshinaka was a high-ranking court official of protocol who held the title Kōzuke no Suke (上野介). Yoshinaka was charged with instructing Asano Naganori, the lord of Akō, in the proper etiquette for entertaining an imperial envoy to be received by the shōgun. Dissatisfied with the customary gifts Naganori gave him in return for his instruction, Yoshinaka sought to make a laughingstock of the lord, insulting and demeaning him during their daily sessions at Edo castle. Naganori bore the insults with patience and grace, which only enraged Yoshinaka. On the day of the envoy's ceremony, Yoshinaka's insults reached their most degrading: "Here, my lord of Akō, the ribbon of my sock has come untied; be so good as to tie it up for me." Burning with rage, Naganori did as he was asked. At this, Yoshinaka delivered the most demeaning insult of all: "Why, how clumsy you are! You cannot so much as tie up the ribbon of a sock properly! Anyone can see that you are a boor from the country, and know nothing of the manners of Edo." This indignity was too much for Naganori to bear. As Yoshinaka turned to leave, Naganori drew his sword and leveled it at him. Deflected by Yoshinaka's court cap, the blow only grazed the startled man's head. A second blow narrowly missed the terrified Yoshinaka as he fled, and Nagonori's blade was embedded in a pillar of the Matsu no Roka (松の大広間, Hallway of Pines). The commotion drew the attention of the court officers, who restrained and disarmed Naganori, allowing the bleeding Yoshinaka to escape with his life. Naganori was arrested for drawing his sword within the shōgun's castle and, after an investigation, was ordered to commit seppuku. The lord of Akō's estates were confiscated, and his samurai retainers reduced to masterless rōnin.

The story of avenging the lord of Akō, originally titled *Chūshingura* (忠臣蔵, *The Treasury of Loyal Retainers*) but better known as *The Tale of the Forty-Seven Rōnin*, has been retold for over three hundred years. Taking place during the opening of the 1700s, when the samurai were increasingly impoverished paragons of moral virtue with only their honor to fight for, *The Tale of the Forty-Seven Rōnin* serves as a historic parable illustrating the warrior code of Bushidō and its values of loyalty, courage, honor, and discipline. After almost one hundred years of peace, the warrior class had assumed roles as aristocratic administrators, and a vibrant new class of affluent townspeople had arisen. As the stoic samurai made annual treks to Edo, commoners prospered in castle towns along the way, as well as in the entertainment districts of the new capital. Reflecting these sweeping societal changes, the aristocratic art of incense found its way to the indulgent "floating world" through commerce, popular culture, and a new form of incense.

By 1700, as the forty-seven rōnin were planning to avenge their lord, approximately one million people lived in Edo, nearly as many as in London and Paris combined, making it the largest city in the world. What began as the voluntary movement of daimyō households to Edo as a sign of fealty and practicality had evolved into the Tokugawa policy known as *sankin-kōtai* (参勤交代, alternate attendance). As officially decreed by Tokugawa Iemitsu in 1635, all daimyō, both fudai and tozama, were required to spend alternating years living in Edo. Their families, however, were to remain there permanently, essentially as hostages. This ensured daimyō loyalty with the added benefit of depleting their resources through the maintenance of households in both their domains and the capital. Daimyō were awarded plots of land near the castle commensurate with their status, and most maintained multiple palatial mansions there, one for their family and others for their principal vassals and staff.

The annual migration of daimyō to and from Edo occurred via a series of national highways, known as the Gokaidō (五街道, Five Highways), that connected the capital to the domains in the countryside. Originally begun as a roadway-improvement project by Ieyasu for rapid deployment of the military to the provinces, the Gokaidō had developed roadways that connected castle towns with the Tokugawa capital. Positioned at regular intervals along the roadways, nearly 250 *shukuba* (宿場, post stations) served as rest stops and transportation centers where travelers could find lodging, meals, and all manner of goods for their journey. The most famous of the Five Highways was the Tōkaidō (東海道, Eastern Sea Route), which ran largely along Honshu's Pacific coast and connected Edo to Kyoto. At 320 miles in length with fifty-three post stations, the Tōkaidō was the most traveled of the routes taken in the annual migration of daimyō from their castle towns in the countryside to their required residency in Edo.

In order to project the strength and status of their clans, processions of daimyō households made the annual journey along the Tōkaidō with ever-increasing pomp and ceremony and as much as half of their household in tow, a parade-like cultural performance for those lining the roads to watch the great lords pass by. As the pageantry grew, so too did the expense of transporting thousands of individuals from the provinces to Edo, further straining the resources of the daimyō and impoverishing the samurai. Within a generation, the heirs of every domain in Japan were born and raised in the capital, children of Edo more than of their own domains, which they often saw only after being invested as lords. The samurai were increasingly dispossessed, wholly dependent upon their lords, and removed from the art of war, ending up instead in roles as aristocratic bureaucrats.

This posed an existential threat for the samurai. The Tokugawa had created Edo as a samurai-run military enclave embodying the Bushidō values of the warrior class, but after nearly a century at peace, the military focus had waned. Even the Tokugawa mandates of Buke Shohatto (武家諸法度, Various Points of Laws for Warrior Houses) were revised, redefining the samurai as aristocratic administrators loyal above all to their lord. However, as the samurai grew no crops, produced no products, and profited without engaging in trade, to justify their place at the top of the Confucian shi-nō-kō-shō class system, they turned to stoic observance of Bushidō, existing as moral exemplars for the lower classes. In a romanticization of the past, samurai, most of whom had never known battle, studied books on Bushidō voraciously. *Hagakure-kikigaki* (葉隠聞書, *Dictations Given Hidden by Leaves*) became the most acclaimed of those books with its famous passage that emphasized the ultimate duty to one's lord: "The way of the warrior is to be found in dying." In many ways, *Hagakure* was critical of the shift of the samurai from highly skilled warriors to perfumed bureaucrats in service of the Tokugawa government, lamenting that by 1700 there were more calligraphy teachers than swordmasters in Edo.

The samurai's role as an example of loyalty and moral virtue is at the heart of *The Tale of the Forty-Seven Rōnin*. Led by Ōishi Yoshio, Asano Naganori's loyal retainer in charge of administering his Akō estate during the lord's required attendance in Edo, the forty-seven rōnin masterfully lulled the wary Yoshinaka into complacency. Feigning a fall into drunkenness and debauchery, for almost two years the rōnin of Akō publicly appeared to abandon their duty to their lord, enduring ridicule and humiliation for their actions as they secretly planned to avenge his death. At great personal sacrifice, Yoshio even publicly divorced his wife and left his family. Eventually, Yoshinaka's guard was lowered, and in January 1703, Yoshio led the attack on Yoshinaka's residence in the Honjo district of Edo. Before attacking, they warned neighboring households that they meant them no harm, respectfully informing them of their intent.

Capturing Yoshinaka alive, they identified him by the scar on his head where their lord had tried to strike him down nearly two years prior. Yoshio declared their purpose of avenging their lord and offered Yoshinaka the honor of committing seppuku, treating him with great courtesy and respect in consideration of his rank and title. Trembling with fear, Yoshinaka was unable to die with honor. Acting as his second, Yoshio took Yoshinaka's head using the same blade with which his master had committed seppuku. Their mission complete, as an act of courtesy, Yoshio then sent word to Naganori's widow that the lord of Akō had been avenged.

As the samurai increasingly venerated the values of Bushidō as exemplified by Yoshio and the forty-seven rōnin, the sankin-kōtai and its annual parade of daimyō households increasingly depleted their finances. As the fortunes of the samurai declined, those of the townspeople who catered to them in the castle towns of the Gokaidō and pleasure district of Edo grew. Providing lodging, eating and drinking establishments, houses of entertainment, and shops selling all kinds of gifts and specialty products, the *chōnin* (町人, townsman) class rose as an increasingly affluent economic force. Serving the needs of the migrating samurai, a boom of artisans and merchants opened establishments in the castle towns and pleasure quarters of Edo. Of the one million inhabitants of Edo, it is estimated that as many as two-thirds were merchants, artisans, and entertainers who flocked to the capital to make their fortunes providing for the younger generation of samurai seeking diversion.

As the samurai passed along the Tōkaidō, the revival of the arts of Kan'ei culture traveled with them, uniting Japan into a cohesive cultural experience that crossed social boundaries. The beauty found in Kan'ei culture was expressed by chōnin in ways that contrasted the stoic values of the samurai. Rather than be restricted by samurai morality, they were to enjoy and treasure the fleeting passage of the beautiful. Life was too short to be distracted by the serious nature of the samurai! The Buddhist term *ukiyo* (憂世) referred to the world of illusion and suffering, but the meaning was turned upside-down by changing its first kanji to create the homophone *ukiyo* (浮世), meaning "to float."

For the chōnin and the samurai they entertained, embracing the illusion of "the floating world" by living in the moment, enjoying life's pleasures, and ignoring life's sorrows was paramount. In what is considered the earliest work to express the chōnin urban ideal of Edo, *Ukiyo Monogatari* (浮世物語, *Tales of the Floating World*), written in 1666 by Asai Ryōi, captured ukiyo this way:

> Living only for the moment, turning our full attention to the pleasures of the moon, the snow, the cherry blossoms and the maples, singing songs, drinking wine and diverting ourselves in just floating, floating; caring not a whit for the poverty staring us in the face, refusing to be disheartened, like a gourd floating along with the river current: this is what we call ukiyo.

The floating world of the chōnin not only provided pleasurable distractions from the world's sorrows, but it also gave rise to a heightened appreciation of aesthetics and new forms of art. Chōnin developed a unique sense of style, known as *iki* (粋), that was fresh, youthful, and chic. For the merchant and artisan classes, being able to display a sense of style discreetly was a way to assert their growing economic influence in a society based upon rigid social class structure. Subtle displays of iki refinement could be found in forbidden colorful patterns allowed to peek from beneath a somber kimono, or in the way one rolled up one's sleeves. Despite the Tokugawa restrictions on displays of wealth, both time and money flowed into Edo's Yoshiwara (吉原) pleasure quarters where iki permeated the floating world and chōnin and samurai mixed more freely.

In a cultural renaissance, new forms of popular culture and art flourished in the floating world, and no form concentrated and amplified iki more than Kabuki (歌舞伎) theater. Kabuki was a bold, energetic, dynamic celebration for the senses. It contrasted the formal, stoic, restrained movements of the Noh (能) drama favored by the shōgunate with the fun and excitement of vibrant colors, flamboyant costumes, elaborate sets, and traditional Japanese instruments and drums, all of which heightened the emotion of the stories told on stage. Initially intended as entertainment for the lower classes, Kabuki took pop culture to its highest art form, where all classes mixed to enjoy the show. Synchronized with the schedule of public festivals, Kabuki was a staple of Edo life. No greater paragons of iki were there than Kabuki actors—the superstars of their time. Fans wore their favorite actors' crests to packed performances and cheered their heroes as they entered the stage. Kabuki stars incorporated their crests into their costumes, advertised products during their performances, opened their own retail shops, and sold their own lines of hair care and makeup products as well as personal brands of incense. Using dynamic, exaggerated movements and striking red and blue makeup, the *aragoto* (荒事, rough) "wild warrior" acting style was considered the height of Edo entertainment.

Kabuki portrayed classical literature and war tales as contemporary dramas, highlighting themes of love and loss, intrigue and betrayal, loyalty and personal sacrifice. *The Tale of the Forty-Seven Rōnin* was first performed as a Kabuki play shortly after the events occurred, but it was shut down by Tokugawa censors for dramatizing current affairs. In 1748, it again found its way to the Kabuki stage as *Chūshingura* (*The Treasury of Loyal Retainers*) after aligning the setting and characters to the fourteenth-century classical period of the *Taiheiki* (*Chronicles of the Great Peace*) to avoid Tokugawa censorship. Gunki monogatari and literary classics like *Genji Monogatari*, once reserved for the social elite, were rewritten in the vernacular of Edo's floating world and dramatized into Kabuki plays where they became part of Edo's popular culture.

As many scenes included the practices of the elite, theatergoers witnessed for the first time acts of the geidō, the use of incense, and the service of tea. Seeing an actor portray Lord Genji blending incense or witnessing the incense game Jūshūkō as part of a Kabuki play revealed the once-secret world of incense to lower samurai and chōnin alike. In some Kabuki plays, incense was even blown over the audience members from the stage to enchant them with the fragrances worn by the characters portrayed. As the art of incense joined the pop culture of the lower classes, incense terms became part of common speech. One popular saying, "He neither lights jinkō nor passes wind," had the meaning of an action that does neither good nor bad. And when a famous Kabuki character wore kyara clogs (kyara being the highest quality aloeswood), "kyara" was adopted as an adjective meaning something esteemed to be of the highest quality. Describing a woman as a "kyara woman" meant she exuded the highest expression of elegance and beauty, further infusing incense culture into the vernacular.

Ukiyo-e (浮世絵, "pictures of the floating world") was a sophisticated form of woodblock printing that captured scenes from the floating world—famous Kabuki actors, beautiful courtesans, and sweeping landscapes from Japan's most celebrated vistas. Ukiyo-e prints were available as individual images or as series on a single subject, and were a form of art accessible and affordable to a mass audience. The forty-seven rōnin was a popular theme, but the most famous series of ukiyo-e was probably Hokusai Katsushika's *Fugaku Sanjūrokkei* (富嶽三十六景, *Thirty-Six Views of Mount Fuji*), which included the unmistakable *Kanagawa oki nami ura*, or *The Great Wave*. Like Kabuki, ukiyo-e popularized classical texts; for example, scenes from *The Tale of Genji* rendered in serialized form were eagerly collected by the general public. Through prints depicting scenes of incense preparation, the playing of kumikō, and the ritual appreciation of Kōdō, the art of incense was popularized among those who had never before had access to such experiences. Through its use in ukiyo-e, Genji-mon became fashionable design motifs for decorating a variety of items from lacquerware to kimono fabrics, a practice that continues to this day.

The popularity of ukiyo-e coincided with a commercial printing boom that fed the appetites of newly wealthy chōnin for whom literature was now an affordable luxury. Books written in kana with little or no kanji, known as *kanazōshi* (仮名草子), were printed instead of being copied by hand, placing them within the economic reach of the masses. Initially written by more literate upper-class authors, in time, kanazōshi covered a wide range of topics, from adaptations of war tales and classical works to religious texts, diaries, and travel guides written by chōnin. *The Tale of the Forty-Seven Rōnin* proved to be an in-demand topic for such literature, and books of biographies of the loyal samurai combined dramatic illustrations with kana to form complete chronicles of Ōishi Yoshio and his men. *Ukiyo-zōshi* (浮世草子, "books of the floating world") further developed this trend, with authors writing entirely in kana using the colloquial language preferred by chōnin and lower-ranking samurai alike. The first popular genre of Japanese fiction, ukiyo-zōshi depicted life in the pleasure quarters of Edo and included erotic love stories, lively dramas, ghost stories, and tales of samurai honor and valor. Often vividly illustrated with ukiyo-e prints, ukiyo-zōshi felt more like a portrayal of real life than the sentimental nostalgia of previous literature, with stories filled with the irony and tragedy experienced in the lives of chōnin. Incense featured prominently in many leading authors' ukiyo-zōshi, such as Saikaku Ihara's books romanticizing illicit love affairs in the pleasure quarters and Ryūtei Tanehiko's complete rewriting of *Genji Monogatari*.

The commercial printing boom also spurred the study of the classics, as newly affluent chōnin sought to elevate their status through knowledge of the refined literature of the upper classes. Previously, classical literature had taken the form of manuscripts copied by hand in flowing calligraphy using both kana and kanji—far beyond the literacy levels of the lower classes. The new printed classics were adapted to the spoken language of the time, written in kana, and often filled with woodblock illustrations; sometimes the books held only illustrations with brief captions, or even just illustrations with no writing at all. Instructional books on subjects such as beginning poetry and etiquette, along with books filled with pictorial examples on topics like flower arrangement and the service of tea, transferred knowledge once available only to the upper classes to upwardly mobile chōnin. Incense culture also became accessible as literary classics like *Genji Monogatari* were translated, complete with illustrations of the incense practices of the nobility.

Accompanying and contributing to the expansion of mass printing was the rise in the education of women. Due to the Tokugawa decree that all Japanese should be educated commensurate with their status, by the 1700s, multiple temple schools were available for all commoners in every district of Edo. Although the women of the floating world were fixed within their social class, the refinement of the geidō held great appeal, and they eagerly studied the arts of tea and incense as ways to effectively emulate the upper classes and appropriately display their newfound economic status and style.

Education on the refined arts typically took place via the *iemoto* (家元, house head) system in which the hereditary head of the *ryu* (流, school) controlled both the curriculum taught and the license to teach. Teachers paid the iemoto according to their rank for the right to teach the curriculum they had mastered; in turn, their students paid them, which led to a progressively widening pyramid of students in the lower ranks.

This pyramid structure provided financial stability for the iemoto houses and helped safeguard the wisdom associated with the geidō. Information was passed primarily orally as a form of control, with the most secret teachings shared only with students who had risen through the curriculum by continued study and payment of fees. But those fees also put the study of the geidō out of reach for the lower classes and increasingly even for mid-ranking samurai. Handwritten manuscripts were also passed from teacher to student as a means of limiting information to private readership, but such information was mostly lower-level rote knowledge regarding specific tools or the sequence of steps in the art. With respect to Kōdō, little was included on the finer points of fragrance or the properties of fragrant woods. Nor was the deeper nature of the art of incense, its philosophical underpinnings, or the spiritual nature of practices such as monkō shared in writing. As basic texts found their way into mass-printed versions that were rewritten into the vernacular, the more profound aspects of the art of incense were often lost. Instead, the focus returned to the use of incense as a pastime that emphasized competitive games and the ability to identify fragrance.

While the samurai continued to live on fixed koku stipends set generations ago, chōnin were able to increase their income, earning profits from the wares they sold to the migrating samurai, and eventually their wealth began to outstrip that of many of the samurai they served. As a class of wealthy chōnin arose in the castle towns and the Tokugawa capital of Edo, their newly sophisticated practices traveled with the samurai along the Gokaidō, spreading to the countryside, where a class of rural elite keen to practice the arts arose as well. Participation in the refined arts was no longer restricted to those of status or birth, but was now available through the iemoto for those with the means to afford the fees or through printed guidebooks for those of lesser means.

This accessibility led to a level of participation in the refined arts never before experienced.

Through the opening of the geidō, the refined arts became a sort of cultural salon where people of different social standings were free to interact. By practicing the geidō, one learned to refine one's manner and expression, and to display status in a socially accepted form that transcended rigid class designations. Gatherings to appreciate incense were first and foremost about a common interest in fragrance, which allowed class distinctions to fade into the background as participants enjoyed playing a kumikō. Although the Tokugawa bakufu frowned upon such mixing of society, in the pleasure quarters of Edo, the appreciation of incense brought people together regardless of rank.

As Kōdō became popularized among commoners, the ritual appreciation of incense began to include contributions from chōnin. A member of the lowest social class, Yonekawa Jōhaku was a merchant with a talent for fragrance. Said to have never made a single mistake during a kumikō performance, Jōhaku is credited with developing a system of fragrance categorization known as the Gomi (五味, Five Tastes), which is based on the five basic tastes of sweet, bitter, sour, spicy, and salty. Resting as much on his reputation as on the intuitive link between the senses of smell and taste, Jōhaku's system was quickly adopted and then integrated with the Rikkoku of Sanjōnishi and Sanetaka to form the Rikkoku-Gomi (六国五味, Six Countries, Five Tastes) still employed to this day. Jōhaku would go on to found Yonekawa-ryu Kōdō, which now exists as a branch of the Oie School of Kōdō.

Incense found its way into the lives of commoners not only through the study of the geidō but also through a new form of incense imported from China. Known as *senkō* (線香), stick incense had been utilized in China for centuries before arriving in Japan. Produced in blended formulas akin to takimonō or in forms that highlighted a single fragrant wood such as jinkō, stick incense was created by crushing fragrant ingredients into powder, then mixing them with a binder known as *tabu-no-ki* (椨の木), which became a sticky dough when warm water was added. Kneaded together with aromatic ingredients, the clay-like dough was rolled or extruded into thin spaghetti-like strings of incense and then dried. The dried stick was economical, simple to use, and easy to carry. This popular new form of incense was quickly adopted by the chōnin of the floating world.

While senkō is thought to have been imported to Japan as early as the mid-1300s, it was not until the dawn of the Tokugawa shōgunate that its manufacture began there. During the Tokugawa shōgunate, the center of production of stick incense was Sakai. After the Tokugawa bakufu eliminated clan doctors' exclusive rights to the production and distribution of traditional medicines, chōnin merchants began to establish medicinal wholesale businesses to meet the needs of the growing urban population. As a rich port where fragrant woods and aromatic spices arriving from Nagasaki were concentrated, Sakai was a haven for merchants specializing in aromatics that were used in both traditional Chinese medicine and incense. Familiarity with the ingredients and their import led these apothecary merchants to manufacture incense sticks alongside selling the constituent fragrant woods and spices. At its height, the incense makers' cooperative in Sakai included more than sixty merchant establishments that supplied an estimated 70 percent of Japan's stick incense for the next two centuries.

Many of the best-known incense houses today trace their lineage back to this time of economic prosperity among the growing merchant class. Baieido and Shoyeido are just two well-known examples of the many incense manufacturers who originated at this time. Baieido traces its origin to its founder Yamatoya Kakuuemon, who was a medicinal wholesaler in Sakai. In 1657, Kakuuemon adopted the name Jinkoya Sakubei and began to sell fragrant woods and incense sticks. His name choice was intentional, as Jinkoya, which meant "aloeswood trader," was allowed for use only by Sakai merchants authorized to specialize in incense. He named his business Jinsaku, an abbreviation of his name *Jin*-koya *Saku*-bei, and developed the business into one of the three major incense manufacturers in Sakai. Not all of the best-known incense manufacturers originated from Sakai, however. Shoyeido can trace its origins back to 1705, when its founder, Hata Rokuzaemon Moriyoshi, a village chief of Tanba-Sasayama, created an incense business named Sasaya. When Hata Rokubei Moritsun, a member of the third generation of the Hata family, worked at the Imperial Palace, he learned the secret traditions of incense blending and began incorporating the traditions of the Imperial Court, once reserved only for the nobility, into Sasaya's products.

Stick incense quickly found a home within the Zen Buddhist practices of the chōnin and the samurai. In an effort to eradicate Christianity from Japan, the Tokugawa Registry of Religious Affiliation Edict required all Japanese to register with their local Buddhist temples. In response, the number of Sōtō Zen Buddhist temples surged, with over 17,500 parish temples constructed by the 1700s. However, the majority of Zen monks' time became occupied not with meditation, but with the many rites and rituals associated with the purification and veneration of the deceased. Funerary Buddhism became an important part of life for the Japanese, with the assignment of posthumous Buddhist names and elaborate funeral rites deifying the dead. According to these rites, the living members of the household were obligated to observe rituals to transform deceased relatives into enlightened spirits who had successfully completed Buddhist funerary rites, some even being posthumously ordained as Zen priests. The most common practice, known as the Thirteen Buddha Rites, required a series of elaborate rituals to be performed over the first forty-nine days after death, the traditional number of days required for rebirth. Additional rites were then required on the seventh, thirteenth, and thirty-third anniversary of the deceased's death to fully honor them and elevate them as a venerated ancestor within the household. All of these rites involved incense for purification and adoration of the ancestors, and stick incense became ubiquitous at the household *butsudan* (仏壇, Buddhist altar) and *haka* (墓, family grave) where ancestors were revered.

The importance of Buddhist funerary rites was highlighted in *The Tale of the Forty-Seven Rōnin*. After they extinguished all lamps and cooking fires to avoid any accidental damage to the neighborhood, Yoshio and his men proceeded to the Asano family graves located next to the temple at Sengaku-ji. There, Yoshinaka's severed head was laid upon their master's grave as an offering of respect and loyalty. Engaging the temple priest to read prayers, Yoshio and each of his men in turn burned incense as an offering to their lord. Afterward, Yoshio gave the priest all the money in his possession, humbly requesting that upon their deaths the priest give them a proper burial with full funerary rites. Moved by their courage and loyalty, the priest agreed to honor their wishes. Their lord avenged and their honor restored, the forty-seven rōnin surrendered themselves to the authorities without incident, knowing they would certainly be put to death as criminals for their actions.

Yet, incense was used not only to commemorate the dead but also to measure each moment of the living. Although Western mechanical clocks were well known in Edo, imported through the nanban trade or presented by nanban traders as gifts to daimyō lords in hope of striking lucrative trade deals, they were seen less as timekeeping devices and more as decorations and objects of status. Instead, the hours were gauged with incense. For centuries, monasteries kept time using a *jikōban* (常香盤), a clock that used an incense seal, a set of patterned lines of powdered incense that were burned atop a smoothed and flattened bed of ash. With the arrival of stick incense, the sticks were marked at even intervals and burned, the time announced by a drum or bell as the incense stick reached each mark. In the pleasure quarters of Edo's floating world, incense sticks were used to measure the amount of time a geisha entertained guests. A wooden box with holes drilled in it held a drawer of incense sticks. The proprietor would start the meter running by lighting an incense stick and placing it in the hole in the box that corresponded to the geisha who was entertaining. The time spent with the guest was measured and billed based upon the number of sticks consumed during the visit.

An unusual amount of time elapsed between the arrest of the forty-seven rōnin and their sentencing. For over a month and a half, the Tokugawa bakufu debated their fates. On one hand, the rōnin had committed a criminal act, forcefully breaking into the residence of a high-ranking court official and murdering him. For this, the punishment was an honorless criminal's death by decapitation. On the other hand, the rōnin had shown great devotion and loyalty to their lord, suffering great personal indignity to restore their lord's honor and avenge his death. In a world in which the samurai's role was to be examples of moral virtue and loyalty for the lower classes that were beginning to outstrip them economically, the forty-seven rōnin had captured the attention of the masses with their selfless act of loyalty. Finally, on March 20, 1703, the rōnin were sentenced to commit seppuku, an honorable death befitting loyal samurai retainers. The sentence was carried out the same day with all rōnin accepting the sentence with honor, providing a final example of moral virtue for the lower classes to emulate. The honor of their lord restored, the forty-seven rōnin were interred alongside his grave, serving their lord in death as they had in life.

The Tale of the Forty-Seven Rōnin is so enduring that it has been retold in numerous plays, movies, and television dramas both in Japan and in the West. Known as the "Righteous Samurai of Akō," the forty-seven rōnin are revered to this day by a steady stream of worshipers who bring incense to their graves. Edo continued to thrive long after the floating world and the forty-seven rōnin had passed. Known today as Tokyo, it remains the largest city in the world.

CHAPTER 12

尊皇攘夷

SON'NŌ JŌI
The decline of the art of incense

IN THE SWELTERING SUMMER HEAT OF AUGUST 1864, REBELS marched on the Imperial Palace in Kyoto. Rallying around the emperor's call to repel the Westerners who were increasingly landing upon Japan's shores, their goal was to seize control of the Imperial Court, overthrow the shōgunate, and restore the emperor as the supreme power in Japan. With cries of *"Son'nō jōi!"* (尊皇攘夷, "Revere the emperor, expel the barbarians!") and armed with antiquated matchlock rifles, three thousand men focused their attack on the Hamaguri Gate (蛤御門). Located in the western wall of the heavily fortified palace complex, the Hamaguri Gate was wide enough to allow a large number of troops through to storm the nearby Kyōto-gosho (京都御所, Kyoto Imperial Palace), the residence of the imperial family. Outgunned nearly seven-to-one by shōgunate defenders, the rebels suffered heavy losses as their attack on the gate was repelled. Pursued in retreat through the streets of Kyoto, the fleeing rebels set fire to the Chōshū estate and other residences to create a diversion for their escape. Amid the chaos of battle, a great fire known as the Dondon-yake (どんどん焼け, "quick-quick burning") arose, engulfing the ancient capital in a massive blaze and leaving more than half of it in ashes. Among the dwellings ravaged by the fire was that of the Shino School of Kōdō. The iemoto escaped the blaze, carrying what rare jinkō he could, before the entire Shino family residence and the rest of the Shino jinkō collection burned to the ground, leaving behind only magnificently fragrant ruins.

Known as the Kinmon no Hen (禁門の変, Forbidden Gate Incident), the attempt to restore the emperor and the near destruction of the Shino School of Kōdō in its wake were harbingers of what was to come for both Japan and its art of incense. Not quite three years after that hot August day, "men of high purpose" succeeded in wresting political control from the shōgunate and restoring the emperor as the supreme authority in Japan. In the frenzy of modernization that followed, Japan would nearly abandon 1,400 years of cultural refinement in its zeal to compete militarily and economically with the Western powers that threatened its shores with colonization. The sweeping political, cultural, and economic changes introduced during what would be called the Meiji Restoration had profound effects upon the refined arts of the geidō, nearly destroying Japan's art of incense—the ramifications of which still echo to this day.

By the early 1800s, more than two centuries after the Sakoku policy had closed Japan's borders to outsiders, incursions by Western ships on Japanese shores had steadily increased, posing a threat to Tokugawa rule. While fudai (insider) daimyō were concentrated near Japanese centers of power, tozama (outsider) daimyō were concentrated along the routes of Western whaling and merchant ships, placing them in the position of first contact with the Western powers. The tozama, especially the Satsuma, Chōshū, and Tosa, were largely anti-Western, viewing the Westerners as "barbarians," and any attempt by the shōgunate to treat with the Westerners threatened to spark a tozama rebellion.

To ensure control over Japan's foreign policy, in 1825, the Tokugawa shōgunate issued the Ikokusen Uchiharai-rei (異国船打払令, Edict to Repel Foreign Vessels), which amounted to a "shoot-first" policy toward Western ships other than the Dutch. As a result, in 1837, the American merchant ship *Morrison* was fired upon by land batteries and dozens of smaller ships as it entered Edo Bay. Led by Charles W. King, under the pretense of returning seven shipwrecked Japanese sailors picked up in Macau, the expedition was likely attempting to establish trade. Fleeing Edo Bay, King took the *Morrison* to Kagoshima in Kyūshū, where the Japanese sailors onboard were repatriated; shortly thereafter, the *Morrison* was again fired upon and driven away.

The Tokugawa were well aware of the Western powers' penchant for expansion and colonialization, needing only to look at China for an example of what opposing the West might bring. Seeking to turn its trade imbalance with China in its favor, the British had shifted their trade with China from Indian cotton to highly profitable opium. The social ills associated with opium addiction resulted in the Chinese banning the drug in 1813 and severely cracking down on its use and importation in 1836. The British retaliated and the Chinese resisted, leading to the First Opium War. Lacking a modern navy and armed with outdated firearms, the Chinese were no match for modern British warships and their superior weapons, and by 1842, China was forced to sign the Treaty of Nanjing. Completely one-sided, the treaty provided no benefits to the Chinese. It ceded control of the deep-water port of Hong Kong—the "fragrant harbor" at the center of incense production in China—to the British and opened five major trading ports, including Canton and Ningbo, to British trade. The treaty also required the Chinese to repay the British government for the costs of the war. It was a humiliating defeat for the Chinese and demonstrated the overwhelming military and naval strength of the West.

It was against this backdrop that Commodore Matthew C. Perry steamed American warships into Edo Bay in July 1853, raising concern of a potential war with the Americans as well as heightening Tokugawa fears of a tozama uprising should negotiations be opened. Perry knew nothing of Japan's internal political divide, nor was he particularly interested in Japan as a trading partner. An ardent proponent of steam power, Perry's goal was to secure Japanese coal for American steam-ships. American steam-powered clipper ships engaged in the China trade were capable of delivering tea and goods from newly opened British-Chinese ports in as little as ninety days—half the time it took British ships—but whaling was much more profitable. America was the global leader in the production of whale oil, which was in demand worldwide. But the most profitable byproduct of whaling was ambergris, a pungent, waxy substance found in the digestive system of only one percent of whales, and highly sought after for its uniquely light, sweet, floral fragrance when refined for use in perfumes and incense. The American Pacific whaling fleet needed ports at which to repair its ships and take on coal. Northern Japan was near the rich northern Pacific whaling grounds and rumored to have the richest coal deposits in the Pacific. In short, Japan was located right in the middle of American shipping lanes and economic interests.

For the Tokugawa, this presented a difficult balancing act: how to avoid an unwinnable war with the Americans while retaining the sup-port of tozama daimyō by restricting Western influence on Japan's shores. Although the Sakoku policy had closed the country to Western influence, Japan was not isolated from the world. Through its trading partnerships with the Dutch and Chinese, the Tokugawa were well-informed of the activities of the Western powers. In 1810, the shōgunate had commissioned a highly detailed map of the world that included the boundaries of American states, geographic landmarks such as rivers and lakes, and descriptions of native tribal lands. Recognizing that the British and Americans landing upon its shores universally spoke English, the shōgunate commissioned Japanese scholars to create an English–Japanese dictionary. The required annual reports from the Dutch kept the Tokugawa abreast of world events such as the Mexican-American War, the California gold rush, and the elections of American presidents.

The shōgunate was aware of Perry's mission before the American warships even arrived in Edo Bay, and knew the names of the ships and their commanding officers as well as the aims of the mission. Perry had clear instructions to prioritize securing a source of coal for American steamships. Americans like Perry felt the Japanese had treated the castaway sailors on the Morrison with disrespect, and their firing on the ship had received widespread negative coverage in the American press. A veteran of the War of 1812 and commander of U.S. forces during the Mexican-American War, Perry, in his hubris, believed the Japanese needed to be taught a lesson in humility. Leaving little room for compromise, Perry threatened that if he was not allowed to present a letter from the president of the United States to shōgunate officials of substantial authority, he would land troops and proceed to Edo to deliver it to the shōgun personally. On July 14, Perry was allowed to land and deliver the letter to sufficiently high-ranking shōgunal officials. He did so with considerable pomp and ceremony, surrounded by 250 sailors, accompanied by a marching band, and marking the occasion with a thirteen-gun salute. Noting that he would return for an answer within the year, he departed to wait in Hong Kong, the port the British had seized in the defeat of the Chinese, as a symbolic gesture.

Complicating the response to Perry's demands was the severe illness of Shōgun Tokugawa Ieyoshi, who died shortly after Perry's arrival and was succeeded by his son Tokugawa Iesada. Iesada did not fit the mold of a strong warrior, having been born frail and suffering a host of severe health complications, including the lasting effects of smallpox and debilitating cerebral palsy. His ascension to shōgun was not universally supported, and his fitness for office was questioned, stoking division between tozama and fudai daimyō further. Because of Iesada's poor health, his duties as shōgun were limited, placing the political reigns in the hands of a council of elders led by Abe Masahiro. In an unprecedented move, to provide legitimacy to any decision taken by the shōgunate, Masahiro surveyed both tozama and fudai daimyō on how to deal with Perry's demands. His action was perceived as indecisive and weak, and the result was a disastrous public debate in which shōgunal supremacy was lost to factions that formed along three general lines: agreeing to Perry's demands and opening the country to the West, opposing Perry's demands and going to war with the Western powers, or dragging out negotiations and gradually opening to trade with the West while buying time to modernize Japan's military.

When Perry returned in February 1854 with a larger force than before, it was clear to the Tokugawa that they could not defend the entire coastline from Western incursion; nor could they withstand internal dissent from tozama daimyō. As a result, they sought a middle ground. Negotiated in little more than a month, the Treaty of Kanagawa granted American merchant and whaling ships the ability to resupply in the ports of Shimoda and Hakodate, and Japan agreed to provide hospitality and protections for American seamen stranded upon its shores. It also gave the United States the right to appoint envoys to reside in these ports. For the shōgunate, the treaty avoided starting an unwinnable war with the Americans, and it slowed the opening of Japan to the West by not agreeing to trade and by recognizing the shōgunate as the sole authority for negotiations. But the treaty only spurred the West to press for more, and in 1856, Townsend Harris, the first U.S. consul to Japan, arrived in Shimoda with imminent threats of naval action by the British and Americans as he belligerently demanded further concessions from the Japanese.

Still seeking to quell internal opposition, in another unprecedented move, the shōgunate consulted Emperor Kōmei for his insights on how to deal with the Western powers' aggression, expecting the emperor to defer to the shōgun's authority, as was customary, and voice support for the treaties it had negotiated. But the tozama daimyō had the emperor's ear, and instead, Kōmei voiced his opposition to treating with the West in favor of a war to expel them from the country. Stunned, the lead negotiator for the shōgunate resigned rather than defy the wishes of the emperor. He was replaced by Ii Naosuke, who, despite the emperor's opposition, signed the Treaty of Amity and Commerce in July 1858. Known as the Harris Treaty, it opened Shimoda, Hakodate, and four other Japanese ports to foreign trade. It also allowed U.S. citizens to purchase land, build, and permanently reside in these treaty ports. With Japan now coerced into opening to the West, the Japanese were soon forced to negotiate a flood of similar treaties with Russia, France, the Netherlands, and Great Britain, with the Harris Treaty serving as the model.

Although these treaties avoided war and bought Japan time to modernize, the shōgunate came under fierce criticism from tozama daimyō and the Imperial Court. Seen as appeasing the West and capitulating to foreign demands, especially by allowing foreigners to reside permanently on Japanese soil, internal opposition grew louder, and the shōgun began to be openly mocked. The shōgunate's inclusion of the emperor in the governing process created a rival center of political power for its opposition to rally around. Believing foreigners and their nanban religion polluted Japanese soil, samurai—mainly from the western Satsuma, Chōshū, and Tosa clans—declared themselves rōnin, which freed them to act upon their own will. Known as *shishi* (志士, men of high purpose), these young, ambitious samurai turned from the shōgun to the emperor under the rallying cry of *"Son'nō jōi!"* (尊皇攘夷, "Revere the emperor, expel the barbarians!"). As they saw it, the way to deal with Western incursion was to restore the emperor as the supreme power in Japan, overthrow the Tokugawa shōgunate, and modernize the military to strengthen their position against the West. Emperor Kōmei increasingly agreed with the anti-Western sentiments of the shishi, and began to actively speak out against the treaties with the West, his dissent reaching its peak with his Jōi Chokumei (攘夷勅命, Edict to Expel the Barbarians) issued in 1863.

The decision of the shōgunate to ignore the will of the emperor and its inability to expel Westerners from Japan as the emperor had decreed amplified the anti-shōgunate loyalists' view that the Tokugawa bakufu was an illegitimate government and intensified the political divide. Spurred on by Kōmei's edict, a series of violent attacks on both foreigners and shōgunate officials followed. Attacks on foreigners were met with swift and overwhelming military retribution by the Western powers, demonstrating that Japan was no match for the modern navies and superior weapons of the West. With the shōgunate weakened by Japan's internal political divide, reaction to attacks upon its officials garnered much less response. In 1860, Ii Naosuke, the negotiator of the Harris Treaty, was attacked and killed by shishi loyalists right in front of the Sakurada Gate of Edo Castle while en route to a meeting with the shōgun. Unlike the West, the shōgunate was unable to respond to the violence, even though it took place on its own doorstep. Instead, it tried to conceal Naosuke's assassination by feigning his resignation due to illness and then announcing his death several months later. Soon afterward, shishi loyalists exacted retribution by assassinating more bakufu officials. As the shishi loyalists attracted followers to the Son'nō jōi movement, bolder moves, such as the attack upon the Hamaguri Gate in 1864 that burned the majority of Kyoto to the ground, left no doubt that the shōgunate had to respond. This resulted in punitive military expeditions by shōgunate forces against the Chōshū in 1864 and 1866.

As Japan's political divide moved it toward civil war, a series of rapid events significantly altered Japan's history as well as its relationship to incense. Succumbing to his many health issues in 1866, at age twenty, Shōgun Tokugawa Iemochi died without an heir. In August of that year, he was reluctantly succeeded by Tokugawa Yoshinobu, known as Keiki, who would be the fifteenth and final Tokugawa shōgun. Yoshinobu immediately began modernization of Japan's army and navy, using trade agreements with the West to purchase modern Western warships and weapons. Less than six months later, in January 1867, Emperor Kōmei suddenly succumbed to smallpox and was succeeded by his second son, Imperial Prince Mutsuhito. After Yoshinobu made several attempts at significant shōgunate reforms and recon-ciliation with the Imperial Court, all of which failed due to shishi opposition, he resigned the position of shōgun in November 1867, ending 264 years of Tokugawa rule. Less than a month later, shishi loyalists flooded Kyoto and seized control of the Imperial Palace. In January 1868, the restoration of imperial rule was proclaimed, and formal documents were sent to all foreign powers stating that the emperor was now the supreme authority in all of Japan's internal and external affairs. Imperial Prince Mutsuhito's coronation took place in September 1868, with his taking the name Meiji, and the "enlightened rule" of the Meiji Restoration began. Following the example of previous power shifts, the capital of the Meiji government was moved from Kyoto to Edo, and Edo renamed "Tokyo" meaning "eastern capital." The selection of Tokyo as the capital of Japan's new modern government was intended as a symbolic break from the old traditions and customs that Kyoto embodied. Tokugawa holdouts resisted in a brief rebellion known as the Boshin War but by June 1869 had submitted to Meiji government rule.

Unlike previous emperors, who infrequently left the Imperial Palace and were rarely seen, Emperor Meiji was much more visible, attending cabinet meetings of the new government and traveling throughout the country. In 1877, he visited Tōdai-ji, and the Shōsō-in Repository was opened for the special occasion of his visit. Once inside, Meiji expressed interest in viewing the legendary incense Ranjatai. Later that evening, in an expression of rulership seen only twice before, the last having been by Oda Nobunaga nearly four hundred years earlier, Meiji requested a piece of the ancient jinkō, and a small portion of Ranjatai was ritually cut from the fragrant log—symbolically distant from the previous notches made by the samurai Ashikaga Yoshimasa and Oda Nobunaga. The young emperor then broke the treasured jinkō in two, burning one piece immediately, its rare fragrance filling the temporary palace. The remaining piece of Ranjatai returned with the emperor to Tokyo.

Replacing "Son'nō jōi!" with the slogan *"Fukoku kyōhei"* (富国強兵, "Enrich the country, strengthen the military"), the new Meiji government enacted a series of sweeping institutional and social reforms to modernize Japan as quickly as possible to overcome the country's deficit with the West. Instead of seeking to expel the barbarians and return to seclusion, the new government looked to the West as its model, pursuing policies that prioritized national unity, a centralized government, and involvement in global affairs, with the goal of remaking Japan into a modern nation equal to that of the Western powers. For the "good of the country," old institutions, traditions, and customs were vigorously eliminated. Issued in 1868, the Gokajō no Goseimon (五箇条の御誓文, Charter Oath) spelled out the new government's Westernization aims, noting that the "evil customs of the past" were to be discontinued in pursuit of modernization. The effects upon the centuries-old geidō were devastating and for the art of incense nearly fatal, as Meiji reforms converged directly upon the traditions at its very core.

One tenet of the Meiji Charter Oath was the creation of national unity by eliminating the shi-nō-kō-shō class system that had placed the samurai atop the social order. This decimated the samurai's monopoly on power, and participation in the military, once the sole domain of the samurai, was now opened to all Japanese regardless of their prior social class. The "evil habits" of the past, such as traditional dress and the wearing of the *chonmage* (丁髷, topknot) hairstyle of the samurai, were discouraged as antiquated, unpatriotic, and divisive to national unity. In a blow to the social status of the samurai, the Haitō-rei (廃刀令, Sword Abolishment Edict) banned the wearing of swords for all but former daimyō. And in a direct blow to the financial base of the samurai, the feudal *han* (藩) system of daimyō domains was eliminated in favor of a new prefecture system that was directly subordinate to the national government and the emperor. The resulting decrease of koku stipends, the samurai's financial lifeblood, to ten percent of their former value significantly impoverished many former samurai. Finally, to emphasize the historic supremacy of the emperor, the Meiji government decreed that during the Northern and Southern Courts period, Emperor Go-Daigo of the Southern Court had been the legitimate ruler, and that the Ashikaga shōgunate of the Northern Court had usurped the rule of the true emperor.

As the samurai were the primary patrons of the refined arts, the end of the samurai class had a significant effect upon the geidō, especially the art of Kōdō. Viewed as passé, elitist, and incompatible with modernity, the ritual appreciation of incense fell into steep decline. Without its primary patrons, the iemoto system collapsed and the majority of schools of incense ceased to exist, leaving only the Shino and Oie schools clinging to life. After the Kinmon incident and the fire that destroyed the Shino family residence, the Shino School of Kōdō left Kyoto for Nagoya, where it was given refuge by the Owari house of the Tokugawa and continued under the Hachiya family line of masters. The Oie School of Kōdō continued with three masters—Tsuzuki Soboku, his son Tsuzuki Kosai, and Shikimori Kagyu—who trained disciples throughout the Meiji period. Tsuzuki Kosai went on to teach maki-e at the Tokyo School of Fine Arts as a means of support, making exquisite maki-e incense utensils treasured for their refined beauty.

As the samurai class was eliminated, Buddhism also came under intense attack. Buddhism and incense had been linked for over a thousand years in Japan, with Zen having significant influence in the development of the refined art of Kōdō. However, the Meiji government viewed Buddhism as an imported Chinese religion, and therefore inherently unsuited for Japanese national unity. Japan was the land of the kami, and the emperor was descended directly from

Amaterasu, the sun goddess and highest of the kami, and therefore the ultimate godlike authority in Japan. The importation of Chinese Buddhist religions like Zen was viewed as causing the destruction of the relationship between the kami and the Japanese people. The Meiji government therefore promoted Shintō, the ancient Japanese "way of the gods," as the official state religion, making the emperor both the political and religious leader of the nation. Through a series of edicts known as Shinbutsu bunri (神仏分離, Separation of Shintō and Buddhism), restrictions on Buddhist shrines and institutions increased. Meiji edicts removed Buddhist shrines and ceremonies from Shintō shrines where they had previously coexisted, forbade Buddhist statuary representing images of the kami, and eventually ordered the removal of all traces of Buddhism from Shintō shrines. Promoted as a means of returning to the ancient way of the gods, the anti-Buddhist edicts were in fact designed to build a national identity that was free from what was viewed as the polluting influence of China.

In the aftermath of these edicts, violence erupted in a movement known as Haibutsu-kishaku (廃仏毀釈, "abolish Buddhism and destroy Shākyamuni"). Across Japan, anti-Buddhist rioters destroyed Buddhist temples, seized temple lands, and forced Buddhist priests to convert to Shintō. Within a decade of the beginning of the Meiji Restoration, more than twenty thousand Buddhist temples had been burned or demolished, countless works of Buddhist art destroyed, and Buddhism pushed to the brink of eradication. By the time the Japanese constitution was ratified in 1889, it was considered the patriotic duty of all Japanese to pay their respects to the kami at Shintō shrines throughout the country, despite the guarantee of religious freedom the new constitution provided. Zen temples suffered terribly under the anti-Buddhist reforms, and the inclusion of Zen spiritual ideals in the art of incense declined accordingly. However, the vast infrastructure and census data collected by the Tokugawa Buddhist temple system proved to be too significant to be discarded. The census data in particular was recognized as important in helping the new Meiji state govern, and thus its position on Buddhism softened, not "abolishing" it, but clearly demoting it from being Japan's primary religion to playing a subservient role to Shintō and the Meiji state.

Shintō, though, was more a code of conduct than an organized religion, and it possessed few beliefs about the afterlife and virtually no funerary procedures. Death was viewed as the ultimate source of uncleanliness, with the soul having left the deceased, no longer present or able to serve the kami. In addition to providing census records, Buddhism provided a useful alternative to Shintō in removing the deceased and purifying the body and those encountering it. During this period, the association of incense with Buddhist rites for purification of the dead altered the Japanese relationship with incense. Instead of being something to enjoy or view as an art form, incense became something considered a Chinese import associated with the utilitarian role of purifying the uncleanliness of death. Incense was offered in stick form at gravesites and family shrines, and its use and any spiritual connotations became linked with death rather than personal expression, entertainment, or art. The new relationship between Buddhism and the Meiji state religion was starkly captured by the saying "Live Shintō, die Buddhist."

The ritual appreciation of incense had strong ties to literary classics dating to the Heian period, and that literature, too, fell under the scrutiny of the new Meiji government. Heian classics such as *The Tale of Genji* and the *Kokin Wakashū*, knowledge of which was foundational for participation in the kumikō of Kōdō, were viewed by the Meiji government as works polluted by Chinese influence and the decadence of the Heian elite and thus deemed unsuitable. Instead, inspired by reading Western literary histories, Meiji leaders sought to reveal the pure Japanese spirit by establishing a curriculum of national literature to be the "flower of a people" (*kokumin no hana*, 国民の 花) rather than the writings of the elite. Through the application of *kokugaku* (国学, national learning), Heian classics were discarded from the national curriculum in favor of a new imperial mythology built upon the two oldest books of Japanese history, the *Kojiki* (*Records of Ancient Matters*) and the *Nihon Shoki* (*Chronicles of Japan*), both of which placed the emperor at the center of the Japanese universe.

The *Kokin Wakashū* was discarded and replaced with a new national anthology of poetry, the *Man̄yōshū* (万葉集, *Collection of Ten Thousand Leaves*). Believed to be compiled by poet Ōtomo no

Yakamochi in the eighth century, the *Mańyōshū* is the oldest Japanese anthology of waka poetry and fit the Meiji government's model for verse suitable for its national curriculum. Unlike the recited verse of the *Kokin Wakashū*, the poems of the *Mańyōshū* were intended to be sung. With more than 4,500 poems in twenty volumes, the *Mańyōshū* was divided into three poetic themes: songs for banquets and trips, songs about love, and songs of mourning. Also unlike the *Kokin Wakashū*, whose authors were Heian elite, the *Mańyōshū's* authors came from all social classes—from the emperor to aristocrats, soldiers to peasants, and street performers to folk-song composers—with nearly half the authors being unknown. For the Meiji, the *Mańyōshū* was the perfect choice, as it revered the emperor, emphasized Shintō themes, and was inherently Japanese. The *Kokin Wakashū*, which had been at the center of the art of incense for nearly a thousand years, was relegated to the category of Chinese-inspired works unsuitable for Japanese study.

Today, the Hamaguri Gate still stands, open to welcome tourists to the Kyoto Gyoen National Garden on the former Imperial Palace grounds. The still-visible scars left by bullets in its ancient wooden timbers echo the effects of the Meiji reforms upon Japan's art of incense. "Live Shintō, die Buddhist" continues to form a considerable association between incense and death, and each August, the Buddhist holiday Obon (お盆), which commemorates ancestors' spirits believed to temporarily return to this world, drives incense sales. Although both Chadō, the Way of Tea, and Kadō, the Way of Flowers, are well known around the world today, after a generation of decline under Meiji reforms, Kōdō, the Way of Fragrance, is far less known in the West and, despite a growing interest abroad, remains the least-known of the three geidō in Japan as well.

CHAPTER 13

再生

REBIRTH

Incense blooms into Japanese fragrance culture

A S RAPID MODERNIZATION LED TO EMPIRE, JAPAN EMERGED AS
a world power with victories over China in the First Sino-
Japanese War in 1895 and over the Russian Empire in the
Russo-Japanese War in 1905. As a wave of nationalism followed
in the early decades of the 1900s, Japan's reliance upon the West
as a model for modernization was questioned, and the traditional
Japanese culture that had been so quickly dismissed in the Meiji pursuit
of Westernization was reevaluated. Through a modern, scientific,
nationalistic lens, the cultural traditions of the refined arts were re-
examined as part of the new government's definition of what it meant
to be Japanese. The West's discovery of the traditional Japanese arts,
the revival of Heian literary classics, and a postwar economic boom
would lead to the Japanese art of incense rising from the ashes of
near destruction, the almost-forgotten geidō blooming into a modern

expression of Japanese fragrance culture, like plum blossoms appearing upon ancient wood after the snows of winter.

Even as the art of incense fell into steep decline, its literary, poetic, and spiritual foundations stripped by Meiji reforms, there were still those in Japan who sought to revive it and who continued to enjoy the ritual appreciation of incense. New life was breathed into the arts of tea and incense through women's education. By the 1890s, girls' schools began to include Chadō in their curriculum, with the Urasenke School of Chadō encouraging this trend by donating tea utensils as well as its iemoto's time and skill in teaching classes in the art. Books on Chadō and Kōdō began to be published, largely in the mold of the Tokugawa primer texts and picture books of the Edo period. For the art of incense, these books focused on the rudimentary aspects of the Kōdō ceremony, basic movements and etiquette, and the more simplistic kumikō. As these books were written for women, the art of incense became associated with women's play rather than viewed as a refined art form.

A perceived distinction developed between Chadō and Kōdō that reflected the different approaches used in their respective revivals. From the early days of the Meiji Restoration, the art of tea was promoted as more than just "play"; Chadō was positioned as having historical ties to the emperor through "rediscovered" traditions attributed to Rikyū. Emphasizing these traditions made Chadō suitable for the education of women, and the art of tea was promoted as creating appropriate traditional values for imperial subjects to display. However, no substantial ties were promoted between Kōdō and the emperor or Japanese tradition.

Just as they emerged concurrently at their inception, Chadō and Kōdō reemerged concurrently, largely through influential writings associating the refined arts with Japan's cultural traditions. Seeking to revive interest in the ritual appreciation of incense through articles written for Japan's major newspapers, beginning in 1903, Mizuhara Suikō provided suggestions to revive the incense ceremony, describing it as a more lofty, elegant, and literary-driven pursuit than the tea ceremony. In

1908, she published the book *Chadō to Kōdō* in which she expressed her regret that the ritual appreciation of incense had been largely forgotten, even by refined women like herself who were well-versed in the tea ceremony. Introducing the art of incense to a new generation, Mizuhara noted that she was saddened that she had only recently learned about the art of incense and its deep literary connections.

Attempts to revitalize incense as an art form promoted it as a way to appreciate "olfactory beauty," much in the way one would appreciate a beautiful painting or a fine sculpture. The influential painter Kubota Beisen studied the European masters in Paris, and his uniquely Japanese works graced rooms in the newly constructed Imperial Palace in Tokyo and were given as official gifts of Japan to Queen Victoria. Beisen painted in the Nihon-ga (日本画) style that incorporated Western techniques yet still maintained traditional Japanese approaches and motifs. He described beauty as that which pleases any of the five senses, expanding the appreciation of the arts beyond merely the visual sense. In his writing on the appreciation of beauty, Beisen described the ritual appreciation of jinkō as an example of the appreciation of olfactory beauty, highlighting the incense ceremony as an example of a fine art appreciated through the sense of smell, reflecting a new and modern view of the art form.

While Meiji reforms had rapidly abandoned the old in favor of the new at home in Japan, the traditional arts exported from Japan's newly opened ports caused a sensation in the West. Known as *Japonisme*, a term attributed to French art critic Philippe Burty in the 1870s, a craze for Japanese art and design swept Europe. As Japanese arts and crafts flooded into European ports, the bold colors, simple use of negative space, and striking beauty of Japanese porcelain, metalwork, and crafts provided an inspiration for European artists that is difficult to overstate. The uniquely Japanese aesthetic was fresh and antithetical to the neoclassical perfectionism in vogue, and it inspired European artists seeking a new way of seeing the world, ultimately giving life to the impressionism, art nouveau, and art deco movements. Japonisme influenced the Western art and design world for nearly half a century, inspiring works in leather by Hermès, cloisonné and silver by Boucheron, luggage by Louis Vuitton, jewelry by Lucien Gaillard, and wallpaper designs by Émile-Jacques Ruhlmann. Japanese Kōdō incense sets and their highly ornate utensils, once the centerpiece of samurai wedding dowries, increasingly found their way into the collections of Western museums and private collectors, valued as exquisite works for their beauty, superior craftsmanship, and refined maki-e decoration.

But beginning in the 1860s, it was the traditional images of Japan's floating world, the ukiyo-e prints made popular in the Edo period, that captured Western artists' imaginations. The simple, asymmetrical compositions, bold use of color, and dramatic foreshortening of subjects in ukiyo-e created a fresh visual language for a changing world, inspiring Western artists even as the traditional subjects of the prints were being modernized in Japan. Works by ukiyo-e masters Kitagawa Utamaro, Katsushika Hokusai, and Utagawa Hiroshige were highly sought after and collected by art dealers and artists alike. The artists influenced by ukiyo-e went on to become luminaries of the art world, and included the impressionists Edgar Degas and Claude Monet, post-impressionist Vincent van Gogh, the American painter and printmaker Mary Cassatt, modern artist Paul-Élie Ranson, and American architect Frank Lloyd Wright.

As the Meiji government promoted industrialization and Westernization at home, it was Japan's traditional arts, crafts, and architecture that were presented to millions of people worldwide through a series of world's fairs. At the International Exposition of 1867 in Paris, Japan first presented its classical arts to the world, exhibiting traditional paintings, ukiyo-e prints, byōbu (屏風, folding screen), metalwork, silks, and ceramics in uniquely Japanese buildings constructed for its national pavilion. But it was at the 1893 World's Fair in Chicago that Japan would truly stun the Western world. In the wake of growing nationalism, the Meiji government saw the Chicago exposition as an opportunity to highlight Japan's dignified culture, architecture, arts, and customs, strengthening Japan's image as a world nation while providing a clear differentiation from China. One of the first countries to enthusiastically express interest in participating in the Chicago exposition, Japan appropriated over $600,000 for its display, by far the largest investment of the foreign countries involved.

It was the construction of the Hōōden (鳳凰殿, Phoenix Hall) as the centerpiece of the Japanese national pavilion that proved to be the most influential and inspiring at the fair. Nestled among trees on an island in Jackson Park by Lake Michigan, the unique site embodied the Japanese love of nature. The Japanese pavilion provided a peaceful oasis away from the crowds penned in by the gleaming faux-white-marble neoclassical buildings of the other foreign pavilions. Unlike these temporary structures built for the exhibition, the Hōōden was a permanent, authentic example of traditional Japanese architecture, its design modeled on the ancient Buddhist temple Byōdō-in that was commissioned in 1052 by Regent Fujiwara no Yorimichi and located outside Kyoto.

Twenty-four Japanese carpenters, who traveled from Japan at considerable expense, erected the Hōōden on-site from pieces previously prepared in Japan then shipped to Chicago. The Hōōden highlighted three periods of Japanese history: its north wing was decorated in the style of the Heian court with rich traditional byōbu paintings; the central hall was decorated in the style of the Edo period of the Tokugawa, with elegant lacquer and gilded decoration; and the south wing was decorated in the style of the Muromachi period of the Ashikaga and featured a tearoom where the tea ceremony was performed. At the close of the exposition, the Hōōden was gifted to the City of Chicago.

Tea and incense featured prominently in Japan's exhibition at the Chicago World's Fair. In addition to the Hōōden, the Japanese pavilion also included a free-standing tea house and a Japanese bazaar, highlighting traditional Japanese life with demonstrations of Japanese art and culture. Not only were authentic tea ceremonies carried out in the south wing of the Hōōden, but the tea house located on the northern shore of Jackson Park's lagoon also provided traditional Japanese tea and wagashi (elegant sweets) to fair visitors so they could rest and enjoy an authentic Japanese experience in a tranquil natural setting. In the Japanese bazaar, all manner of arts and crafts were sold to visitors eager to return home with a memento of their encounter with the Japanese, and Japanese incense was formally introduced to the West through a display by incense manufacturer Shoyeido. The fragrance of incense wafting from the bazaar filled the Japanese pavilion, enchanting visitors with Japan's centuries-old traditional art. The response by fair visitors was tremendous, and Shoyeido soon developed a cone form of incense that could better survive an arduous journey at sea, exporting it to the United States for the first time in 1897. Demand soon outpaced the manufacturer's production capacity.

As Japanese incense was making an impression on eager Western markets, Western essential oils and liquid perfumes were making an equal impression on Japanese incense makers. Incense masters studied French perfume culture and added perfumes and floral essences to the list of ingredients used in Japanese blended incense. The creation of a "modern" incense culture that integrated Western perfumes with Japanese traditions led to a new form of blended incense. In 1911, the first Japanese floral incense, Hana no Hana (花の花, Flower of Flowers), was introduced to Japanese markets. Created by the gifted incense master Yujiro Kitō, the founder of the incense house Kitō Tenkundō, Hana no Hana incorporated Western perfume culture with Japanese incense-blending techniques; it would become one of Japan's most beloved floral incenses and lay the foundation from which Japanese floral incense grew.

In 1912, Yujiro Kitō returned to Japanese incense tradition as the inspiration for Mainichikoh (毎日香, Everyday Incense), a blended sandalwood incense based on the *kōjū* (講中) tradition. The kōjū was the court official charged with the offering of incense for purification and ceremony on auspicious days of the traditional calendar at the Imperial Court. Derived from the poem "Kō no Jittoku" ("The Ten Virtues of Incense"), the title had an almost priestly quality associated with it. Established in 1575, the position of kōjū was eventually inherited by the Takai family, and its eighth-generation master, Kōjū Jūemon, was particularly renowned for his incense-blending ability. Yujiro's Mainichikoh built on Jūemon's work in a modern expression of traditional sandalwood incense intended to "nourish the hearts of those who live hard day after day, so that people use it every day." Elegant and economical, Mainichikoh would go on to be one of the best-selling and most-produced incenses in Japan.

As the popularity of "modern" blended incense grew, the production center for incense shifted from Sakai to Awaji Island. The manufacture of stick incense had begun in Awaji in the 1850s, centered in the port of Ei, a hub for the import and sale of raw incense materials. When the strong seasonal west winds that buffeted Awaji dampened the local fishing industry, the fishers turned to incense making, because although the warm wind hampered fishing, it was perfect for the drying process of incense manufacturing. As Sakai rapidly modernized under the Meiji government, incense makers who continued with a traditional hand-crafted approach to incense began to relocate to Awaji, seeking the advantage of its favorable winds, and by the early decades of the 1900s, Awaji Island had become Japan's center of incense manufacturing.

By the start of the Shōwa period (昭和時代), which began with the ascension of Emperor Meiji's grandson Crown Prince Hirohito to the Chrysanthemum Throne in 1926, Japan had risen from a feudal nation unable to resist the demands of the Western powers to a powerful nation on the world stage. Within a single generation, Japan transformed from having virtually no naval defense to possessing one of the most powerful naval forces in the world, surpassed only by the United States and Great Britain. The Shōwa period saw Western modernization increasingly questioned and traditional Japanese culture revitalized. In the wake of escalating militarism and ultranationalism, *kokutai* (国体), the strict defining of a Japanese national identity and uniqueness of Japanese spirit, rose to prominence.

In his 1933 essay *In Praise of Shadows*, the preeminent Japanese author Jun'ichirō Tanizaki discussed traditional Japanese aesthetics, using the contrast of lightness and darkness to compare Western and Asian cultural identities. Over a wide range of topics, Tanizaki questioned taking the West as the model for Japan's modernization and promoted the traditional Japanese cultural aesthetic as that of the subtlety and simplicity of *sabi* (寂), an ineffable quality that could be likened to the "patina" achieved with age—a deep tranquil beauty that emerges through the passage of time and that reminds us of the fleeting nature of things. Using the example of writing utensils, Tanizaki wondered what would have happened if Japan had been able to modernize without the influence of the West, perhaps developing a modern version of the brush used in Japanese calligraphy rather than adopting the Western fountain pen, a modernization of the quill used in the West. Turning from his youthful infatuation with Western modernity to a deep reverence for traditional Japanese aesthetics, Tanizaki's interest in classical Japanese literature led to his translation of *The Tale of Genji* into modern Japanese.

Within the hypernationalism of kokutai, the "Japanese-ness" of traditions such as the geidō began to be reevaluated as elements of the Japanese spirit to be revived. Largely building upon the work of Mizuhara Suikō's *Chadō to Kōdō*, in 1929, Sugimoto Fumitarō's book *Kōdō* explicitly linked the incense ceremony to Japanese tradition as a refined art that evoked the national spirit. Appealing to the nationalistic flavor of the prewar years, Fumitarō channeled the samurai purity of ichibokudaki (one-wood burning), decrying modern blended incenses as "artificial" and criticizing the use of Western perfumes as detracting from the purity of the natural fragrant woods that epitomized the Japanese love of nature. Lamenting the decline of Kōdō, Fumitarō blamed the downturn in the popularity of the ritual appreciation of incense on an aristocratic decadence that reduced it to ceremonial gesture and produced an overreliance on literary classics to express the ineffable nature of fragrance.

In the decades preceding the Second World War, the ministry of education commissioned a group of prominent scholars to create a series of documents on kokutai, formally defining for the Japanese people the official interpretation of the Japanese national spirit. Published in 1937, the ministry's *Kokutai no Hongi* (国体の本義, *Cardinal Principles of the National Entity of Japan*) was considered required reading for Japan's teachers, especially those at the middle school and high school levels. Initially published in a run of three hundred thousand copies, over two million were eventually printed and distributed throughout the Japanese empire. Representing an official definition of national polity, the *Kokutai no Hongi* reaffirmed the emperor's divine status as a descendant of the sun goddess Amaterasu and the center of Japanese life. It blamed Japan's social ills on aspects of European and American culture that had been imported too rapidly during the Meiji government's hasty pursuit of modernization, and it mandated that the advancement of Japan instead be based on modifying Western practices to fit within traditional Japanese culture. It also recognized the traditional refined arts as vital expressions of the Japanese national spirit, highlighting the three geidō of Kōdō, Chadō, and Kadō as striking aspects of "our national way." After nearly seventy years of decline and attempted revitalization, the ritual appreciation of incense was reaffirmed by the *Kokutai no Hongi* as part of the official ideology of the government and, by extension, the emperor.

The first modern history of incense, *Kōsho* (香書, Book of Incense), was compiled in 1943 by Rikyō Isshiki, a disciple of the Tsuzuki branch of the Oie School of Kōdō. Written during the Second World War, his book included a preface by prominent Japanese author Rohan Kōda, one of the first persons to be awarded the Order of Culture, presented by the emperor himself in 1937, for his contributions to the advancement and development of Japanese culture. Kōda had a considerable interest in the incense ceremony and is believed to have selected the source material for the book and contributed notes on its drafts. In *Kōsho*, Rikyō Isshiki highlighted the incense ceremony as a means of spiritual training, enhancing concentration through the appreciation of fragrance. Looking through the moral lens of the time, he argued that the use of kumikō should be reduced, as many "frivolous" games used poems about love affairs, which promoted immorality. *Kōsho* emphasized the incense ceremony as being the precursor of the modern science of olfaction, connecting Japanese tradition to modernity by highlighting the Rikkoku-Gomi as an example of the refined art predating modern science. *Kōsho* had an influential effect on the perception of Kōdō and was reprinted four times before the end of the war. While Isshiki hoped to contribute to the science of olfaction, other wartime authors went so far as to stress Kōdō's olfactory training as a useful wartime skill in distinguishing poisonous gases on the battlefield.

In the aftermath of the war, the Allied occupation forces "demilitarized" the Japanese national curriculum, removing more than half of its wartime subjects as well as its focus on the glorification of military histories, Shintō legends, and mythic war heroes. Once eliminated from textbooks entirely, the classical literature of the Heian period began to reappear. In the decades following the Second World War, excerpts from Heian classics such as *The Tale of Genji* again made their way into textbooks as part of a new national curriculum. By the 1960s, literary scholars also began to reevaluate the *Kokin Wakashū*, which had been abandoned in favor of the *Manyōshū* for nearly a century. Although awareness of classical literature increased, after its having been nearly erased for a generation, proficiency with it and deep knowledge of it fell far short of that in the Edo period.

As the classical literature at the heart of kumikō returned to public awareness, the art of incense also reasserted itself, with both participants and scholars highlighting the relationship between the incense ceremony and newly reinstated literature. The head of the Oie School of Kōdō, Kimimasa Sanjōnishi, was also a professor at the Jissen Women's University and worked diligently toward the revival of the art of incense. Published in 1955, his book *Kōen Gayū* (*Play Elegant at Incense Ceremony*) described the fragrant categories of the Rikkoku and elaborated on the etiquette and rules of Kōdō. In his book, he also questioned the prewar "propaganda" that relegated the incense ceremony to little more than a competition to distinguish smells.

In 1957, Kimimasa expanded upon this assertion in his contribution to the first issue of *Jissen Bungaku*, a literary journal published by the humanities faculty of Jissen Women's University. Kimimasa lamented the loss of direct connection to classical literature in modern Japan. Highlighting the ability of the six classifications of fragrant woods in the Rikkoku to create a fragrant image that expanded on classical texts, he emphasized that the incense ceremony was about much more than olfaction; it was a method to bring the classics to life through fragrance. As the direct association of Kōdō with classical literature had been nearly erased in the wake of Meiji reforms, Kimimasa's assertion as the head of the Oie School of Kōdō represented a major step in the restoration of the art of incense to its literary foundations.

Buddhism and its use of incense was also revitalized after the war. In Japan's postwar constitution, government support for Shintō as the state religion was eliminated, the divinity of the emperor was repudiated, and Shintō institutions were reorganized into the Association of Shintō Shrines supported by private contributions. Buddhist institutions also saw a rebound in their fortunes as they turned to a new source of support: tourism. As views on Buddhism softened and Shintō returned to its pre-Meiji role of offering moral guidance rather than moral absolutes, the use of incense began to be accepted again for ceremony, appropriate once more as an offering to the Buddha and pleasing to the kami.

Zen also began to grow in popularity in the West through the efforts of the influential Sōtō Zen priests Shunryu Suzuki and Taizan Maezumi. Arriving in the United States in the late 1950s, their focus on supporting the Zen community brought a new awareness of meditation to Western thought and exposed students to the use of incense in spiritual development. Suzuki's students established the San Francisco Zen Center in 1962, and Maezumi founded the Zen Center of Los Angeles in 1967. The first Zen monastery outside Japan, Zenshinji (Zen Mind Temple) at the Tassajara Zen Mountain Center, opened in 1967, with Suzuki serving as its first abbot. The introduction of Zen to America reintroduced incense to the West much as Buddhism had introduced incense to Japan more than a thousand years earlier.

Capitalizing on the expanding market in the United States, the Nippon Kōdō Group was established in 1965 with offices in New York and Los Angeles. Begun as a branch of longtime Osaka incense manufacturer Kōkandō, Nippon Kōdō became an independent manufacturer in 1942. In 1947, when esteemed incense house Kitō Tenkundō was without an heir to assume the family business, Nippon Kōdō stepped in, inheriting the rights to the popular Mainichikoh and Hana no Hana incense lines. Less than a decade later, Nippon Kōdō inherited several priceless documents from the kōjū tradition of the Takai family, including documents from the influential and gifted incense master Jūemon. The company went on to develop many fragrances based on the recipes of Kitō Tenkundō's founder, Yujiro Kitō, and the kōjū traditions of Jūemon, extending its roots back to the first kōjū in 1575. Television commercials for Mainichikoh and the company's modern floral Seiun fragrances would make Nippon Kōdō a household name in Japan. By the 1990s, Nippon Kōdō began to acquire other well-known Western brands, such as French perfume-maker Esteban and American incense manufacturer Genieco, the maker of the well-known Gonesh brand.

With the postwar economic boom of the 1950s leading to the rise of leisure activities in the 1960s, Japan's art of incense continued to gain in popularity. As fascination with the geidō grew, a renewal of interest in Kōdō followed, accompanied by the Shino and Oie schools once again offering classes on the incense ceremony and the art of incense.

New handbooks were produced that presented Kōdō in a simpler, more approachable fashion, introducing the appreciation of incense to a generation less familiar with classical literature. Emphasis shifted from the intimidating formality of manners and etiquette to a focus on creating opportunities to learn about and appreciate fragrance as a wonderful gift of nature.

The emphasis on the appreciation of fragrance fit well with the use of incense as a means of relaxation and leisure, and created a growing culture of fragrance that was less reliant on the classics and more in line with the new concept of aromatherapy. Initially described in the 1920s by French chemist René-Maurice Gattefossé, aromatherapy's use of fragrance for relaxation and healing was little known outside of France until the late 1970s. Robert Tisserand was the first to introduce aromatherapy to a wider audience, publishing his groundbreaking book *The Art of Aromatherapy: The Healing and Beautifying Properties of the Essential Oils of Flowers and Herbs* in 1977. His book blended ancient wisdom with modern science, laying the groundwork for present-day aromatherapy.

Originally written for an English audience (in fact, the first aromatherapy source written in English), *The Art of Aromatherapy* went on to be published in ten languages and was translated into Japanese in 1985. Tisserand's book gave new meaning to Japan's art of incense, and the development of "room" or "hobby" incense gave the Japanese a way to enjoy fragrance by scenting their homes. The Shino and Oie Schools of Kōdō were increasingly featured in publications centered on the growing culture of fragrance in Japan. Articles written by the heads of each school introduced Kōdō, often accompanied by illustrated scenes from *The Tale of Genji* or photographs of exquisite incense utensils. As awareness of Kōdō rose, publications began to treat the ritual appreciation of incense as less about competition or play, and more as part of a worldwide fragrance culture that included wine, perfume, and gourmet foods.

As the art of incense experienced a resurgence in Japan, Japan's fragrance culture made its way to the West, and interest from abroad grew. Incense masters from both the Shino and Oie schools traveled to the United States to demonstrate the incense ceremony, with events held in New York, Los Angeles, and San Francisco in 1982 and throughout the world in the decades that followed. The first book available in English detailing the Japanese art of incense, *The Book of Incense: Enjoying the Traditional Art of Japanese Scents*, was written by Kiyoko Morita and published in 1992. Focused on introducing Japan's art of incense to a new audience, *The Book of Incense* covered incense ingredients, Japanese incense origins, traditional incense games, and an overview of Kōdō. Morita's approachable and easy-to-read book became Western audiences' introduction to the Japanese use of fragrance for enjoyment in daily life. Morita went on to be a founding member of the Boston branch of the Shino School of Kōdō and had a significant role in introducing the Japanese art of incense throughout the U.S.

Today, as the art of incense continues to gain in popularity in Japan and abroad, the Shino and Oie Schools of Kōdō offer classes to train a new generation of incense masters and provide Kōdō experiences for curious Japanese and tourists alike. Most major incense manufacturers offer space for classes on incense blending and Kōdō sessions in their retail stores, and Nippon Kōdō, Baieido, and Shoyeido all have branches located in the United States.

Awaji Island is now home to the Awaji Island Kōshi, a group of fourteen incense masters who oversee the entire process of incense production for their incense houses. Manufacturers based on Awaji Island are now the leading source of incense in Japan and produce 70 percent of all Japanese incense. Worldwide, Nippon Kōdō is now the largest manufacturer of incense, with sales of nearly $100 million in 2015. Today, their rarest and most expensive kyara is sold overseas, especially to Chinese and Middle Eastern markets, rather than in Japan. The company's fourth president, Masayoshi Konaka, believes the future of Nippon Kōdō, and that of the Japanese incense industry as a whole, rests in its ability to attract international customers.

As we conclude the epic story of the origin of the Japanese art of incense, we end where we began—with the most famous piece of fragrant wood in the incense world: Ranjatai. Nearly 1,300 years after Empress Kōmyō dedicated the emperor's incense to the Great Buddha at Tōdai-ji, Ranjatai continues to be carefully preserved in the Shōsō-in Repository at Tōdai-ji under the conservancy of the Imperial Household Agency. Put on public exhibition by the Nara National Museum only every ten to fifteen years, Ranjatai draws thousands eager to view it. As befits its relationship with the rulers of Japan, the last time Ranjatai was publicly displayed (as of this writing) was by the Tokyo National Museum in 2019 as part of a special exhibition celebrating the enthronement of Emperor Naruhito. Titled *Shōsō-in: Essential Treasures of Ancient Japan Passed Down by the Imperial Family*, an entire section of the exhibition was dedicated to incense and featured exquisite incense burners, ornate incense tools, and brilliant lacquerwork incense containers. Ranjatai, however, was the jewel of the show, attracting tens of thousands eager to view for themselves the fragrant piece of jinkō at the very origin of the Japanese art of incense.

II: SELECTION

Although your blossoms
elude our gaze, their color lost
amid flakes of snow,
send forth, at least, your fragrance
that men may know you are here.

KOKIN WAKASHŪ, BOOK 6: POEM 335

CHAPTER 14

KŌBOKU
Aromatic woods

K NOWN AS KŌBOKU (香木), RARE AROMATIC WOODS LIE AT THE
heart of the Japanese art of incense and are the centerpiece of
the incense ceremony of Kōdō (香道, the Way of Fragrance).
A rare and precious gift of nature, kōboku's aromatic properties often
transcend fragrance, possessing historic, cultural, and spiritual associations capable of transporting the listener beyond the mere sense of
smell. (See chapter 23 for a full discussion of "listening" to incense.)
Unlike the familiar floral fragrances expressed in a single season of
nature's flower blooms, the fragrance of kōboku is mysterious, taking
decades to ripen, with no two aromatic woods having exactly the same
scent. An enigmatic repository for nature's expression of fragrance,
kōboku has been a highly sought-after commodity for centuries,
treasured not only for its redolence, but as an expression of wealth
and social status. As such, there is no more appropriate place to start

169

a discussion of the selection of Japanese incense than by exploring the rare fragrant woods at the heart of it.

JINKŌ: ALOESWOOD

Known by many different names—aloeswood, agarwood, and oud among them—*jinkō* (沈香) has a wonderfully rich and mysterious fragrance that can vary from sweet to spicy to sour to bitter to an amazing blend of some or all of these characteristics in the same piece of kōboku. Because of its exceptional fragrance, jinkō also carries deep spiritual significance and is mentioned in some of the world's oldest religious texts, including the Torah, the Bhagavad Gita, the Sushruta Samhita, Islamic scriptures, and the Christian Gospels. Highly prized for over a thousand years in Japan, jinkō has been collected by emperors, shōguns, and *daimyō* (大名, feudal lords) alike for its fragrance and as an expression of wealth and power.

Jinkō is formed from a dozen or more species of trees in the *Aquilaria* genus as well as several species of the *Gyrinops* genus native to the jungles of Southeast Asia. Sourced primarily in Laos, Cambodia, Malaysia, Indonesia, and Vietnam, jinkō can also be found over a wider area, including parts of the Philippines, India, and China, with the tree species themselves found even outside the jinkō-producing regions. Dependent on the hot humid climate near the equator, the quality of jinkō is less related to the botanical classification than to the fragrance possessed. Producing a bell-shaped fruit with few seeds, these trees grow fast and bear fruit within a few years, and have white wood that is soft and easily damaged.

However, the wood of these trees is not fragrant. Instead, it is the resin the trees produce in response to injury—and the resulting resinated wood—that is considered jinkō. The precise way in which jinkō is formed is still uncertain and is considered by the Japanese to be a miracle of nature. Generally, however, when a tree sustains an injury—whether from a storm breaking off a limb or an animal piercing the trunk bark—it responds much like our own immune system, producing a dark resin to protect the damaged area, forming a sort of scar tissue. Over time, as the weakened area continues to be damaged through wind, weather, animal, or insect, more resin is produced, collecting in the damaged area or even deeper within the heartwood of the tree. In time, the weakened area may come under attack by mold and fungal infection, causing further immune response and accumulating additional resin. The effects of humidity, rainfall, altitude, and even fog and morning dew are all thought to contribute in some way to the fragrance of the resin.

Formally known as *jinsuikōboku* (ち沈水香木), meaning "sinking incense wood," though more commonly called by its shortened name, it is the density and quality of the resin produced that gives jinkō its name and its sought-after fragrant quality. The more resin that is produced, the more densely resinated the wood becomes, causing the jinkō to sink rather than float in water. However, it is the quality of the fragrance that is paramount, and even if jinkō does not sink in water, it may still be considered of high quality. Today, sinking and non-sinking grades are used as guidelines rather than absolutes regarding the quality of jinkō; however, the density of resin produced is generally correlated to the quality of fragrance.

To judge the quality, incense masters use all five senses, evaluating the wood's visual qualities such as pattern and color; feeling the wood's weight, texture, and hardness; listening to the wood's density by tapping; smelling the wood both at room temperature and heated; and putting a small piece in their mouth to taste the relative bitterness and sweetness to assess its sugar content. Regardless of quality, naturally resinated wood is very rare, with estimates that only 1 to 2 percent of wild *Aquilaria* trees produce the fragrant resin, even within the same area under the same conditions. When resin *is* produced, jinkō has a wide range of fragrances, even among wood produced in the same area. It is still unclear what causes one tree to produce jinkō while another does not, and factors such as location, climate, soil, and even the genes of the individual trees remain potential factors.

The harvesting of jinkō can take several forms. Over years, decades, or centuries, as the resin accumulates and ages within the tree, the resinated part of the tree may be cut, or the tree may die naturally. Generally, the greater the age of the tree, the longer it has for accumulating resin and for the resin to age, which enhances the depth of its fragrance. For meaningful amounts of jinkō to form, repeated damage over many years or decades must occur. As the resin accumulates, much like scar tissue in our own bodies, the weak area that is created can eventually shorten the life of the tree. If the tree dies naturally, after it falls to the ground, its white wood decomposes, leaving the resinated wood behind as a kind of fragrant fossil. Buried in the earth, the jinkō interacts with water and soil, which adds another layer to its fragrant qualities. In this way, the nonfragrant wood is removed by nature, leaving behind only the pure resin-infused incense wood of jinkō. If, on the other hand, the tree is harvested while still living, the resin-infused parts may be cut out with an axe or saw, allowing the tree to continue producing jinkō, or the entire tree may be felled and collected. Either way, much work remains to carefully scrape away by hand any remaining nonfragrant white wood that surrounds the resin-infused jinkō.

Demand for jinkō worldwide has increased significantly during the past century, leading to a depletion of jinkō-producing species of trees due to overharvesting, poaching, and deforestation. Vietnam, a significant source of high-quality jinkō, was particularly hard hit with damage by bombings and the spraying of defoliants during the Vietnam War. In 1995, the primary species harvested for jinkō, *Aquilaria malaccensis*, was listed as a potentially threatened species by the Convention on International Trade in Endangered Species of Wild Fauna and Flora (CITES), an international trade agreement originally signed by 184 parties in 1973. By 2004, CITES classified all *Aquilaria* species as potentially threatened. Accordingly, the majority of jinkō-producing nations no longer allow the harvesting of wild trees, while a few allow only limited harvesting under tightly controlled international trade restrictions. All trade in jinkō is heavily monitored internationally, with restrictions on the exportation of raw jinkō and related products. But the highly profitable nature of this fragrant resource makes illegal trade in jinkō ripe for poachers and corruption.

Although jinkō is the foundation for the Japanese art of incense and core to the refined art of Kōdō, primary demand comes from the Middle East and China. In the Middle East, jinkō, known as oud, has long-standing cultural and religious affiliations and is in demand for its fragrance. Large pieces are burned directly upon hot coals to produce fragrance that is used for enjoyment and relaxation and to scent clothing. In China, demand is driven by a financial nature, and jinkō is collected as an investment commodity and hoarded for its value while only rarely displayed as art or used for its fragrance. In contrast, the Japanese treasure jinkō as a rare gift of nature, and its use is carefully considered. During the ritual appreciation of Kōdō, for example, only a tiny piece of jinkō the size of a grain of rice is used. Even then, it is heated rather than burned to ensure the purest release of fragrance for as long as possible.

Since the 1970s, when the collection of jinkō in the wild was at its peak, the decline in wild jinkō has accelerated at a pace that has exceeded projections, and high-quality jinkō found in nature has become increasingly rare. Experts estimate that due to unsustainable harvesting and illegal poaching, jinkō-producing species have declined by over 80 percent in the past 150 years. In response, to ensure the continued availability of jinkō for future generations, several Japanese manufacturers and representatives from the Shino and Oie Schools of Kōdō have begun programs of afforestation in jinkō-producing regions such as Vietnam. In some countries, such as Indonesia, the planting of jinkō-producing species has been encouraged by the government as well. It is unknown if these afforestation trees will ever produce the type of resinated wood found naturally in the wild, but the goal is to plant thousands and allow nature to take its course, in hopes of providing a new sustainable source of jinkō for the future.

Another approach being tried in several countries is the artificial production of jinkō by intentionally damaging commercially farmed trees. In this method, jinkō plantations are filled with *Aquilaria* trees that are intentionally wounded by drilling holes into their trunks and injecting a solution of molds and fungus to encourage the production of resin. However, the Japanese, for whom a love of nature is at the core of the valuation of this fragrant wood, consider commercially created jinkō to be unnatural and inferior to wild jinkō. In the Buddhist tradition, the way the tree is treated in life is said to affect the energy of the tree's wood and resin; thus, the intentional harming of the tree is believed to taint the resin produced.

Today, jinkō is one of the most valuable commodities in the world, with the price per gram exceeding that of gold. The global market for jinkō was estimated to be $32 billion in 2020 and expected to double to $64 billion by 2030. Perhaps the most valuable tree in the world sits on the grounds of a temple on the Cambodian border. Over two hundred years old, the local villagers celebrate the tree as holy and constructed the temple to honor the tree. A military checkpoint has been erected to protect the tree from poachers, as its value in the current market has soared. Temple officials noted that in 2016, Japanese buyers offered the temple $23 million for its fragrant wood. They turned down the offer, as it would have required the tree to be harvested, killing what they revered as a holy expression of nature.

KYARA

Kyara (伽羅) is one of the most enigmatically fragrant and exceedingly rare substances on earth. Traditionally considered the highest grade of jinkō, kyara is the rarest of kōboku and the most prized. With a fragrance that is often described as eloquent, deep, and multifaceted, kyara is treasured not only for its inexplicable fragrance but also for a perceived connection with the divine. The Japanese have long associated a rich spirituality with kyara due to the difficulty in describing its scent, inspiring poetic allusions that attempt to express kyara's transcendence of fragrance, emphasizing the need to experience it directly.

Although kyara is most often considered a type of jinkō, the connection between kyara and jinkō remains mysterious, as the process through which jinkō reaches such a sublime state is still unclear. In fact, there are discussions about whether kyara is a higher grade of jinkō, something formed from jinkō, or an entirely different fragrant wood altogether, known as "kynam." The term "kyara" itself is a relatively recent term. In ancient Japan, there was no term differentiating the highest quality jinkō from ordinary jinkō. As the samurai began to focus exclusively upon the one-wood burning of *ichibokudaki* (木薫), jinkō with more complex fragrances possessing a greater quantity of softer resins was judged to be superior and began to be referred to as kyara, which may have been derived from the Sanskrit word for "black," translated through Middle Chinese.

Although kyara is believed to be created by the same *Aquilaria* genus of trees as jinkō, a key difference is that it is found in a considerably smaller area. Whereas jinkō is harvested throughout the equatorial jungles of the South Pacific and throughout Vietnam, the highest quality kyara is found primarily in the mountain plateaus of a few dozen square kilometers where the Vietnamese provinces of Dak Lak, Lam Dong, and Khanh Hoa meet. It is unknown what local factors create this miraculous fragrant gift of nature, be it the mountainous terrain, soil composition, temperature, humidity, rainfall, prevailing winds, or a combination of some or all. But the area has been known for centuries for its production of superior kyara.

In addition to location, a second key distinction between jinkō and kyara is the viscosity of the oil present in its resin. Although fragrance is considered first and foremost, it is the hardness or softness of the resin that is used to determine the quality of kyara. In general, the resin found in kyara is softer than that of jinkō and releases its fragrance at a lower temperature when heated. The viscosity of the resin found in kyara ranges from the dense oils of iron oil kyara and black oil kyara to the soft oils of yellow, blue, and green oil kyara. Even on the hardest side of this scale, the resin of iron oil kyara still remains softer than the resin found in typical jinkō. Green oil kyara is especially prized, as it is considered young and soft and it has the highest sugar content, which gives it an elegant, woody, floral sweetness and a strong sense of connection to nature. Dubbed "liquid gold" by traders, in its purest form, aged green oil kyara essential oil can command $80,000 per liter. The grade of kyara oil and its overall quality closely align with the sugar content of the resin and the bitter quality that tempers its fragrance. However, there are no specific measurements for this subjective quality, and accurately assessing kyara's quality, similar to a sommelier evaluating fine wine, requires considerable skill and experience.

As jinkō production has declined, so too has kyara production, making kyara one of the rarest substances on earth. Unlike jinkō, kyara has not been successfully cultivated, and its fragrance continues to be a miracle of nature that eludes artificial replication. As such, sources of kyara continue to decline rapidly, and no wild kyara of note has been found in Vietnam in more than a decade. Today, virtually all kyara is sourced from domestic supplies that have been collected over decades and that are held by various incense houses and private collectors. Whereas the largest consumers of jinkō are found in the Middle East, Japan remains the largest consumer of kyara. After the Vietnam War, many collections of kyara also found their way overseas to collections in America and Europe. As these supplies dwindle, there is, unfortunately, no other source available. Incense manufacturers have responded accordingly, increasing the price of their highest quality kyara products significantly, cutting the quantity of kyara in their incense, and/or reducing the number of sticks in the package. In recent years, several well-known manufacturers have had to discontinue some of their highest quality products and eliminate even well-known flagship products entirely. It is now feared that kyara will disappear entirely by the end of the century, if not sooner.

BYAKUDAN: SANDALWOOD

Known for its sweet, creamy, relaxing fragrance, *byakudan* (白檀), or sandalwood, is one of the oldest known fragrant woods, with a history of more than four thousand years of use in Southeast Asia. Declared a "Royal Tree" by the Sultan of Mysore, a kingdom in South India, in 1792, it became illegal for individuals to grow it, and to this day all sandalwood trees in India are owned and controlled by the government. Revered as a sacred tree, sandalwood has been used in the cremation of royalty as well as in a position of prime importance in Hindu and Buddhist religious ceremonies. It is said that when the Buddha died, his body was cremated using sandalwood, a tradition that continues today with a small amount of the valuable fragrant wood added during cremation to escort the soul of the deceased to the next life. Considered sacred in many religions, sandalwood traveled with Buddhism to Japan, and serves as a primary ingredient in many Japanese incense recipes. Prized for its fragrant heartwood, byakudan is used extensively in Japanese blended incense. The essential oil distilled from the heartwood is also widely used in perfumes, soaps, candles, cosmetics, aromatherapy, and increasingly in incense.

Sandalwood can be categorized into three primary areas of production—Australia, Africa, and India—with each sourcing it from a different species of plant. Sandalwood from the South Pacific Islands and Australia is collectively referred to as "Australian sandalwood" and is derived from *Santalum spicatum*, a parasitic tree native to the semiarid regions of the state of Western Australia. African sandalwood is found throughout a wide area of tropical east Africa, including Tanzania, Kenya, and Uganda, and is sourced from *Osyris lanceolata*, a parasitic small shrub-like tree that grows in rocky soil at the edge of dry forests. Indian sandalwood is what is commonly referred to as "true" sandalwood. Harvested from the heartwood and roots of *Santalum album*, a slow-growing evergreen tree native to India and Southeast Asia, Indian sandalwood grows up to 30 feet in height and is hemiparasitic, meaning it is dependent on a host plant for nutrients and water. Capable of using up to three hundred different species as hosts, *S. album* grows without any detrimental effect to the host plant. Taking fifteen to twenty years to reach harvestability, or sixty to eighty years to reach full maturity, Indian sandalwood is prized for both its rich, sweet, woody fragrance and its superior essential oil.

Unlike the fragranceless wood of the *Aquilaria* tree from which jinkō is produced, the heartwood and roots of *S. album* produce the essential oil that gives byakudan its fragrant properties. To harvest sandalwood, the tree is usually uprooted during the rainy season, when the soil is softer and extracting the roots from the ground easier. Next, the sapwood and bark are removed, as they are not fragrant and contain no essential oil. Byakudan intended to be used as fragrant wood is then cut into short logs of about 3 feet in length and left to dry naturally in the sun for up to a year, intensifying the fragrance in the wood itself. If harvested for sandalwood essential oil, the oil is extracted from the heartwood by steam distillation over a period of several days totaling 3 percent to 6 percent of the volume of wood.

Sandalwood oil has a sweet, powerful, long-lasting woody fragrance that serves as a base note in incense and perfumes. Oil from Indian sandalwood has the highest concentration of *santalol*, the organic compound that gives sandalwood its distinctive sweet creamy fragrance, at up to 90 percent of the oil's content. African sandalwood has the lowest santalol concentration in its oil and is increasingly used as an economical alternative to Indian sandalwood oils. Australian sandalwood has a softer fragrance than African sandalwood and is becoming popular for use in dipped incense sticks that use a bamboo core. One of the most widely used ingredients in incense, in addition to its fragrance, sandalwood oil also offers excellent fixative properties that extend the life of other aromatics, and it blends extremely well with a variety of fragrant materials.

Known as Rozan sandalwood, Indian sandalwood from Mysore in South India is considered the highest quality sandalwood in the world and produces the highest quality sandalwood oil. Grown in the rocky red soils of the northern slopes of the mountains in the area, sandalwood from Mysore has been renowned for its quality throughout Asia for centuries and is referred to as "Old Mountain sandalwood" by the Chinese. Highly sought for its rich, sweet, resinous fragrance, Rozan sandalwood is used as a premium ingredient in Japanese incense. In the past, Mysore sandalwood was harvested from ancient trees, often more than fifty to one hundred years in age. Today, however, this is no longer the case, as due to immense corruption, a patchwork of bureaucracy, and illegal and unsustainable harvesting practices, Indian sandalwood is rarely harvested from trees older than twenty years of age and the Royal Tree is on the brink of extinction in India. The increasingly young harvest age is a significant factor in the declining quality of both sandalwood and sandalwood oil, as the older the tree becomes, the greater the production of superior oil from its heartwood.

This has provided an opportunity for other regions, especially in Australia, to offer alternatives to the Indian sandalwood market. Accordingly, exports of sandalwood from countries other than India are rapidly increasing. As demand for sustainably harvested sandalwood grows, countries like Australia have put laws in place to ensure the future of the sandalwood industry. In the early twentieth century, the Western Australian government passed the Sandalwood Act of 1929, which strictly controlled the harvesting and planting of these endangered trees to ensure their sustainability, though their production did not ramp up dramatically until the twenty-first century. Limiting the harvest of *S. spicatum* to only a small percentage of trees each year, the Forest Products Commission (FPC) plants over ten tons of seed annually to replace harvested trees. The FPC is now the largest supplier of "wild" sandalwood, each year supplying over 50 percent of the *Santalum* traded in the world. For the Chinese who refer to Mysore sandalwood as Old Mountain sandalwood, this new reliable source of sandalwood from Australia is called "New Mountain sandalwood."

Wild *Santalum album* in India is now severely threatened due to overharvesting, corruption, and poaching, and the Indian sandalwood and sandalwood oil industry, once the world leader, has fallen into decline. Cultivation and harvesting are now completely under the control of the government, and since 2002, individuals have not been allowed to grow or harvest sandalwood. The Indian government now grants specific permission to select government officials who are then allowed to harvest and sell the fragrant wood. Harvested Indian sandalwood is sold only domestically, as the Indian government has banned the export of raw wood. To control the illegal production and export of sandalwood oil, the government registered the oil for protection under the Agreement on Trade-Related Aspects of Intellectual Property Rights (TRIPS agreement) and patented the trade name "Mysore Sandalwood Oil" under the Geographical Indications of Goods (Registration and Protection) Act of 1999 with the World Trade Organization. The Indian government has also begun to take a more aggressive approach to illegal harvesting and smuggling. However, regardless of these actions, due to rampant illegal poaching, government corruption, and black-market smuggling, wild trees are increasingly scarce, high-quality products are becoming more difficult to obtain, and the source of Indian sandalwood is shifting toward commercially farmed trees.

Commercial growth of sandalwood is challenging, however, as unlike *Aquilaria* trees that produce jinkō, *S. album* is a difficult tree to cultivate. Sandalwood is a large, slow-growing tree, and its hemiparasitic nature makes commercial farming of the tree difficult to initiate. Yet despite these difficulties, Indian sandalwood plantations are beginning to develop, especially in Western Australia. In 1982, the Australian government began testing various trees in a regional development program, and *S. album* showed considerable promise. The first commercial plantations of *S. album* were begun in 1999, with the largest one today located in Kununurra, in the northern part of Western Australia. Kununurra, with its subtropical climate featuring distinct dry and rainy seasons, hosts a plantation of over thirty thousand acres and began its growing with rare seeds of *S. album* imported from Mysore, India. By creating the best possible growing conditions and using seeds from the highest quality trees for its nursery stock, the Kununurra plantation produces harvestable trees in as little as fifteen years, compared to more than twice that time in the wild. Following a sustainable model, the Kununurra plantation ensures the future of Indian sandalwood by planting a new tree for each one that is harvested.

HINOKI: JAPANESE CYPRESS

Although jinkō, kyara, and byakudan have the longest history and are the most widely used in the Japanese art of incense, the invigorating fragrance of *hinoki* (檜), Japanese cypress, should not be overlooked. Used for centuries to build imperial palaces, Buddhist temples, and Shintō shrines, hinoki is considered sacred by the Japanese. Used in Shintō purification rituals since the eighth century, hinoki is revered for its beautiful, durable wood and fragrant essential oil. Naturally resistant to rot and insects, hinoki has a beautiful, tight grain structure and a lovely, pure fragrance that ranges from fresh evergreen to warm pine. Considered an exceptional building material, high-quality hinoki timber can last as long as a thousand years and is found in some of the oldest surviving wooden structures in Japan.

Unlike jinkō, kyara, and byakudan, which are imported commodities, hinoki is found throughout Japan. Sourced from the species *Chamaecyparis obtusa*, hinoki is a type of evergreen cypress with red-hued bark that grows to 50 to 75 feet in height at maturity. Old-growth trees can reach heights of 150 feet, and are considered sacred and thus protected by the Japanese government. In an effort to prevent defor-estation of old-growth hinoki, such trees can no longer be harvested in Japan today. Instead, hinoki is widely cultivated as a timber crop for its high-quality wood.

Hinoki is naturally fragrant with a fresh, evergreen, citrusy-sweet, woody scent. Hinoki essential oil contains many aromatic agents, including *hinokitiol*, a compound found in many members of the cypress family. Hinokitiol is known to absorb toxins and possesses strong antibacterial properties capable of inhibiting the growth of fungus, bacteria, and viruses. Hinoki essential oil is used in aromatherapy and is considered a natural air freshener in Japan. The fresh evergreen fragrance released by hinoki is believed to both stimulate and relax the mind, calming and focusing the intellect while reducing stress and fatigue. As other fragrant wood resources continue to decline, hinoki has seen an increase in popularity and in its use in a range of cypress, pine, and cedar incense fragrances.

TABU-NO-KI

No discussion of kōboku used in the Japanese art of incense would be complete without *tabu-no-ki* (椨の木). Often referred to as *makkō* (抹香, incense powder), unlike fragrant woods, tabu-no-ki is prized for having no fragrance at all. Without it, many of the fragrant woods above would be difficult or impossible to shape into the most common forms of incense, such as sticks or coils. In the production of incense, makkō refers specifically to tabu-no-ki, the powdered bark of *Machilus thunbergii*, the Japanese Bay tree, a large broad-leafed evergreen tree that can reach 90 feet in height, with a trunk over 3 feet in diameter at maturity. Its powdered bark forms what is known as a "binder," which acts as the glue that holds together the fragrant materials in Japanese incense. When warm water is added, makkō forms a sticky claylike paste that is easily processed and extruded into incense sticks or coils or formed into cones.

Tabu-no-ki has four grades, the highest of which is nearly odorless when burned. When combined with other fragrant materials, tabu-no-ki is almost imperceptible, making it a perfect neutral base upon which to build a fragrance. Makkō also exhibits properties as a burning agent, allowing it to burn completely and consistently and ensuring uniform combustion of all fragrant materials within the incense mixture. Nearly all Japanese extruded or pressed incense (stick, cone, or coil) is a mixture of aromatic ingredients bound together by tabu-no-ki. In general, the higher the quality of incense, the higher the proportion of high-grade fragrant materials to makkō, whereas more economical incense generally uses a high proportion of makkō with less and/or lower-grade fragrant ingredients.

Although presented here separately, it is not uncommon to find the three main woods of jinkō, kyara, and byakudan blended within incense recipes to enhance or moderate the fragrant qualities of each. Jinkō and kyara are often combined to elevate the fragrance of aloeswood and to reduce the cost of kyara products. Sandalwood and aloeswood are often blended together, utilizing sandalwood's sweetness to temper the sharp and bitter qualities of jinkō. By contrast, hinoki is most often presented alone to highlight the fresh and invigorating nature of its fragrance. Together or alone, these woods serve as the base for the majority of Japanese incense.

CHAPTER 15

六国五味

RIKKOKU-GOMI

Classifying jinkō

AT THE HEART OF THE JAPANESE ART OF INCENSE LIES JINKŌ, which, as a commodity imported to Japan, has developed a rich history associated with its selection and classification. Just as wines are named for the region in which they are produced—regions that play an important role in their bouquet—the region where jinkō is sourced also affects the character of its fragrance. But as no two pieces of fragrant wood have the exact same scent, jinkō's "personality" also has a role in its classification. Combining jinkō's country of origin with specific enigmatic fragrant qualities, the centuries-old aloeswood classification system known as the Rikkoku-Gomi (六国五味, Six Countries, Five Tastes) provides a useful framework for the selection and description of jinkō.

GOMI: THE FIVE TASTES

To begin understanding the Rikkoku-Gomi, it is beneficial to approach jinkō in terms of the sense of taste rather than smell. A gifted fragrance expert, Yonekawa Jōhaku was a merchant during the Edo period (1603–1868) with the reputation of having never made a single mistake during the many *kumikō* (組香, incense games) he attended. To achieve this feat, Jōhaku is credited with having developed a system of fragrance categorization known as the Gomi (五味, Five Tastes) based on the five fundamental tastes: sweet, spicy, bitter, sour, and salty. Jōhaku defined the character of a wood's fragrance through its association with taste to distinguish the various fragrant woods used during different incense games and to recall them effectively. As smell and taste are linked in the brain, with signals from one sense commingling with those from the other, using taste to describe fragrance was an intuitive and effective expansion of the senses used to appreciate incense. It is important to note, however, that the five traditional tastes of the Gomi were representative of those familiar to people of the Edo period; as our modern tastes have shifted, today the five tastes are used as guidelines rather than rote absolutes.

The classic tastes of the Gomi are:

Amai (甘, sweet): Traditionally likened to sugary, concentrated honey, the Gomi's "sweet" taste is less like the candy sweetness of today and more akin to the natural sweetness found in honey, sweet spices, or sweet fruits.

Karai (辛, spicy): Traditionally likened to grilled chili peppers, the Gomi's "spicy" taste may be displayed as a piquant, zesty quality with a sharp, warm overtone, such as the warmth of clove or cinnamon, or the heat of curry or pepper.

Nigai (苦, bitter): Traditionally likened to a medicinal or sharp brewed herbal fragrance, the "bitter" tastes of the Gomi may be compared to the bitterness of coffee, dark chocolate, grapefruit, or green tea.

Suppai (酸っぱい, sour/acidic): Traditionally likened to acidic fruits, the taste of "sour" in the Gomi shows up in the sourness of fruits like plums or nectarines, or the cool tartness of citrus fruits like lime, lemon, or yuzu.

Shiokarai (塩辛, salty): Traditionally likened to the briny fragrance of dried perspiration or seaweed, the Gomi's "salty" taste may be displayed as sharp and savory as well as salty.

A final taste quality that is sometimes used to denote an indescribable combination of tastes is written as *mu* (無, nothingness). An important concept in Zen Buddhism, mu is beyond reason and description and defies categorization.

The five tastes of the Gomi provide not only an intuitive connection to multiple senses, but also an easily accessible language capable of descriptions both simple and complex from which to discuss the fragrance of Japanese incense.

RIKKOKU: THE SIX NATIONS

With its roots in fifteenth-century Higashiyama culture, which emerged from the cultural salons of Shōgun Ashikaga Yoshimasa, the origination of a system to classify aloeswood is attributed to Sanjōnishi Sanetaka, renowned calligrapher, literary scholar, and master of courtly etiquette, and Shino Sōshin, an incense master and samurai military advisor to the Ashikaga shōgunate. Charged with organizing and cataloging Yoshimasa's large collection of fragrant woods, Sōshin and Sanetaka are credited with leading roles in creating the Rikkoku (六国), the "Six Nations" framework used extensively to classify jinkō.

During the Ashikaga shōgunate, jinkō was imported to Japan from relatively few countries throughout the South Pacific. Just as the region where grapes are grown affects the taste and character of a fine wine, the origin of jinkō similarly influences its fragrance. In the same way that wines are classified as Bordeaux, Burgundy, and Champagne—names derived from the regions of France where they were originally produced—the six countries from which jinkō was imported (or was believed to be imported) were adopted as classifications for organizing fragrant woods of diverse character. Although the two schools of Kōdō, Oie-ryu and Shino-ryu, assign tastes of the Gomi to the Rikkoku nations, it is now jinkō's fragrance more than its country of origin that drives its classification.

The Rikkoku continues to be used today as a framework for the classification of aloeswood within the following six nations:

Kyara (伽羅): The most highly sought-after grade of jinkō, Kyara is believed to come from the ancient Sanskrit word *karaaguru*, a combination of *kara* (black) and *aguru* (wood), meaning "black wood," even though Kyara can range in color from dark brown to a lighter golden brown. Kyara is found in nature only in a very small geographic area in present-day central and southern Vietnam and is exceptionally rare. The primary taste associated with Kyara today by both Oie-ryu and Shino-ryu is bitter.

Rakoku (羅国): Rakoku is originally believed to be an abbreviation of Shorakoku, the ancient name for the country of Thailand, and the consensus today is that Rakoku refers to jinkō originating from Thailand. Rakoku is usually soft pale yellow to warm tan in color, and according to Oie-ryu, the primary taste associated with it is sweet, while Shino-ryu associates it with spicy.

Manaban (真南蛮): Often very dark in color, Manaban is believed to be derived from the name Malabar, the coastal region of India. Manaban is thought to have been brought to Japan through Portuguese trade in tea, spices, and sandalwood. Today Manaban is generally considered to be jinkō imported from Cambodia. The primary taste associated with Manaban is salty (Oie-ryu) or sweet (Shino-ryu).

Manaka (真那伽): Manaka is thought to be a lingual adaptation of Malacca, the former capital and port city in present day Malaysia, near the southern tip of the Malay Peninsula. Rich brown with dark resinous streaks, Manaka is recognized by the oil left behind on the mica plate used during Kōdō and a fragrance that is short-lived and dissipates quickly. The primary taste associated with Manaka today is subtle or without taste (Oie-ryu) or salty (Shino-ryu).

Sasora (佐曽羅): The origin of Sasora is unknown, but the nation this classification represents is believed to have been either a region in India or the western portion of Southeast Asia near Myanmar and Bangladesh. Oie-ryu classifies sandalwood as well as jinkō as Sasora. Sasora is typically a warm pale yellow with brown resinous streaks, and the primary taste associated with it today is spicy (Oie-ryu) or sour/acidic (Shino-ryu).

Sumatora (寸門多羅): Sumatora is an alliteration of Sumatra, an island just south of the Malay Peninsula in the present-day island nation of Indonesia. Ranging from chocolate brown to warm tan in color, Sumatora today is generally considered jinkō of Indonesian origin. The primary taste associated with Sumatora by both Oie-ryu and Shino-ryu is bitter.

Oie-ryu adds to the six nations a seventh classification: Shin-kyara (新伽羅). This additional kyara classification is based on the era of a wood's origin, with kyara that came after the Keichō period (慶長, 1596–1615) recognized as Shin-kyara, the fragrance believed to have not matured to the level of ancient kyara.

Although over five hundred years old, the Rikkoku continues today to provide a useful framework for describing the unique and multifaceted character of one of nature's most mysterious and enigmatic fragrances.

SIX NATIONS. FIVE TASTES.
ENDLESS POSSIBILITIES.

At this point, it is important to emphasize that the Rikkoku-Gomi today is a classification of jinkō driven by fragrance more than by location. This distinction is critical, as it is easy to jump to rote memorization and assume all Kyara will display as primarily bitter and all Manaban will be salty or sweet. However, with the enigmatic fragrance of jinkō, classification is much more complex than the basic framework might at first indicate. Distinguishing fragrance at the level of the masters of the Rikkoku-Gomi takes years of training and experience, as there are myriad factors that make classification of jinkō highly complex.

First, the countries named in the Rikkoku are artificial lines on a map—lines that change over time and do not reflect the natural world. Many of the countries that existed when the Rikkoku was established now have different borders or no longer exist. For example, the port of Malacca, from which Manaka takes its name, ceased being a major exporter of incense over two hundred years ago when trade moved to Singapore, and Manaban is now accepted as jinkō from Cambodia rather than from the coast of India. Confining jinkō to shifting human-drawn lines on a map is not how nature works.

Second, our sense of smell is capricious, mutable, and unpredictable. No two people have the same sense of smell or perception of fragrance. Affected by temperature, humidity, wind, allergens, and personal preferences and associations, one person might notice certain notes more than another does, leading to completely different experiences even with the identical piece of jinkō. The same can be said for the sense of taste the Gomi represents. Over time, our palates change and shift, not only from infancy to childhood to adulthood, but also from generation to generation. The tastes of the Gomi are not absolutes, as the original definitions are based upon the sense of taste of the Japanese people of the Edo period, and do not necessarily align with that of modern Japanese or Western tastes. Even within each of the five tastes of the Gomi, the specific nation has an influence, producing

Kyara with bitterness different from the bitterness of Sumatora, or a sweetness in Rakoku distinct from the sweetness of Manaban.

Finally, jinkō itself adds to the difficulty with classification. One of the most magical characteristics of jinkō is the complexity of its fragrance. High-quality jinkō rarely has a single note that describes it. The flavor of fragrant wood is subtle, mutable, and often contains multiple tastes that present over time as the wood is heated. For example, it is not unusual for Kyara to start off bitter, warm to a soft sweetness, and continue to blossom with the addition of sour tones. The three notes together form a chord that creates an indescribably complex new character for the wood, with a delightful floral or exquisite gourmand fragrance that far exceeds the simple "bitter" attribution.

Because it is difficult to express the Rikkoku-Gomi in words or through a simple chart of region and taste, Sanjōnishi Sanetaka and Shino Sōshin also sought to convey the innate character of jinkō by ascribing archetypal characteristics of the social classes of the time to the wood groups of the six countries. Archetypes such as "samurai," "monk," "peasant," and "aristocrat" were invoked to describe the aromatic qualities of jinkō that transcended their fragrance, giving fragrant woods personalities and roles to express during kumikō. In this approach, the origin, taste, mental imagery, and disposition the wood evoked all would be captured in a manner as nuanced and complex as the jinkō itself.

Detailed in *The Book of Incense: Enjoying the Traditional Art of Japanese Scents* by Kiyoko Morita (1992), these five-hundred-year-old descriptions may seem quaint and even off-putting by today's social norms. But the goal was to transcend fragrance and arrive at a comprehensive expression of jinkō's character in humanistic terms readily understandable to the nobility of the fifteenth century:

Kyara: "Like an aristocrat in its elegance and gracefulness."

Rakoku: "Generally bitter and reminds one of a warrior."

Manaka: "Changing like the mood of a woman with bitter feelings."

Manaban: "Coarse and unrefined, just like that of a peasant."

Sasora: "So light and faint that one may think the smell has disappeared. It reminds one of a monk."

Sumatora: "It has something [...] distasteful and ill-bred about it, like a servant disguised as a noble person."

Today, descendants of Sanjōnishi Sanetaka and Shino Sōshin in the Oie and Shino Schools of Kōdō use the classic Rikkoku-Gomi as a traditional framework, allowing the character of the individual jinkō to seek its own classification. The *iemoto* (家元, house head of school) listens repeatedly to the fragrance of a specific wood over the span of nearly a year before applying a classification from both Rikkoku and Gomi. Afterward, the wood is named, allowing the perfect essence of its character to shine forth beyond any classification. Incense names are chosen from the mental imagery the fragrance evokes, such as a landscape, a season, or a classical *waka* (和歌) poem from the famous tenth-century *Kokin Wakashū*. The goal of this difficult task is to express the wood's fragrance in terms that reflect its true spirit, beyond any limitations, using the Rikkoku-Gomi as a guiding framework only.

Although jinkō was once classified based on its source nation, this is no longer the case. Much as wines classified as Bordeaux or Champagne are now produced worldwide, the Rikkoku-Gomi is used today as a framework, not an absolute classification. The Buddha noted that the finger pointing to the moon is not the moon; likewise, the Rikkoku-Gomi is a helpful guide for expressing in words the true nature of jinkō, but it is only a guide. Our true aim, akin to the brilliance of the moon, is to enjoy the enigmatic fragrance of jinkō.

CHAPTER 16

香原料

PRIMARY AROMATICS
Traditional ingredients in Japanese incense

J APANESE INCENSE IS FAMOUS FOR THE RARE AND FRAGRANT woods featured in its often-centuries-old recipes and celebrated in the ritual appreciation of Kōdō. But the majority of Japanese incense is blended with aromatic ingredients that have been used throughout history. As with kōboku, most of these ingredients are not native to Japan, having traveled from China with Buddhism over one thousand years ago. Used for their fragrance as well as their medicinal properties, the use of aromatics in blended incense in Japan dates back to the fragrance culture of the Heian period (794–1185 CE) and the kneaded incense of *takimonō* (薫物). Even today, many of the blended incense formulas are based on recipes that date back to the 1500s. Discussion of the selection of Japanese incense would not be complete without exploring the aromatic ingredients most commonly found in Japanese incense blends.

KEIHI: CINNAMON

Keihi (桂皮, cinnamon) is one of the oldest spices known to humankind. Traded on the Silk Road of antiquity from Egypt to China, it was written about by the ancient Greeks and mentioned in the Bible, and has long been used in traditional Chinese medicine. In the Napoleonic era, wars were fought for control of its sources and thereby the cinnamon trade itself. But what most of us commonly refer to as cinnamon today is in fact not true cinnamon at all. Created from the bark of the *Cinnamomum* genus of trees, there are two types of cinnamon in use today. Ceylon cinnamon, often called true cinnamon, is native to Sri Lanka and comes from the *Cinnamomum verum* tree. Cassia cinnamon, sometimes called Chinese cinnamon, comes from the bark of the *Cinnamomum aromaticum* tree native to southern China.

An evergreen tree that can achieve mature heights of 50 to 70 feet, *C. aromaticum* is widely cultivated for its bark throughout Southeast Asia and is the most common form of cinnamon in use today. Ceylon cinnamon saw a significant decline in use among the Allied countries during the Second World War, as Japan's military occupation of the Dutch East Indies led to a severe disruption in production. A decline in postwar colonialism led to a further shift away from the import of increasingly costly Ceylon cinnamon in favor of its less costly cousin, cassia cinnamon from China. Today what most in the West refer to as cinnamon is actually cassia cinnamon.

Cassia cinnamon is generally darker and possesses a stronger fragrance than the less common Ceylon cinnamon. Ceylon cinnamon, in turn, is generally milder and sweeter than its more common cousin. Used for its warmth and sweetness in incense, its sharp, woody, sweet fragrance is a staple in many traditional Japanese incense recipes and commonly paired with sandalwood or aloeswood.

CHŌJI: CLOVE

One of the primary ingredients in traditional Buddhist incense, *chōji* (丁子, clove) has been traded for more than two millennia along spice routes from China to India to Europe. The spice was highly valued in Roman society, and possession of it was a mark of social standing. As with cinnamon, wars were fought between European nations for control of the clove trade, especially between the Dutch and the British. In Japan, clove was a primary ingredient in the blended takimonō of the Heian period, and later, samurai would mix clove oil with the lubricating oil applied to their swords not only to prevent corrosion but also for its sweet fragrance.

Cloves are the aromatic flower buds of *Syzygium aromaticum*, a small evergreen tree native to the Maluku Islands of Indonesia, historically referred to as the Spice Islands. While clove is widely cultivated throughout Southeast Asia and East Africa, Indonesia is by far the leading producer today, producing over 110,000 tons of clove annually. Harvested while still unopened, the flower buds are collected and dried, turning from pink to their familiar deep earthy brown color. The name clove comes from the French word *clou* which means "nail," as the shape of the dried bud resembles cut iron nails.

A natural antiseptic and antibacterial, clove has many fragrant properties that make it one of the most renowned spices in the world and a staple of Japanese incense. Potent and woody, clove's fragrance is an enigmatic blend of earthy, sweet, and spicy. With a subtle camphoraceous quality, clove is warm and autumnal, reminiscent of holiday desserts and rich spiced drinks. Unique and mutable, clove can also display a slight acidity, cooling medicinal qualities, or even an exotic citrus top note that complements its sweetness. As an incense ingredient, clove also has a burning-agent quality, aiding in smooth and complete burning of all ingredients in the incense blend.

ANSOKUKŌ: BENZOIN

Ansokukō (安息香)—known thousands of years ago in Arabic as *luban jawi*, or frankincense of Java, and now commonly known as benzoin—has a long history of use as both an incense ingredient and as incense itself. Called *smyrna*, which literally means "incense" in Greek Orthodox traditions, it was used in ceremonial rituals of the church. The Romans prized benzoin as incense and traded for it along the spice routes of antiquity. Its fragrance is a staple in many blended Japanese incense recipes.

Native to the tropical islands of Sumatra, Indonesia, and Malaysia, benzoin is a balsamic resin produced by several trees of the *Styrax* genus in the Styracaceae family. Known originally as gum benjamin, the resin today has two primary source species: *Styrax benzoin* and *Styrax tonkinensis*. Often referred to as Sumatra benzoin, *S. benzoin* is similar to a rubber tree, and at maturity can reach heights of up to 90 feet. Also called Siam benzoin, *S. tonkinensis* is a semi-deciduous tree that at maturity also reaches heights of up to 90 feet and is cultivated extensively for both its aromatic resin and for its pulp wood. To harvest the resin, the trunk of the tree is scored and the white sap that flows from the wound is left to harden for a period of up to six months. The solidified resin is then harvested and cleaned to remove impurities prior to export.

As a fragrance, benzoin has a warm, creamy, vanilla-like bouquet. Rich, woody, and sweet, benzoin possesses a layered fragrance featuring a strong vanilla top note with subtle, powdery floral tones beneath. Sumatran benzoin adds to this a cinnamon-like quality akin to a warm, sweet caramel, with a slightly floral background note. Used not only for its fragrance, benzoin is well known for providing fullness and warmth to the full composition of incense ingredients as a fixative. By slowing the release of other fragrant materials into the air and extending the life of other aromatic ingredients, benzoin aids in creating long-lasting and far-reaching fragrances.

RYŪ-NŌ: BORNEOL

Known as *ryū-nō* (龍脳) in Japanese, borneol was once referred to as "dragon brain," because it was a rare and mysterious spice that came from over the distant seas, the home of mythical dragons. The Chinese thought borneol to be auspicious due to its uniquely cool fragrance. T'ang Dynasty officials revered borneol so much that they not only used it for incense but also shaped it into elaborate amulets to be worn for the cooling fragrance. Traded along the spice routes between East and West, borneol was a main source of camphor, worth more than gold for its use in perfume and incense.

Borneol is an aromatic crystalline resin that accumulates in clefts in the trunk of *Dryobalanops aromatica*, commonly known as the camphor tree. Native to Borneo, Sumatra, and Malaysia, *D. aromatica* is a giant tropical evergreen that reaches mature heights of over 150 feet, preferring hillsides in primarily coastal lowlands. Prized for its production of borneol resin, the camphor tree is also sought for its hardwood, known as *kapur*, which is regarded as being on par with teak. Records of trade in camphor wood date back more than a thousand years. Due to its high quality, kapur has been overlogged, and populations in Indonesia have declined by as much as 80 percent. As a result, *D. aromatica* has been placed on the International Union for Conservation of Nature (IUCN) list as an endangered species. Today the main fragrance component of borneol is increasingly synthesized from camphor, which possesses similar qualities.

Colorless, clear, and crystalline, borneol has a sharp, cool, uplifting, medicinal fragrance. There is no doubt of its presence when a box of incense is opened: its fresh camphor-balsamic character and sharp, mint-like cooling note make borneol quickly recognizable. Often used in Japanese incense, borneol sublimates the notes of other fragrant ingredients, carrying them upon its uplifting camphor coolness. Borneol is prized for its invigorating and refreshing nature, making it a common ingredient in incense created for meditation.

KAKKŌ: PATCHOULI

Kakkō (藿香), or patchouli, is often recognized as the "scent of the 1960s," but the use of patchouli's calming, earthy fragrance is measured in millennia rather than decades. Egypt's famous pharaoh Tutankhamen, who lived circa 1341–1323 BCE, had gallons of patchouli oil placed in his tomb for the afterlife; patchouli was grown in China for its medicinal properties over two thousand years ago; and Romans used patchouli for its fragrance and medicinal properties over a thousand years ago.

Patchouli was highly valued by early Europeans, who traded aggressively and paid handsomely for it, considering it to be worth as much as gold. During the Victorian era of the British Empire, dried patchouli leaves were inserted into textiles and silks exported from the East to ward off moth damage during shipping to Europe. The leaves scented the fabrics with their familiar musky fragrance, which became associated with fine-quality textiles of Eastern origin. The earthy scent soon became a symbol of "exotic" luxury from the Far East.

Yet today, patchouli is still associated with the "flower power" era of the 1960s. With many "tuning in and turning on" to meditation and Eastern philosophies, patchouli incense was often used for immersion in these new practices, as well as to hide the smell of marijuana that became a popular diversion at the time. In fact, the fragrance of patchouli is still so widely associated with the flower child era that is often used to recall the period by drawing on fragrance's ability to trigger memories and moods. For example, pop superstar Madonna had the packaging of her 1989 album, *Like a Prayer*, scented with patchouli to bring to mind the feeling of a 1960s church.

Patchouli is made from the dried leaves of *Pogostemon cablin*, a type of herbaceous mint native to tropical Southeast Asia. Now cultivated throughout tropical India, Indonesia, China, and South America, patchouli is a bushy evergreen perennial reaching approximately 30 inches in height and bearing small white to light pink flowers in late fall. The plant thrives in warm tropical climates, preferring indirect sunlight to produce the largest amount of fragrant material. Harvested by hand, patchouli is often left stacked to dry or bundled to encourage the start of fermentation prior to use.

The fragrance of patchouli is intensely rich, deep, earthy, and musk-like. Its sweeter green notes are long-lasting, as is its notorious warm, woody fragrance. Often described as "wet," patchouli presents an intense fragrance of dark, rich, earthy soil. As an incense ingredient, patchouli is used for both its fragrance and its excellent fixative properties, which help extend the life of other fragrant ingredients, providing a solid and steady base note upon which to build a fragrance.

KANSHŌ: SPIKENARD

Used as a fragrant spice for centuries and prized for its fragrant oil, *kanshō* (甘松), or spikenard, has long been a fixture in religious rituals. It is sung of in the Old Testament's Song of Solomon, and in the Christian New Testament, Mary used it to anoint the feet of Jesus at the Last Supper. In fact, spikenard is so entwined with Catholic history that it is used to represent Saint Joseph and is included in the coat of arms of Pope Francis. Spikenard's use is not unique to Christianity, however, as it finds a home in many cultures and religions, including Ayurvedic and Chinese traditional medicines, and has a long history of inclusion in Japanese incense, where it is often listed as "sweet pine."

Called by many names—including nard, nardin, sweet pine, and muskroot—spikenard comes from the rhizomes (shoots from tuberous root nodes) of only one species: *Nardostachys jatamansi* of the Valerian family. Native to the Himalayan regions of Nepal, China, and India, *N. jatamansi* is a small flowering plant that grows at altitudes above 9,800 feet, reaching a height of up to 3 feet and producing pink, bell-shaped flowers. Spikenard is cultivated for the fragrant, amber-colored oil derived from its rhizomes, with its botanical name, *jatamansi*, coming from the Hindi phrase "lock of hair" due to the appearance of its harvested rhizomes. Cultivated commercially today, its production is heavily regulated, as it is the only species to produce such intensely fragrant oil and, as such, has seen overharvesting and its natural environment depleted.

Spikenard has a sweet, animalic fragrance that is spicy and herbal, making it a natural alternative to musk. With slightly bitter, woody, earthy, and heavy tones, spikenard is sometimes likened to the smell of moss or the damp soil of the forest floor. Natural and warm, spikenard contains several chemical compounds similar to those found in borneol and patchouli, making it one of the most highly prized incense ingredients.

DAIUIKYŌ: STAR ANISE

Used medicinally for centuries in China, India, and Egypt, *daiuikyō* (大茴香, star anise) is also a key ingredient in many Eastern culinary traditions. One of the five ingredients of five-spice powder at the core of Chinese cooking, it is also used in Vietnamese *pho* (soup) and is common to Indian cuisine. It has also become a popular spice to flavor a wide variety of products, from liqueurs to toothpaste, and as a breath freshener after meals.

Star anise is the dried seedpod of *Illicium verum*, commonly known as Chinese anise. Native to the region of the Chinese-Vietnam border, and routinely cultivated in the southern provinces of China, star anise is a small evergreen tree that reaches a height of up to 16 feet at maturity, flowering from March until May. The fruit, in the form of an eight-pointed star-shaped seedpod, is then harvested in autumn just prior to ripening. After harvesting, the seedpod turns a deep rust brown as it is dried prior to use. Both the seed and the pod are fragrant. In Japan, a botanical cousin of star anise, *Illicium anisatum*, is viewed as sacred by many Buddhists due to its ability to remain fresh long after pruning. Known in Japan commonly as Japanese star anise, or sacred anise tree, *I. anisatum* is inedible and dangerously toxic.

Star anise contains the natural compound anethole, the same chemical compound found in peppermint, wild celeries, nutmeg, and coriander. The licorice fragrance of star anise is quickly recognizable. With an intense, warm, spicy sweetness, star anise also presents a balsamic, woody, and slightly floral undertone that enhances its licorice top note.

SANNA: GALANGAL

Known commonly as aromatic ginger, sand ginger, or resurrection lily, *sanna* (山柰, galangal) is a member of the family of flowering plants closely related to ginger and turmeric. Used throughout China and India both medicinally and as a culinary spice, galangal root has many well-documented uses that date back over a thousand years.

A member of the Zingiberaceae family of gingers and known botanically as *Kaempferia galangal*, galangal's genus is named in honor of German botanist Engelbert Kaempfer, who wrote extensively on the topic of Japanese flora in the late 1600s. A small, perennial, rhizomatous plant, galangal has flat, spreading leaves of 3 to 6 inches that grow low to the ground and that produce stemless white blooms marked with pink. Native to India and Burma and cultivated for its root stock throughout Southeast Asia, galangal thrives in humid tropical climates, growing in shady, forested understory locations.

Galangal's unique fragrance and spicy taste come from its high concentrations of the flavonoid galangin in its rhizomes. Sweeter than other ginger varieties, galangal has a warm, spicy, camphoraceous scent with rich woody and bitter notes. Galangal's bright, subtle, earthy fragrance often displays notes of citrus or pine sharpness with a camphoraceous acidity tinged with peppermint, giving it a sharp, peppery, piquant quality.

MOKKŌ: COSTUS

Mokkō (木香), commonly known as costus, has been used as traditional medicine and for its fragrance for centuries and is known by many names—saussurea, kuth, *kustha*, and *mù xiāng* among them. Like licorice, costus is one of the fifty fundamental herbs in traditional Chinese medicine and is also used widely in Tibetan and Ayurvedic traditions as both medicine and incense. In rabbinical texts, the root was called *kosht* and it was used in ancient Israel as an incense. Shipped from China to early Rome, costus was used as a culinary spice and fragrance. The root's name costus comes from the Sanskrit *kustha*, which translates as "that which stands in the earth."

A species of perennial alpine thistle, *Dolomiaea costus* is native to the Kashmir region of India near the borders of Pakistan, Afghanistan, India, and China. In India, it is believed to be of divine source, as it thrives in the high altitudes of the Himalayas, growing between 8,000 and 12,000 feet above sea level. A perennial herb, costus has heart-shaped leaves with jagged toothed edges and flowering stems that reach from 3 to 6 feet in height.

Primarily prized for its root stock, costus is cultivated commercially in mountainous regions of the Yunnan Province of China. The root is approximately the size of a finger, with off-white bark and yellow wood, growing up to 16 inches in length. *D. costus* in the wild is listed as critically endangered by the Convention on International Trade in Endangered Species of Wild Fauna and Flora (CITES) due to overexploitation and illegal trade. However, the biggest factor threatening the herb has been the increasing demand for its use medicinally. As a result, the government of India has prohibited the export of *D. costus* as either oil or processed product.

As an incense ingredient, in addition to being used for its fragrance, costus is used as a fixative to extend the life of other fragrant materials and as a diffusing agent to expand the overall fragrance. Costus has a bold, exotic fragrance with a distinct animalic quality, described as ranging from the smell of fine wool to that of a wild goat or wet dog, and it functions aromatically as a botanical musk. With woody, herbaceous notes of sweet tobacco or sage, costus has a beautiful musky fragrance that is soft yet long-lasting. *Mù xiāng*, the Chinese name for costus, translates as "wood fragrance," which is appropriate, as costus often presents as richly aged wood.

NYŪKŌ: FRANKINCENSE

Nyūkō (乳香)—also known as *luban* in Arabic and olibanum in English—is most commonly known as frankincense, from the Old French words *franc* (noble) and *encens* (incense). Long treasured for its sacred, ceremonial, and medicinal properties, frankincense has been used for over five thousand years. Presented to the baby Jesus by the Magi as part of the gift of gold, frankincense, and myrrh, it was frankincense that was the most valuable of the three.

Frankincense is obtained from the resin of several species of *Boswellia* tree that thrive in the arid climates of northeast Africa, Somalia, and the Arabian Peninsula near the coasts of the Arabian Sea. Although there are as many as twenty-five different species of *Boswellia* tree that produce the sought-after resin, *Boswellia sacra* is the genus to which frankincense is most often attributed, as it is believed to possess the most sublime and enduring fragrance. Native to Oman and Yemen in the Arabian Peninsula and Somalia in northeast Africa, *B. sacra* is a small deciduous tree with peeling, papery bark and densely tangled branches. Reaching heights of up to 15 to 20 feet at maturity, *B. sacra's* ability to tolerate harsh, arid conditions allows it to grow in the poorest soils, even seemingly out of rock. It is not unusual for *B. sacra* to grow on steep, rocky cliffsides, often making harvesting the trees somewhat dangerous.

In recent years, the population of frankincense trees has been declining due to increasingly frequent harvests to accommodate the demand for their fragrant resin. As the trees are being pushed to exhaustion, the lack of rest time between harvests has caused germination rates of *Boswellia* seeds to drop by as much as two-thirds, which is resulting in far fewer new trees. Several species of *Boswellia* are now listed as threatened species due to overharvesting and elimination of their natural habitat, with cultivation and production increasingly being strictly regulated.

The harvesting of frankincense begins with stripping off a portion of the bark with a sharp knife. The injury triggers the tree to start the process of gummosis, a natural reaction in which a milky white sap is produced to prevent infection. Stripping the bark is a delicate process, as injury stresses the tree and too much injury could reduce future production or even kill the tree. Once the bark is stripped, the resin is left to bleed out and harden for a period of several weeks. The hardened resin forms into droplets called "tears," which are then harvested by hand.

Much like grapes grown for wine, the shape, color, and quality of the tears are affected by many factors, such as the species of tree, region of growth, soil type, climate, and season of harvest. All these factors combine to create significant variety in frankincense resin, even from the same species of tree. For many people, especially in the Arab Gulf states, the trees of the Najd region near the Dhofar Mountains in Oman are considered to produce superior resin due to the trees' slow growth, the fog-prone environment near the seacoast, and the large tears produced.

Just as no two fine wines are alike, describing the fragrance of frankincense is not straightforward. Depending on the region and grade of resin, frankincense can be any combination of rich, sweet, woody, warm, fresh, and fruity, and may even possess delightful citrus and balsamic green notes. In addition to its heavenly fragrance, frankincense is used in Japanese incense for its fixative properties, extending the life of other fragrant ingredients in the recipe.

JAKŌ: MUSK

Used medicinally and as a fragrance for over five thousand years, *jakō* (麝香), or true musk, is one of the rarest and most luxurious commodities known to exist. Over the centuries, musk has been displayed in pouches to ward off evil, carried into battle by samurai, added to ink by scholars to create fragrant works of calligraphy, and worn by royalty as an aphrodisiac. The origin of the word musk comes from the Sanskrit *muskah*, which means "testicle," referring to the assumed source of this fragrant material. Although musk today generally refers to a wide range of animalic fragrances derived from plant materials, or more often a synthetic approximation known as white musk, musk originally was the name given to the secretions from a gland of the musk deer.

Musk deer are in fact not actually deer, but seven distinct species of *Moschus* of the Moschidae family. Standing only twenty inches tall and weighing in at a scant twenty-five to thirty pounds, musk deer are nocturnal and live primarily in the mountainous alpine regions of southern Asia across the Himalayas. They differ from true deer in several anatomical ways, such as producing tusk-like canine teeth instead of antlers and the male's having a musk gland. Only mature male musk deer produce musk, which is stored in a hairy sack about the size of a golf ball. Although resembling a testicle, the gland is used to secrete a pheromone to attract a mate.

Today, natural musk from musk deer is rarely used, and sale of wild musk is illegal. Due to hunting and poaching, musk deer were driven to the brink of extinction, with populations nearly vanishing from their original habitat across the Himalayan range. Musk deer are now listed as an endangered species and their conservation is strictly controlled under CITES. Natural musk was used as a fragrance extensively as late as the nineteenth century; however, due to the astronomical price of natural musk, a synthetic alternative was sought well before concerns for the preservation of the musk deer began. Today, nearly all musk fragrance used is a collection of synthetic white musk.

Given the exotic and unique fragrance profile of natural musk and the emphasis on natural ingredients used in Japanese incense, other aromatics with similar fragrance profiles, such as spikenard, are often substituted for it. However, recent efforts in China and Russia to produce musk sustainably through commercial farming of musk deer have proven promising. Recent studies have concluded that musk deer are able to be farmed sustainably through proper management and breeding of the animals. With over sixty years of experience, the Chinese have mastered the craft of extracting this "soft gold" without harming the deer. Labeled as "musk from breeding deer" by the Chinese government, this form of natural musk is available for legal trade.

Raw musk is quite unpleasant and strong smelling and requires processing before it can be used for its fragrance. Initially a sepia-colored paste, once dried, the content of the musk gland is referred to as musk grain due to its black, granular consistency. The musk grain is then powdered and soaked in grain alcohol for several months up to several years. At this point, musk takes on an extraordinary and unique fragrance that is surprisingly light, powdery, and sensual. Contrary to common belief, musk is not heavy or dark, but rather sweet, complex, floral, and earthy. Often described as the fragrance of baby skin, even in small quantities, true musk possesses an extremely powerful aromatic presence that is at the same time subtly light—in complete contradiction to its dark and overbearing reputation. As an incense ingredient, musk is treasured for both its fragrance and superb ability as a fixative to enhance other aromatics and create long-sustaining fragrances.

KAIKŌ: ONYCHA

Like musk, *kaikō* (貝甲香, onycha) has been used as an incense ingredient for over a millennium. But unlike natural musk, onycha is still widely in use today. Often listed as "shell fragrance" in Japanese and Chinese incense, onycha has been used throughout the Mediterranean,

Middle East, India, and Tibet as both incense and perfume. Used since biblical times, onycha is specifically mentioned in the Bible and is believed to be the source of the blue dye used to color Jewish prayer shawls and the robes of high priests. Onycha is used not only in the incense traditions of Japan, but also in the premium incense of Indian, Tibetan, Middle Eastern, and African traditions. During Japan's Heian period, onycha powder comprised up to one-quarter of the ingredients used in the Mukusa no Takimonō (Six Kneaded Incenses) enjoyed by the Imperial Court.

Onycha is the operculum of various species of sea snail of the Gastropoda class of mollusks. In ancient Greek, onycha represents the word for "fingernail" or "claw," as the operculum looks like fingernails when dried. Essentially, the operculum can be thought of as a door or lid that the mollusk uses to close the opening in its shell to protect itself from predators or to prevent drying. The operculum consists of proteins extruded at the foot of the sea snail, much like a fingernail, and is removed from the fleshy part of the mollusk during processing. The shape, which ranges from circular to oval, and the size vary depending upon the species and type of shell opening produced. As an incense ingredient, onycha may come from the operculum of many different species located in Southeast Asia, South America, and Africa. Today much of the onycha used in Japanese incense is of South African origin.

People who have hunted for shells on a beach and forgotten a fresh find in their car know firsthand the pungent smell of shellfish. Therefore, prior to being used as an incense ingredient, the operculum must be heavily processed. After cleaning, opercula are soaked in a mixture of vinegar and water, grain alcohol, or even wine, and then slowly baked to remove any remaining proteins that create an unwanted shellfish scent. Once they are completely dried, the opercula are ground into onycha powder for use as an incense ingredient.

As a fragrance, onycha has been used as a natural musk since ancient times, as high-quality onycha has a leathery, animalic, musk-like fragrance. Onycha can also impart a soft, powdery quality prized in both incense and perfume. With salty, mineral, and medicinal notes, onycha is often used to provide a savory element, invoking a marine fragrance. Onycha also possesses a binding and harmonizing aspect that stabilizes and preserves fragrance, increasing the depth and longevity of the incense blend it is part of. Prized for its fixative effect upon other fragrant materials, onycha is often used for prolonging fragrance duration and shelf-life.

In a practice refined over centuries, Japanese incense masters have used these primary aromatics to create incense with an almost infinite range of fragrances. Each ingredient offers a unique character for an incense, and when combined with a featured wood base, the resulting fragrance is greater than the sum of its parts.

CHAPTER 17

形状

FORMS
Different types of Japanese incense

D RAWING ON CENTURIES OF EXPERIENCE CREATING FRAGRANCE, Japanese incense takes many forms, ranging from raw wood to fully blended incense. The most common type of Japanese incense made today is stick incense, but many forms have been used for centuries and reflect historical and cultural practices that have been carried forward. When selecting Japanese incense, it is helpful to have some basic knowledge of the many different forms available, their uses, and their origins. As befits its popularity, special emphasis is placed on the characteristics and manufacture of stick incense.

KŌBOKU: FRAGRANT WOOD CHIPS

Intended for the appreciation of fragrant woods, chips of *kōboku* (香木) are a premium item sold by many manufacturers. Usually no more than 2 millimeters thick, the size of the wood chip varies depending upon the type of fragrant wood. Generally, sandalwood is available in chips 16 millimeters square, aloeswood in chips about 8 to 10 millimeters by 15 millimeters, and kyara in chips not much larger than a grain of rice. Intended to be cut into small, rice-sized pieces and heated on a mica plate over a hot coal buried in ash, fragrant wood chips are the centerpiece of Kōdō and used for the appreciation of incense burned for pleasure in *soradaki* (空薫, "empty burning") and for formal appreciation in *monkō* (聞香, "listening to incense"). Sold by weight and specific wood, many manufacturers offer sets of fragrant wood chips aligned with the seasons or highlighting each of the six nations of the Rikkoku.

SHOKŌ: GRANULATED INCENSE

Known as *shokō* (焼香), literally "burning incense," granulated incense is a dry mixture of incense ingredients cut into very small pieces for burning. Granulated incense can be a mixture of fragrant woods and aromatic ingredients or just a mixture of fragrant woods. Originally intended for use in Buddhist ceremonies, granulated incense is burned by placing a small amount directly upon a hot coal to immediately release its fragrance. As granulated incense is burned directly, little control over the fragrance is achieved, and the incense is rapidly turned to smoke and consumed. Because of shokō's use as a religious offering, smaller amounts of high-quality ingredients are preferred to larger quantities of lower-quality materials, making granulated incense a more premium product. Although not its intended purpose, granulated incense can also be heated to appreciate its fragrance in the same fashion as wood chips.

ZUKŌ: POWDERED INCENSE

Used for both purification of the body and as a personal fragrance, powdered incense, or *zukō* (塗香), is applied directly to the wrists and earlobes like perfume. Powdered incense contains a combination of naturally aromatic spices, such as cinnamon, clove, and camphor, and utilizes body heat to create a unique personal fragrance. Used for centuries, powdered incense is most often blended with sandalwood, as aloeswood does not produce fragrance unless heated significantly.

NIOI-BUKURO: SACHET INCENSE

Used for personal fragrance as well as to scent and protect clothing from insects, *nioi-bukuro* (匂い袋, incense sachets) are intended for use without heating. Sachets range from small, simple paper packets of fragrant ingredients that can be placed in a drawer, pocket, or wallet, to colorful silk brocade or kimono fabric pouches intended as elegant fashion accessories, to large bags of fragrant material used to scent a room. As many traditional aromatic ingredients have insect-repellant qualities, incense sachets have been used for centuries to protect kimonos during storage, much in the way mothballs have been used in the West. Traditionally filled with finely ground ingredients that release their fragrance at room temperature, incense sachets commonly include spices like cinnamon, borneol, clove, ginger, star anise, and sandalwood powder, and they have a useful life of up to one year.

NERIKŌ: KNEADED INCENSE

With roots over a thousand years old, *nerikō* (練香, kneaded incense) is often made following recipes that have origins in Heian-period Japan. An original form of blended incense, kneaded incense combines finely powdered fragrant woods and aromatic spices. Then, using honey, plumb, or apricot as a binder, the mixture is rolled into small balls about 8 to 10 millimeters in diameter. Once formed, kneaded incense is often aged for a period of months up to a year to blend and intensify its fragrance. Kneaded incense recipes are some of the oldest in use today and often consist of more than a dozen ingredients. Nerikō formulas and production techniques are closely guarded secrets of Japanese incense manufacturers. Primarily made by hand, kneaded incense creates a highly unique fragrance that varies depending upon the age of the incense, ambient temperature and humidity, and the season in which it is used. Intended to be heated rather than burned, kneaded incense is placed on a bed of hot ash atop a buried coal to slowly release its fragrance over a period of hours. Producing little smoke, the fragrance from kneaded incense has a magical quality, as it seems to spread invisibly, gently filling the space. For this reason, kneaded incense is often used in conjunction with the tea ceremony or to scent rooms.

ENSUIKEIKŌ: CONE INCENSE

A popular form of blended incense, *ensuikeikō* (円錐型香, incense cones) were first developed in 1897 by the manufacturer Shoyeido as a form of incense that was capable of better withstanding the rigors of being shipped overseas to the West. Cone incense combines fragrant ingredients with tabu-no-ki as a binder, and then the mixture is pressed into a cone-shaped mold. In general, cone incense is approximately 8 to 10 millimeters wide at its base and 20 to 24 millimeters in height, with a short burning time of about eight to fifteen minutes. Intended to be used where a quick and powerful burst of fragrance is desired, cone incense can be burned easily by placing it on a ceramic incense holder and lighting it. Cone incense also has the advantage of producing little ash, which is contained in the small area of the burning cone.

UZUMAKISENKŌ: COIL INCENSE

Invented in Osaka during the Meiji period (1868–1912), *uzumakisenkō* (渦巻き線香, coil incense) was originally intended for continuous use during Buddhist ceremonies for the deceased, from the wake right after death until forty-nine days later when the spirit was reborn. Believed to be a source of nourishment leading the deceased to the next life, incense was to be ritually burned day and night at the home altar without fail. Coil incense was designed to burn for twelve hours at a time, thus requiring the lighting of incense only twice a day, in the morning and the evening. Although coil incense is still used for this purpose today, it has also been repurposed for scenting large spaces or welcoming guests. Made in much the same way as stick incense, coil incense is made by feeding a wet string of incense through a machine that wraps it around a wire pin, forming a spiral-shaped coil. Still available with twelve-hour burn times from some traditional manufacturers, coil incense today more commonly has burn times of only two to three hours.

SENKŌ: STICK INCENSE

Known as *senkō* (線香), stick incense is believed to have been introduced to Japan from China as early as the 1300s, along with Zen Buddhism. At the dawn of the Tokugawa shōgunate in the seventeenth century, its manufacturing techniques were imported from China, making incense more readily available to a mass audience and leading to senkō becoming a popular way for Edo's growing *chōnin* (町人, "townsman") class to enjoy incense. (See chapter 11 for more information.) Today, stick incense is by far the most common form of incense produced in Japan. Unlike the familiar Indian "joss stick" incense that is made by rolling fragrant materials on to a nonfragrant bamboo core like a lollipop, Japanese stick incense is extruded like spaghetti and made with nothing but powdered fragrant materials.

Generally, senkō is available in three sizes, the majority having a diameter of approximately 2 millimeters. Exceptions to this are sticks extruded with a thicker square profile intended to enhance the strength of the fragrance by increasing its burning area. Mini-size sticks (*mini sun*, ミニ寸) are usually 57 millimeters long (2.25 inches), with burning times up to fifteen minutes. Mini-size sticks are usually found for specialty fragrances or those containing high-end woods, but some fragrances are produced in multiple sizes, including mini. By far the most common size of senkō is short-size sticks (*tan sun*, 短寸), which are most often 135 to 140 millimeters (about 5.5 inches) long with burning times of twenty-five to thirty minutes. "Great" or large-size incense sticks (*dai kunkō*, 大薫香) vary in length from 20 to 33 centimeters (8 to 13 inches) up to as much as 74 centimeters (29 inches), the diameter increasing in longer sizes, with burning times of up to eight hours. Sometimes referred to as "temple incense," large-size senkō is meant to be used for Buddhist ceremonies or meditation sessions and, as such, is intended to burn for the entire duration of the event.

The manufacture of senkō is a blending of art, skill, and technology. Although most Japanese manufacturers have centuries of experience making incense, modern technology, laboratory environments, and automated processes are being carefully integrated with traditional methods. Making senkō is a multistep process that requires a great deal of skill and attention to detail, with strict quality control every step of the way.

In general, stick incense is manufactured in the following way.

STEP 1: SELECTING AND FORMULATING RAW MATERIALS

The first step in making stick incense is the act of acquiring the raw materials. With many of the raw materials becoming increasingly difficult to obtain and as most are imported to Japan, this is done through extensive networks of suppliers developed over decades. Additionally, incense manufacturers understand the increasingly rare nature of these raw materials, and many employ researchers to help ensure their continued legacy through performing field research around the globe on cultivation and harvest as well as conservation and afforestation.

Once the materials are acquired, rigorous quality control measures are undertaken. These measures, often conducted under laboratory conditions, include establishing reproducible measurement methods and creating safety standards for those who make and use incense. Emphasis is also placed on developing methods that extend the use of raw materials, use source materials effectively and efficiently, and explore new product potential. These quality control measures are increasingly being elevated to meet the highest international standards.

Raw materials can take the form of plant-based products, oils derived from woods and plants, and whole-wood materials. During inspection, all raw materials undergo strict testing for quality, potency, and consistency of fragrance. Whole materials are carefully crushed and ground into powder. This process is monitored especially for fragrant woods, as any frictional heating diminishes the wood's fragrant properties.

STEP 2: WEIGHING AND COMPOUNDING

Once the raw ingredients have been selected and reduced to powdered form, the manufacturer begins weighing and compounding the various ingredients. Because many incense recipes use a number of different ingredients, each ingredient must be carefully weighed to ensure the proper ratio when mixed with the others. Many of these recipes are tightly held trade secrets, especially for manufacturers' flagship product lines. Often, these recipes can be traced back hundreds of years through blending books, and many of the formulas have seen little variation over time. While traditionally done by hand, weighing and compounding is an area that is becoming increasingly modernized, with some manufacturers using fully automated, computer-controlled blending systems.

Once all the powdered ingredients are measured, they are mixed together. At this stage, binders, colorants, and any remaining materials are added to the powdered mix. Once completely blended, the ingredients are passed through a sieve to remove any impurities and to further refine the uniformity of the powdery mixture. The finer and more uniform, the better the fragrant materials will blend in the following steps.

STEP 3: KNEADING

After sifting, the powdered mixture is put into a kneading machine and hot water is added. Kneading takes a great deal of skill, as the amount of water needed varies based on the type of mix, the ambient temperature, and the ambient humidity. After thirty to forty minutes of kneading, the mixture begins to take on a claylike consistency. Once the mixture solidifies into a single mass of clay called *tama*, it is shaped and readied for the next step by putting it into a mold and pressing it into a cylindrical mass.

STEP 4: EXTRUSION

Next, the tama is placed in a hydraulic extruding machine. With multiple tons of force, the incense in clay form is extruded through a stainless-steel plate with rows of small holes, much like dough through a pasta press. The small holes can vary in size and shape, depending upon the product being produced, but most often the holes are sized to achieve a dried stick with a diameter of 1.8 to 2.0 millimeters. Over time, these holes get worn by the friction of extrusion and their diameter changes, eventually requiring the plate to be replaced. However, any change in diameter does not constitute a quality defect, as the finished product is packaged by weight rather than by the number of sticks.

As the wet strings of incense are forced from the extruder, a skilled artisan collects them by hand on a board called a *bonita*. The incense is carefully captured as straight as possible upon the board's surface, with the ends allowed to hang over the bonita's sides like wet pasta. Immediately after the incense is captured, it is trimmed to the bonita's length using a bamboo spatula, and the trimmed-off wet ends are collected and recycled. Once the bonita is filled with trimmed incense, it is set aside, and another is used to collect more wet strings of extruded incense. This is done many times until a stack of bonita with wet strings of incense is collected.

STEP 5: RAW INCENSE

Once the tama has been extruded and collected, it is considered raw incense. At this point, the wet raw incense from several bonita is combined onto one long board, called a model board, which can be made of wood, metal, or cardboard. This is a very important step and one of great craftsmanship. In one swift motion, the raw incense is lifted by hand from the bonita using a bamboo spatula. Significant skill and training are required, as the incense is quite soft and easily marred at this stage. As the raw incense is transferred to the model board, it is inspected for quality and straightness. Wet sticks that are marred, broken, or not straight are recycled.

Considerable care is taken to ensure the wet incense sticks are lined up straight with no gaps between them. They are also smoothed by hand to ensure uniform consistency. Once the contents of multiple bonita have filled the model board, the number of sticks on each board is made uniform by removing any additional sticks from the ends; as with other discarded sticks, these are collected and recycled.

STEP 6: CUTTING

At this stage, the raw incense is usually longer than the finished product. Once the raw incense has been inspected and prepared on the model board, it is cut to size in multiple rows using a bamboo spatula or rotary knife like a pizza cutter. Once cut, the incense may be transferred from the model board to a drying board made of corrugated cardboard (if it's not already on such). Executed by hand, this process takes great skill so as to not damage the incense when moving it.

STEP 7: DRYING

The individual drying boards are arranged in what is called the laminated drying method, in which they are stacked one atop another. This allows air to pass through the corrugation of the cardboard to slowly and evenly dry the incense and prevent the sticks from warping or bending. Once multiple drying boards have been stacked together, the stacks are transferred to a drying room.

Traditionally, natural drying has been used in the manufacture of incense, and some manufacturers consider this the most appropriate way to dry raw incense. Natural drying usually takes several days in the hotter summer months or up to two weeks in the cooler winter months. However, other manufacturers are moving toward a modern drying method, in which blowers are used to circulate air through the corrugated spaces in the cardboard. In this method, temperature and humidity are carefully monitored and kept constant to ensure even and consistent drying. This method cuts drying time significantly, from weeks to two days or less.

During drying, the incense sticks begin to shrink. To ensure the sticks do not warp, quality checks are conducted to eliminate any gaps caused by shrinkage, keeping the incense tightly together. This ensures that the sticks will dry as straight as possible. Any sticks that are found to be broken or warped are removed and recycled.

STEP 8: OPTIONAL BUNDLING AND AGING

After the sticks have dried, depending upon the desired end product and quality level, they may be collected into bundles and, bundled or not, they may be aged. During collection, the dried incense goes through another inspection, and broken or warped sticks are removed from the drying boards and recycled. If bundled, the sticks are then collected by hand into consistent size bundles as measured by weight. Bundling the sticks together further keeps them from warping and provides rigidity and strength to reduce the risk of breakage.

Either bundled or loose, the sticks may be aged, which allows the ingredients in the incense to further blend together and the fragrance to stabilize. Generally, the higher the quality of the end product, the more likely it is to be aged and the longer it will be allowed to age.

STEP 9: FINISHING AND PACKAGING

The final step in producing stick incense is also the final quality control check. Incense is inspected as it is prepared, wrapped, and packed according to the product line specifications. Incense sticks that are bundled are packed in a box. Incense sticks that are not bundled are gathered and weighed during this step, then packed loosely in a box. Stick incense is packaged by weight, so the diameter of the stick and number of sticks is less important than the total package weight.

Driven by their end use, the many different forms of Japanese incense provide fragrance for any occasion, from the most ordinary to the sublime, and highlight the evolution of the Japanese art of incense over its 1,400-year history.

CHAPTER 18

出発点

WHERE TO START
Beginning the journey with Japanese incense

Hen first selecting Japanese incense, the vast range of price points and myriad fragrances can be intimidating and raise many questions. What makes one Japanese incense cost so much more than another? Is there really that big of a difference between an economical fragrance and a premium fragrance? Which one should I start with? With such an incredible array of Japanese incense available, understanding the subtle and varying qualities of the different levels of incense is helpful in knowing where to start along the Fragrant Path.

THREE GENERAL CATEGORIES OF INCENSE

To generalize, Japanese incense can be roughly divided into three fluid and often overlapping levels, which for the sake of discussion we'll refer to as *mainichi-kō, tokusen,* and premium incense. These generalized categories vary a great deal by manufacturer, and each may have different fragrant characteristics, feature different ratios of fragrant woods and aromatics, and have varying quantities of rare ingredients. Much like fine wine, these categories present different tastes and uses, and appeal differently to each person's unique olfactory palette. As such, these levels should be thought of as general divisions based on fragrance composition and *not* as a value judgement of "good," "better," "best."

MAINICHI-KŌ: EVERYDAY INCENSE

Mainichi-kō (毎日香) means "everyday incense" in Japanese. With its roots in the everyday use of incense in the Buddhist altars found in many Japanese homes, mainichi-kō incense has been created for burning multiple sticks every day. As such, it is generally the least expensive incense, contains the most common ingredients, and has the lowest ratios of fragrant woods to binders. Some brands include perfumes or artificial ingredients to embellish the small quantities of fragrant woods and aromatic ingredients used.

Generally, the fragrant notes of mainichi-kō are more uniform and feature fewer notes overall, with little of the variation often seen in more expensive incense. Often these are "one-note" types of incense in popular, common fragrances, such as lavender, patchouli, or jasmine. When not single-note fragrances, mainichi-kō rarely features more than two or three key aromatic ingredients, with the fragrance usually built on a sandalwood base. Additionally, the fragrance that remains after the incense has extinguished, known as the afternote or residual note, is most commonly shorter and quicker to die off.

But mainichi-kō is not without its beauty and appeal. Many daily incenses are highly regarded and are often some of the best-selling product lines found in Japan. Offering more straightforward fragrant landscapes with less subtlety and shorter learning curves, mainichi-kō is a great way to begin the journey into Japanese incense and to learn various fragrant notes. It is a good choice for adding a background fragrance or setting a mood, or when a long-lasting fragrance is not desired. Some mainichi-kō lines are refined, elegant, and enjoyable just to spend time with.

TOKUSEN: SELECT INCENSE

Tokusen incense can generally be thought of as mid- or upper-mid-range incense, depending upon the manufacturer. *Tokusen* (特撰) means "special" or "select" in Japanese, with its key difference from mainichi-kō being the increased amount of high-quality ingredients, more select fragrant woods, and a higher ratio of fragrant materials to binder. Tokusen incense also tends to more closely focus on its fragrant wood base, using its other aromatic ingredients to emphasize the unique character of the wood. High quality sandalwood, aloeswood, and hints of kyara are often featured in tokusen recipes. Where mainichi-kō has a more consistent fragrant presentation, tokusen incense offers an increasingly rich fragrance score with more depth and life, notes that vary in strength and potency throughout the burn, and often long-lasting afternotes that can be quite changeable as they die off.

As Japanese incense is predominately made from high quality natural ingredients, its aromatics possess a natural ebb and flow of fragrance intensity and consistency. With a tokusen product, this ebb and flow gives the fragrance a life that highlights the quality and rarity of the ingredients used and that often creates an exquisitely complex fragrance. In this way, a single incense can present a variety of subtle fragrance differences throughout the burn or over a range of sticks. Tokusen's dance of fragrant notes sets it apart from more economical incense, but that dance also makes its learning curve more pronounced. Many tokusen fragrances require more active listening and experience to fully appreciate them, as their dance is often content with presenting its fragrant notes through a subtle elegance that can be easily overlooked.

PREMIUM INCENSE

Premium incense is generally made from the rarest and most select fragrant woods, often combined with small amounts of the most precious and highest-quality fragrant ingredients, and features the highest ratio of fragrant material to binder. Often these are manufacturers' flagship incense titles based on secret recipes, many still prepared as they have been for decades or even centuries. As such, these are also the most expensive Japanese incenses, with their rare ingredients often meeting or exceeding the cost per gram of gold. Premium incense may feature rare Mysore sandalwood but more often contains the highest quality aloeswood and the highest concentration of the rarest and most prized fragrant wood in the world: kyara.

Premium incenses are some of the most subtle, complex, and elegant fragrances available. Often producing multiple notes dancing together in an exquisite complexity of rhythms, premium incenses highlight the very best qualities of their rare fragrant ingredients in some of the most stunning and sublime fragrances available. The rarity of these ingredients makes premium incense increasingly in short supply, with several manufacturers eliminating their highest-end products due to the lack of availability of their rare fragrant woods. As such, premium incense is designed to be listened to fully, with care and attention in its use and appreciation. Premium incense is sought for its transcendent fragrance as well as its ability to create a desired mental state. Often producing the most intricate of fragrances, filled with notes active with life, premium incense typically has the longest afternote of the three levels of incense, with the afternotes often considered a key feature and highly desirable.

Although it is easy to try to compartmentalize Japanese incense into these three categories based on their typical attributes, the generalizations above are intended only as shorthand to begin a journey. In fact, thanks to incense's natural ingredients and centuries of development by Japanese incense masters, these categories are often quite fluid. One manufacturer's tokusen product may overlap another's premium product. There are manufacturers whose mainichi-kō are highly regarded and rival other's tokusen fragrances. In the other direction, some manufacturers actually produce kyara mainichi-kō, presumably simulating the fragrance of kyara with economical aromatic ingredients, as it is unlikely any kyara could be included at the typical mainichi-kō price point.

As a general rule, as an incense approaches the premium end of the spectrum, rarer and greater quantities of high-quality ingredients are used. Additionally, as incense approaches the premium end of the spectrum, more direct listening and development of the olfactory palette is required to fully appreciate it, in contrast to incense intended for a supporting role or background use. Finally, as incense approaches the premium level, it is capable of producing more pronounced effects upon mood and mental state, more intricate and subtle fragrances, and longer-lasting afternotes that are often just as pleasant and surprising as the fragrance when the incense is first burned.

BEGINNING SELECTIONS

When it comes to the selection of Japanese incense, there is a clear corollary to the selection and appreciation of wine. Fine wines come at different price points, appeal to different palettes, and often require a certain level of knowledge to appreciate; Japanese incense offers a similar experience and learning curve. But that is its beauty. The development of the olfactory palette is part of the journey to be enjoyed on the Fragrant Path. Just because an incense is intended as mainichi-kō doesn't mean that it can't be greatly enjoyed and used regularly. Conversely, just because an incense falls within the premium category doesn't mean that it will be fully appreciated or even enjoyed when first listened to. Finding fragrances that resonate and are enjoyable is more important than becoming a connoisseur of the most expensive and rare. Most people will find fragrances at all three levels that they enjoy for different reasons and occasions, and favorites often change and evolve over time as the olfactory palette matures.

Regardless of category, an individual's experience and personal taste should be used to determine which fragrances are the most enjoyable for them at the time. The goal is to enjoy the unique gift nature has provided in its fragrant woods, highlighted through centuries of the Japanese perfection of the art of incense. When deciding where to start the journey on the Fragrant Path, many people find the following suggestions helpful.

START WITH INCENSE SAMPLERS

One of the aspects of Japanese incense that often raises concern with those first starting out is the large number of sticks in a box of Japanese incense. While in the West incense is sold in small packs of fewer than thirty sticks, even small boxes of Japanese incense tend to have fifty or more sticks, and in the mainichi-kō category, where most people are likely to start, it's common to get more than a hundred sticks. This often raises the question: What if I don't like it? This is a natural concern, as no one wants to spend money on something they don't like, especially when they've paid for so much of it. When starting out, one of the best ways to find fragrances that resonate is to begin with incense samplers.

Many Japanese incense houses sell sample packs of their best-selling lines that have one or two sticks of up to a dozen different fragrances at a very affordable price. Some of these sample packs are real values, with incense ranging from the most basic to the top-of-the-line product all in the same pack. Some manufacturers even provide sample packs of their premium lines with single sticks of each exquisite fragrance at a price well below the cost of a full box. Incense samplers are an excellent way to explore many different fragrances without the worry of spending money on something that may or may not be liked. Through an incense sampler, one gets the macro-level experience of a wider range of fragrant woods and aromatic spices than a single box could provide, and can identify which fragrances resonate and which do not, allowing more confidence in deciding which direction to take for further exploration.

FOCUS ON A SINGLE FRAGRANCE

In Kōdō, the highest form of ritual appreciation of incense, all distractions are removed from the environment and the participant's complete attention is focused upon listening to incense. This allows the listener to open to the subtle variances and refined interplay of notes that otherwise might be overlooked. However, there are many ways to apply this same focus on the fragrant qualities of Japanese incense that are not as rigid as those required for Kōdō. One of the easiest ways is to enjoy a single incense at a time over an extended period.

When new to Japanese incense, people often try many different brands and fragrances in rapid succession. A few sticks of one are rapidly followed by a few sticks of another in an effort to experience many different Japanese incenses as quickly as possible. This is a completely natural desire, especially when the excitement of discovering new fragrances is kindled. However, listening to too many fragrances in rapid succession can lead to sensory overload, making it easy to overlook an individual fragrance's delicate notes and subtleties or to blur the experience of one fragrance with another.

With this in mind, once an incense sampler has been completed, it can be beneficial to choose a favorite and focus on that one incense, listening deeply and repeatedly over an extended period—at least several days, maybe a couple of weeks—before moving on to another fragrance. Something magical happens when we experience a single fragrance for an extended period: our senses develop, and we find nuances we can't with just a couple of quick sticks. This micro-level practice allows the incense to open to us, and lets us get to know the fragrance on a much deeper, more profound level.

STRENGTHEN THE SENSE OF SMELL

A common concern expressed by those starting out is the ability to perceive the subtleties of the highly refined nature of Japanese incense. Indeed, we tend not to develop our olfactory sense to the same extent as our other senses; additionally, as we age, our sense of smell diminishes. But just as working out at the gym strengthens our muscles, focusing our attention on our sense of smell strengthens our ability to discern subtle fragrant notes, no matter our age. Japanese incense, with its centuries of refinement and high-quality aromatic ingredients, is perfectly situated for strengthening our olfactory palette. But unlike a workout at the gym, strengthening our sense of smell requires only that we be mindful of it.

One of the beautiful qualities of Japanese incense is that it possesses the ability to work subtle fragrant notes back and forth, into and out of awareness. By focusing our attention on this fragrant dance, we can improve our ability to "hear" different fragrant notes and their subtle nuances, strengthening our olfactory palette over time. As each person's sense of smell is unique, and because of the way we perceive fragrance, each incense is unique not only to each person, but also to the moment in which it is experienced. That means that fragrances can shift and develop over time as the moment changes, as our awareness increases, and as our tastes change and become more refined.

Incense samplers help us identify fragrances that resonate from a macro perspective. Spending time with individual fragrances deepens the understanding of them at the micro level. As our olfactory palette begins to mature through simply focusing upon incense, subtle nuances and the interaction of various notes become more apparent, opening us to greater enjoyment of this rare and fragrant gift of nature.

III: USE

*When springtime blossoms
glow on the flowering plum,
we know it at once,
though we travel without light
across the Hill of Darkness.*

Kokin Wakashū, Book 1: Poem 39

CHAPTER 19

使用と安全性

BASIC USE
Safely enjoying stick incense

U PON OPENING A NEW BOX OF INCENSE AND GETTING THE first hints of its fragrance, excitement and anticipation grow. Experimenting with different fragrances and finding a place for them in daily life can be energizing, soothing, and fulfilling. From relaxing after a long day at work, to welcoming guests, scenting spaces, practicing mindfulness, or remembering ancestors, Japanese incense can fill many different roles. When used correctly and thoughtfully, Japanese incense is easy to enjoy safely, enhancing our lives through fragrance. This chapter focuses on the use of stick incense, which is the form of Japanese incense most often encountered today.

THE ENVIRONMENT

As in Japan, most incense sticks in the West are burned in homes and personal spaces. The environment in which incense sticks are burned affects both the fragrance and the personal wellbeing of the inhabitants. With that in mind, the following environmental factors are good to be aware of when using incense.

TEMPERATURE AND HUMIDITY

Atmospheric conditions such as ambient temperature and humidity have a direct effect upon the perceived strength of incense. This has been known by the Japanese for centuries. In *The Tale of Genji*, written over a thousand years ago, Prince Genji schedules the judging of his incense-blending competition for the day after a rainstorm to take advantage of the moist air. During the Muromachi period (approximately 1336–1573 CE), it was common to use a room that overhung a pond to appreciate incense, making use of the increased humidity created by the pond.

The humidity level of the space where incense is burned affects the overall perception of its fragrance. In general, warm, humid air is more efficient at transporting fragrance molecules, increasing their volatility as they evaporate from burning incense. But optimal atmospheric conditions have a "Goldilocks" window where they are "just right," as temperature and humidity that are too high or too low will suppress the fragrance of incense. Full of water vapor, air with high humidity can trap fragrance molecules, depressing their dispersion in the air, whereas low humidity may cause the fragrance molecules to evaporate more quickly, shortening their effective life. Lower humidity levels also increase the speed at which incense burns, thus producing more particulates, which obscure the fragrance and create health concerns. Generally, the lower the humidity level, the lower our ability to perceive fragrance and the greater the number of harmful particulates produced. As temperature and humidity are often linked, colder temperatures tend to be dryer and higher temperatures more prone to stifling humidity. This is why in the cold, dry winter months, fragrances are less pronounced, whereas in warm, moist months, fragrances seem to pack a greater punch.

When using incense, it is best to control both humidity and temperature as much as possible to create an environment favorable for experiencing its fragrance. In the cooler winter months, humidifying the air helps moisturize nasal passages and provides water vapor that increases the air's ability to transport fragrance molecules. In the hot, humid summer months, use of an air conditioner to reduce temperature and humidity aids in maintaining the right balance of heat and moisture in the air. If air-conditioning is not available, enjoying incense in the cooler morning or evening hours better approaches the Goldilocks window by avoiding the high temperatures of the day.

VENTILATION

One of the biggest misconceptions about incense is that its smoke produces the fragrance. This is incorrect. Smoke is a byproduct of burning incense and produces particulates that are considered health hazards. Too much smoke in an environment is not only unhealthy, but it also suppresses the fragrance of incense by crowding out the fragrance molecules with denser airborne particulates. When burning incense, it is important to have a source of fresh air to ventilate the space.

Much like temperature and humidity, ventilation has a certain Goldilocks window where it is just right. Whiskey tasting provides an apt comparison. In whiskey tasting, water is added to spirits to open the fragrance by encouraging the integration and balancing of its flavors during evaporation; adding too little water produces no effect, and adding too much negatively dilutes the whiskey. Ventilation has a similar effect upon incense. Too much fresh air dilutes and disperses the fragrance, and heavy air currents can interrupt and overly disperse the fragrance. At the other end of the spectrum, too little ventilation produces a concentration of smoke that crowds out the fragrance of incense and creates a health hazard through overexposure to harmful particulates. By adding a source of fresh air, incense has room to open, expanding its fragrance.

When using incense, fresh air can be introduced simply by having a window opened a small amount or by having a source of ventilation such as a furnace fan running to circulate the air. However, a fully opened window or the breeze from an oscillating fan may provide too much air movement. By providing a source of fresh air while burning incense, both enjoyment of its fragrance and personal well-being are better protected.

PLACEMENT

Whereas temperature, humidity, and ventilation are not always within our control, the placement of incense within a given space is an important environmental factor we can easily manage. Too often, those who are new to incense place the burning stick close by them to allow its smoke to envelope them, under the mistaken assumption that the smoke produced by incense is the source of its fragrance. In actuality, the fragrance of incense is produced just below the stick's glowing ember. Here, the stick's aromatic materials are heated, causing fragrance molecules to evaporate into the air, thus producing its fragrance. Smoke is a byproduct of the smoldering ember's consumption of the stick. Placing incense directly within one's immediate personal space increases the exposure to its smoke, which has the dual effect of coloring the fragrance with a smokey or "campfire" smell and increasing the user's exposure to harmful particulates.

When using incense, rather than thinking of a fragrance as something to actively inhale, it can be useful to think of it as something that creates a fragrant environment in which one can passively exist. Being too close to incense is like watching television with one's nose an inch from the screen. Just as being that close makes it difficult to watch a TV show and can harm one's vision, placing incense too close makes it difficult to experience its fragrance and offers needless exposure to harmful smoke.

With this in mind, once lit, incense should be placed out of reach and allowed to fill the space naturally, obliging one to relax and enjoy the environment it slowly creates. Placing incense in the corner of a room, away from sources of foot traffic and breezes, allows the space to gently fill with fragrance over time. However, optimal placement depends upon the size and shape of a space, so experimenting with placing incense in different locations is encouraged and can offer different experiences even with the same incense.

LIGHTING INCENSE

Perhaps the most exciting part of enjoying incense, lighting it is especially thrilling when first starting out, and can be as ritualistic or routine as desired. After a little practice, the lighting process becomes as effortless as it is enjoyable. By following a few simple steps, in no time at all, incense sticks can be safely lit and the enjoyment of fragrance begun.

Step 0: Reflect on the use of the incense.

When choosing an incense for use, it may be beneficial to reflect upon the intention for lighting it. Obviously, this step is optional, but pausing to reflect on why the incense is being lit can offer a moment of peace and clarity. This reflection may be as deep or utilitarian as the moment dictates, bringing to mind the enjoyment of fragrance, a special moment of relaxation, the commemoration of an event, or the remembrance of a loved one.

Step 1: Light the incense.

Using a candle, lighter, or other safe source of flame, one end of the incense stick is lit. As Japanese incense does not use a bamboo core, there is no right or wrong end to light, as long as only one is lit. It is not necessary to expose much of the stick to the flame; just the very tip is sufficient to begin the burning process.

Step 2: Extinguish the flame.

Once the tip catches fire, a small flame will begin, like that on a candle. This flame should be extinguished, as incense should never have an open flame. Often the flame will go out on its own, but if it does not, rather than blowing it out like a candle, good etiquette requires gently waving the stick to extinguish the flame. After the flame is extinguished, a glowing red ember on the tip indicates the incense is smoldering and will continue to burn.

Step 3: Place the incense in a holder or burner.

Once the flame has been extinguished and a glowing ember created, the unlit end of the stick is inserted into a nonflammable incense holder or burner. (See chapter 20 for a discussion of holders and burners.) If using a holder, the holder should be placed on a ceramic plate to catch the ash. If using a burner, the incense stick should be inserted vertically into the ash far enough to securely hold the stick. With either a holder or burner, it is important to ensure the incense ash will not fall outside the plate or burner.

Step 4: Place the incense in the environment.

As noted earlier, the best way to experience incense is by placing it in a location where it can naturally fill the space over time. The incense should not be placed right next to anyone or where children or pets might come in contact with it, and it should be placed away from combustible items such as pillows, curtains, tablecloths, and paper.

Step 5: Enjoy the incense.

As the fragrance of incense fills the space, it should be "listened" to not only with the sense of smell but with all the other senses as well. (See chapter 23 for more on listening to incense.) Japanese incense often offers one note from the unlit stick, another note while burning, and yet a final lingering note after the incense has stopped burning. Listeners can delight in the gentle flowing smoke that trails from the burning end and may choose to reflect upon any feelings and memories that arise while listening to the fragrance.

SAFETY PRECAUTIONS

By following some simple common-sense precautions, Japanese incense can be enjoyed safely and without worry. The following is not an exhaustive list, but it provides basic precautions to keep in mind whenever incense is used.

Always be aware that burning incense poses a fire hazard.
- This sounds obvious, but it is easy to forget that incense is burning, because there is no conspicuous flame. Both the burning incense and the ash present fire hazards.
- Be careful not to touch the lit end of the incense! This can cause burns and be quite painful.
- Brushing up against or touching burning incense can start a fire, cause burns, ruin clothing, or discolor furniture. Always be careful around burning incense.

Once lit, never leave incense unattended.
- Burning incense is a fire hazard and should be regularly monitored.
- Lighting incense and then going to sleep is dangerous and should be avoided.
- Incense should always be used with an appropriate incense holder or burner.
- Use only those holders and burners that are designed to safely hold burning incense.
- When using a simple holder, be sure to use a ceramic dish or plate under the holder to catch the ash produced.
- Ensure that the ash is caught by the burner or plate, because it is often hot enough to discolor furniture or create a risk of fire.

Be aware of the placement of burning incense.
- Always make sure the incense burner/holder is placed on a stable surface, out of the flow of traffic, and away from flammable objects.
- Keep burning incense away from places where children or pets might encounter it.

- Keep lit incense away from where a breeze might blow a curtain into contact with it or knock over a lit stick.
- When burning multiple sticks at one time, take extra caution.
- Multiple sticks require extra vigilance, because a common cause of fire is one stick accidentally lighting another in the middle, which then burns through and falls outside the holder/burner with its tip still lit.
- Ensure that ash from one stick will not fall onto another.

Be sure to burn incense in spaces that are well ventilated.
- Burning any incense produces smoke, even in reduced-smoke varieties.
- Always ensure adequate ventilation and a source of fresh air, such as a window kept slightly open.

Do not intentionally breathe in incense smoke.
- The incense smoke is not the incense fragrance. The fragrance from incense is produced just below the smoldering tip where the aromatic incense ingredients are heated, not from the smoke the smoldering tip produces.
- Smoke is a byproduct of burning incense and contains particulates that are potential health hazards.
- Avoid placing incense near anyone or intentionally exposing anyone to its smoke.
- Incense (even a reduced-smoke variety) produces smoke that may impact breathing issues or produce allergic reactions.
- Prior to using incense, anyone with an underlying health condition that may be affected should speak to their medical professional.
- Incense is to be enjoyed for its fragrance and is not intended as a medical remedy.

CHAPTER 20

お香を確保する

HOLDING INCENSE
Using incense holders and kōro

ONE OF THE MORE COMMON QUESTIONS ASKED BY THOSE using Japanese incense for the first time is whether a special incense holder is necessary. Japanese incense sticks are typically smaller in diameter than the bamboo-cored incense common in the West, and, as such, they tend to dangle loosely in common wooden "banana" incense holders made for bamboo-cored incense. In response, countless methods have been improvised to hold Japanese incense, from placing incense in the dirt of potted plants, to using sand, salt, or rice in a shallow bowl, to using an aluminum can with holes pierced into it. (I've even seen photos of an individual who used their gum—eeew!) Although utilitarian, none of these methods enhances the experience of listening to Japanese incense. In fact, many of them will certainly detract from the beauty of the fragrance.

The Japanese art of incense goes beyond the mere burning of incense, extending to the entire experience before, during, and after it is burned. There are two methods traditionally used to safely hold incense that are much more faithful to the Japanese custom: using a specifically designed incense holder, and placing the incense in ash contained within an incense burner, or *kōro* (香炉). Unlike the improvised practices mentioned above, the beauty of a simple incense holder or the timeless elegance of an incense kōro can provide as much allure as the fragrance radiating from it, complementing and enhancing the experience. Both methods have advantages and disadvantages, and both can be found at various price points to fit virtually any budget. When using Japanese incense, deciding between the two is a necessary step to creating a safe and enjoyable experience that goes beyond fragrance.

JAPANESE INCENSE HOLDERS

The easiest way to hold Japanese incense is using a simple incense holder. Usually made of ceramic or metal, Japanese incense holders range in shape from spheres to squares, to miniature ginkgo leaves and cherry blossoms, to rabbits and cats and other small animals. Forms to fit virtually any personality or taste are available, with styles ranging from modern to classical, formal to whimsical. What Japanese incense holders generally have in common is a small size—less than an inch square, a hole (or holes) used to secure the incense stick(s), and a budget-friendly price. In fact, some manufacturers include basic ceramic holders in their boxes of daily incense.

But holders do have several disadvantages. First, they are just weighted holders (for stability) and do not provide a method to catch the ash produced while burning incense. As incense ash is hot, although it rarely starts a fire, it is quite capable of discoloring any surface that it falls upon, not to mention the mess it creates. Some incense holders are sold with companion trays or plates, but most must be used with some sort of dish to safely catch the burnt ash. Using a simple ceramic dish or plate leads to a buildup of ash that is messy and looks like an ashtray if not cleaned often.

Second, most holders do not hold incense vertically. Japanese incense is intended to be burned vertically to achieve the optimal burning temperature. Holders tend to leave the incense at an angle, some more angled than others. Generally, the closer to horizontal incense is, the more quickly and hotly it will burn. As the burning dynamics of the stick are changed, the intensity and consistency of its fragrance are also changed, at least slightly. For simple daily incense, this may not be a concern, but for more complex fragrances with rare *jinkō* or *kyara* (see chapter 14 for more on these fragrant woods), this dynamic should not be overlooked.

Finally, the portion of the incense stick held by the holder does not burn, as oxygen is unable to reach it. This often leaves a small nub of incense that is not consumed. As many fragrant woods used in Japanese incense are increasingly in short supply, regularly leaving a portion of incense to be discarded is an unfortunate use of rare and limited resources.

Lack of optimal burning angle, quicker burning, and small amounts of incense not being consumed may not pose much of an issue with *mainichi-kō* (daily incense). But both are critical considerations for *tokusen* ("special" or "select" incense) and premium jinkō and kyara incense. (See chapter 18 for more information on categories of incense.)

Holder advantages:
- Able to fit any personality or taste
- Small size
- Budget-friendly

Holder disadvantages:
- Need to use with a ceramic plate or dish to catch ash
- Exposed ash can be messy
- Incense not held vertically
- Small portion of the incense wasted

JAPANESE KŌRO (INCENSE BURNERS)

For centuries, kōro, or incense burners, have been considered a refined Japanese art form, prized for their craftsmanship and exquisite detail, and often sought-after collectables in their own right. One of the National Treasures of Japan is the sixteenth-century Iroekiji-kōro (色絵雉香炉) by famed Edo period (1603–1868) potter Ninsei (仁清). On display at the Ishikawa Prefectural Museum of Art, this priceless Kyoto-ware kōro takes the form of a life-size ceramic pheasant, overglazed with brilliant jewel-like enamel feathers with spaces between them to allow the fragrance of jinkō to rise from within its elegant body where the incense is burned. Although rarely so ornate, kōro are often made from ceramic and porcelain, but they are also available in cast iron, copper, or alloy forms. Usually more traditional in style, kōro can range from highly elegant and refined hand-glazed Kutani-ware ceramics to the more natural, imperfect beauty of *wabi-sabi*-esque bowls, to simple, utilitarian glazed cups. Although more expensive than simple incense holders, kōro range from everyday affordable to the heights of luxury.

In general, one advantage of kōro is that they provide a total system for holding incense and catching the ash created while burning. An added advantage is that they can be used to enhance the listening experience with their own beauty. They are a tried-and-true staple of the Japanese art of incense and have been used for centuries to honor the tradition of the art. Often used with the tea ceremony, Japanese kōro can be changed with the seasons or used to reinforce the feeling and mood the listener is trying to capture with incense. Functional works of art, kōro are often collected for their beauty and passed down through generations as family keepsakes.

Used in conjunction with ash, kōro are able to hold incense sticks in a vertical orientation, allowing for optimal burning. The ash, sold as "white ash" or "Kōdō ash," is placed inside the kōro, holding the incense in place while allowing oxygen to reach the entire stick, ensuring the rare aromatic ingredients are fully consumed. Preparing the ash initially takes little effort and is often viewed as a meditative part of the overall listening process. More refined kōro also include lids to conceal the ash when not in use, leaving a tidy, elegant, and sophisticated piece of fine art to be admired before and after burning incense.

The disadvantages of kōro generally center on their price and the use of ash. Where a simple holder and plate can be purchased economically on virtually any budget, Kutani-ware kōro, for example, can range from the low hundreds to upward of tens of thousands of dollars. Both rare antique kōro and new exquisite kōro can reach prices in the thousands of dollars, driven by collectors' demand for fine art. Even so, elegant and simple burners, bowls, and cups are available at prices comparable to that of a box of incense.

The use of ash often scares many away from kōro under the assumption that using it takes specialized knowledge or too much work. Although initially it takes a short time to prepare a kōro with ash, potentially entailing some associated mess, once set up, a kōro can be used repeatedly for an extended period of time with little to no effort. Cleaning is not necessary, and replacement of the inexpensive ash after several months of use is quick and easy. (The use of ash is covered in more detail in chapter 21.)

As mentioned previously, fear of ash has led to many improvised workarounds. Some people prefer the simple method of placing sand in a small bowl; others use small rocks, salt, rice, or even dirt in place of ash. While these alternatives do indeed work, they have several disadvantages. Dense materials such as salt, sand, and dirt do not breathe the way ash does. As a result, they prevent oxygen from reaching the portion of the stick held in the material, leaving that portion of the stick unburned. These materials also look messy, as the ash generated from the incense shows prominently in them, looking especially untidy and unappealing in rice. Finally, and somewhat importantly, none of these improvised methods is faithful to the centuries-old tradition of the Japanese art of incense.

Kōro advantages:
- Elegance and beauty
- Collectable as works of art
- Optimum burning angle
- Entire stick is consumed

- Easy, low maintenance once set up
- Some kōro have lids to conceal ash when not in use
- Remains true to the tradition of the Japanese art of incense

Kōro disadvantages:
- Can be expensive
- Requires rice chaff ash
- Initial ash preparation

When first starting out, it is not uncommon to begin with a simple incense holder on a ceramic plate, as one's focus is on developing the olfactory palette and gaining experience with different fragrances. In time, as experience builds, many people move toward kōro for their ease of use and elegant appearance. As with any art form, collections often grow, with some people preferring multiple kōro to express specific moods or seasons, and others preferring one kōro for daily incense and another for special burns of premium fragrances. Regardless of where one falls on this continuum, the goal of using Japanese kōro is to safely enjoy nature's gift of fragrance before, during, and after the burning of incense.

CHAPTER 21

灰を使って

USING ASH
Holding incense traditionally

FROM MAKING OFFERINGS AT BUDDHIST TEMPLES, TO SCENTING spaces for purification or personal enjoyment, to the ritual appreciation of jinkō through Kōdō, the practice of using kōro (incense burners) with ash has a rich tradition in Japanese incense culture. Kōro have been highly collected for centuries not only for their utility but also for their beauty as works of fine art. An elegant accessory for the burning of incense, a kōro can complement and enhance the incense experience both during and after burning.

Japanese kōro are traditionally filled with ash sold as "white ash" or "Kōdō ash," and this kōro-ash system provides the perfect method with which to enjoy Japanese incense as it was meant to be experienced, fully and completely. One of the more common questions when using incense is how to prepare a kōro with ash. With a little knowledge and some simple preparation, using ash with a kōro is easy to do and contributes to the optimal environment for the full appreciation of the rare and fragrant ingredients used in the Japanese art of incense.

ASH BASICS

Whether for simple daily enjoyment or the ritual appreciation of Kōdō, the ash traditionally used with a Japanese kōro is rice husk ash, often abbreviated RHA, also called rice chaff ash. As noted above, it also may be sold as white ash or Kōdō ash, but it is most frequently called simply "ash."

RHA is produced by incinerating rice husks. During the burning process, the evaporable and organic components of the husk are burned away, leaving residue of primarily silica, the basic chemical building block found in sand. A versatile byproduct of rice production, the resulting amorphous silica ash has many applications in the material sciences. RHA is used extensively in the manufacturing of concrete and as a suspension agent for porcelain enamels. The ash also has a rich tradition of being used in ceramic glazes in China and Japan, lowering the melting point of the glaze.

The burning of rice husks in open air always produces silica ash; however, the temperature of incineration influences the color and quality of silica ash produced. When burned in temperatures up to 1100 degrees Fahrenheit (around 600 degrees Celsius), the ash produced is pink in color and has not yet substantially generated amorphous silica. Between 1100°F and 1500°F (approximately 600°C to 800°C), amorphous silica ash is formed and turns gray in color. At temperatures over 1800°F (about 1000°C), the amorphous silica ash takes on a white appearance. All ash used with incense is at least gray; "milky white" is considered the purest and is the most popular type of ash sold for incense appreciation. The finer and whiter the ash, the higher the quality and purity it represents.

There are many benefits of using ash for listening to incense. The ash provides an excellent thermal insulation material for holding the incense safely within the kōro. Ash is traditionally used in the incense ceremony of Kōdō to cover a burning charcoal used to heat a fragrant wood chip, providing a thermal barrier between the red-hot charcoal and both the kōro and the listener. Fine grained and lightweight, RHA is also breathable, allowing a flow of oxygen to the burning incense while retaining the heat of the burning ember; as a result, the stick of incense is fully combusted, even below the surface of the ash. RHA is also odorless and does not absorb odors, providing a perfect neutral olfactory base that will not color the aromatic notes of the rare fragrant ingredients in Japanese incense.

ADDING ASH TO A KŌRO

Preparing the kōro to receive incense is a simple process that requires little more than adding ash. Each kōro requires a different amount of ash depending upon its size and shape, and a practical guideline is to fill the kōro to no more than 80 percent full or to a depth of approximately two inches of ash. When filling a kōro with ash, it is best to do so in an area that is easy to clean and away from breezes, as the ash is very light and can create a mess if not handled carefully.

Once the ash has been added to the kōro, it is a common mistake to compress the ash flat. This is the leading cause of incense sticks not fully burning, because compressing the ash reduces the flow of oxygen and prevents the incense from burning below the surface. Stick incense utilizes the ash as a simple support and requires the ash to remain uncompressed to allow oxygen to pass through it. If the surface of the ash is uneven after being added to the kōro, instead of compressing it, gently tap the bottom and sides of the kōro to allow the ash to settle slightly until the surface is uniform.

Note that the ash press tool often seen in preparing a kōro for the Kōdō ceremony is used to draw the ash over a piece of burning charcoal rather than to compress the ash. Also, the flat ash presses used to create a pristine flat ash surface (seen in many online videos) are not intended for stick incense but rather to create a base for lines of *powdered* incense that are burned upon the surface of the ash.

Finally, after the ash has been added to the kōro and settled, excess ash must be removed from the top and sides of the kōro. Traditionally, this is done with a feather tool or feather brush, but a soft dry towel can also be substituted. Once this is complete, the kōro is ready to be displayed and used to burn incense.

BURNING INCENSE

Burning incense using a kōro with ash is an easy process that requires little effort. By following some simple steps, not only will incense sticks burn completely and safely, but the smoke rising from an elegant kōro themed to the season or to one's decor will add to the experience of listening to the fragrance before and after the incense is burned.

To begin, if the kōro has a lid, it should be removed and placed safely beside the kōro. One of the most asked questions for those new to Japanese incense use is whether to leave the lid on or off. Simply put, the answer is that the lid is not intended to be left on during burning. Instead, the kōro lid is intended to cover the ash between uses to keep the space clean and neat looking, emphasizing the beauty of the kōro rather than the ash within it. Even if the incense stick is placed horizontally on the ash, or if another form of incense is used that allows the lid to be replaced during burning, removing the lid is still recommended for two reasons. First, burning incense with the lid on restricts the flow of oxygen, which could reduce the temperature of the burning ember; this, in turn, could diminish or alter the fragrance released or even extinguish the incense all together. Second, Japanese lidded kōro are often collectable works of fine art. Replacing the lid during burning will expose the lid to high quantities of smoke very near the heat of the burning incense, leading to staining and discoloration of the lid. It would be a shame to give a beautiful Japanese kōro over to soot gremlins!

Once the lid is removed, the ash should be stirred to add oxygen. This need not be done each time incense is burned in the kōro; however, over time, the ash will settle and absorb moisture from the ambient humidity. That's when stirring is needed. The goal of stirring the ash is to incorporate oxygen and break up any clumps that have absorbed moisture. In more humid months or in environments that are more naturally humid, stirring of the ash is required more often. Traditionally, ash is stirred using metal "fire chopsticks" in a clockwise motion. However, any implement that allows the ash to be broken up and "fluffed" can be used. Stirring is easy and takes less than a minute to do, but it ensures that the entire incense stick below the surface of the ash is consumed. As a general guideline, the ash should be stirred until almost no resistance is felt and it appears soft and fluffy.

Next, it's time to add incense. The incense stick is lit and placed vertically in the center of the kōro with the lit end up, ensuring that any falling ash will be contained by the kōro. The stick should go into the ash effortlessly; if the ash exhibits marked resistance, then it needs to be stirred. How deep to place the incense stick into the ash depends upon the length of the incense stick, with longer sticks requiring more depth in the ash to support them. The goal is to place the stick far enough into the ash that it is securely supported and will not move as the stick's center of balance changes during burning or if the kōro is bumped or encounters a breeze. Placing the stick vertically also ensures that the incense will burn at the optimum temperature and duration. Alternatively, the stick can be broken to fit the mouth of the kōro and placed horizontally directly upon the ash; however, in this orientation the stick will burn more quickly.

Finally, once the stick is consumed, the lid of the kōro is replaced, hiding the ash within it until the next use.

ASH MAINTENANCE

Maintaining the ash in the kōro is often a matter of personal preference. Some people prefer to remove the incense ash from the surface with a sifter or spoon after every burning. This is not necessary, however, as ash can be reused over and over for an extended period with little attention beyond regular stirring. Ash by itself is odorless and will not absorb odors. However, the same is not true of incense ash. As incense is repeatedly burned, incense ash builds up in the kōro. This ash can easily be stirred into the RHA and mixed away. But over a long period of successive burns, mixing the two can lead to the buildup of odor from past incenses in the kōro. Generally, for daily or mid-grade incense, this is not a cause for concern. However, when listening to expensive incense, such as rare kyara or fine jinkō incense, the odor of previous incense would be unwanted, as it may color the purity of these rare and fragrant woods. For these types of applications, some people prefer to ensure the incense ash is new or to reserve a special kōro for burning premium incense.

Regardless, after many successive uses over an extended period, the ash in a kōro will eventually become too dirty and need to be renewed. How often this threshold is reached depends upon the quantity and frequency of use and will differ for each user. When the ash becomes noticeably darker gray or presents a strong odor without incense, it is time to renew.

There are two ways to renew ash. One is to remove the ash from the kōro, sift it through a common kitchen sifter onto aluminum foil, bake it at 450°F (about 230°C) for approximately twenty minutes, allow it to cool, and then replace it in the kōro. But with the economical nature of ash, when it becomes dirty enough to consider renewal, it's usually easier to just replace the old ash with new.

Ash often scares new Japanese incense users away from using a kōro. Without the proper knowledge, it can seem a messy, difficult process that is not worth the effort. But by using the simple approach above, the kōro is easy to set up and even easier to use in the traditional way Japanese incense has been enjoyed for centuries. Once the kōro is prepared with ash, it can be used repeatedly for a significant length of time, adding elegance and beauty to the process of enjoying Japanese incense.

CHAPTER 22

貯蔵

STORAGE
Preserving an incense collection

O NE OF THE MORE COMMON EXPERIENCES WITH JAPANESE incense is how it quickly grows into a collection. Incense to promote specific moods, incense for different times of the day, incense for different seasons, and incense for special occasions all rapidly accumulate into a substantial amount of incense. Over time, collections can quickly outgrow the space next to the incense burner! As Japanese incense is filled with rare and natural ingredients prized for their specific fragrances, the question of how to store a collection to best preserve its fragrant qualities comes into play. Some people go to great lengths and even greater expense to create the "perfect" incense storage system. But such lengths are not necessary if some basic understanding about storing Japanese incense is put into practice.

First, Japanese incense prefers dryness. As such, a top priority when storing incense is the control of moisture and humidity. Storing incense in a basement or refrigerator may expose it to undesirable dampness and higher humidity levels. Over time, this moisture will degrade the incense and may even promote mold growth, a decidedly unwanted addition to the fragrant mix. There are also less obvious ways incense may be exposed to moisture, such as placing incense in resealable plastic bags or glass vials. Often used with the intent of preventing fragrance cross contamination, this practice can trap moisture and cause more harm than good. Japanese incense is, by and large, a natural product that needs to breathe. Incenses made with oils distilled from fragrant woods and other aromatic ingredients need to be able to naturally and slowly release over time. Whereas sealing incense in airtight containers runs the risk of trapping moisture, vacuum sealing, also used with good intent, runs the risk of removing oils or preventing the incense from being able to breathe naturally.

Second, Japanese incense is often presented in beautifully designed packaging that is part of the overall Japanese incense experience. But besides the beauty of the packaging, many tokusen and premium Japanese incenses come packaged in *kiri* (桐, *Paulownia*) wood boxes that expand and contract, naturally controlling humidity levels. Additionally, incense packaging is designed to keep incense sticks closely together to prevent breakage. Removing incense from its packaging and transferring it into glass containers or plastic bags instead of relying on the structure of the original container exposes the incense to breakage during transfer and storage.

Third, Japanese incense likes cool darkness. Taking incense from its packaging and putting it in glass jars or clear plastic exposes the incense to light, which can more readily break down fragrant compounds. Exposing stored incense to direct sunlight may also degrade its fragrance more quickly.

Finally, Japanese incense is, by and large, a natural product and, as such, will absorb odors and other incense fragrances from its surrounding environment. Incense stored where strong odors are common, such as in a kitchen, may absorb unwanted odors that can negatively color the fragrance of the incense. The same is true for storing incense in cigar boxes or humidors, as these may contaminate the delicate fragrances of Japanese incense with their residual odors.

Often the heavy smell of cigars lingers in cigar boxes, and humidors, although attractive, are usually lined with highly aromatic cedar, which can overpower subtle Japanese fragrances. Care must also be taken when storing dissimilar fragrances together, as stronger fragrances, such as florals, may overpower and color more delicate aloeswood fragrances.

With these basics in mind, below are three simple storage practices that will ensure a long life for any collection of Japanese incense.

Keep the original packaging. Keeping Japanese incense in the packaging it came in provides the most favorable conditions for preventing incense breakage, unwanted light exposure, and excess humidity. Plus, the beauty of the various packaging will add elegance to the collection, and any kiri wood packaging will naturally guard against moisture and humidity.

Store it someplace cool, dry, and dark. Storing Japanese incense in a cool, dry, dark place will help ensure it maintains its aromatic qualities for as long as possible. If money is not an object, a kiri wood *tansu* (箪笥, chest of drawers) may be purchased for this use. But for most people, the easiest and most cost-effective place to store incense is in a typical dresser drawer kept in an air-conditioned space. If air conditioning is not available, opt for a drawer at ground level in a space that has good air movement, but preferably not in a basement, where humidity levels are much higher.

Store like with like. When storing Japanese incense, it pays to be mindful of potential environmental odors as well as cross contamination between fragrances. Incense should not be stored in areas where strong odors are created, such as a kitchen or in a chest/box/closet lined with strong scented woods like cedar. Similar incenses should be stored together: daily incense with daily incense, floral incense with floral incense, jinkō with jinkō, and so on. Again, if money is not an object, a multi-drawered kiri wood tansu is a luxury item that will fit this task nicely. However, the easiest and most cost-effective method for storing Japanese incense is in a typical chest of drawers, using separate drawers for each group of fragrances.

By following these three simple best practices, Japanese incense can easily and safely be stored in almost any home with little effort and expense, ensuring long-term enjoyment of it along the Fragrant Path.

IV: APPRECIATION

*The autumnal breeze
has come blowing past places
where maidenflowers bloom:
though our eyes cannot see it,
we know it from the fragrance.*

KOKIN WAKASHŪ, BOOK 4: POEM 234

CHAPTER 23

MONKŌ
Listening to incense

I N THE JAPANESE ART OF INCENSE, THE APPRECIATION OF FRAGRANCE
is known as *monkō* (聞香), translated as "listening to incense." To
those in the West, the idea of listening to something that appears
to center upon the sense of smell may seem a bit confusing. But in the
Japanese appreciation of incense, the expressions "to smell" and "to
sniff" are not used, as they limit the perception of fragrance. Monkō
traditionally refers to the appreciation of *jinkō* during the formal
incense ceremony, Kōdō, but the deep appreciation of incense in any
form is often referred to as "listening" whether it be when burning
an incense stick, heating *nerikō*, or warming a sliver of *kyara* during
Kōdō. The concept of listening rather than smelling incense predates
its introduction to Japan and, like much of Japan's art of incense, has
its roots in Buddhism. Although an understanding of Buddhism or
Zen practice is not necessary, developing an understanding of monkō can

open us to an appreciation of incense that transcends the sense of smell, revealing the true nature not only of fragrance but of ourselves as well.

At the heart of monkō is a view of the world where fragrance is more than just fragrance, stemming from the otherworldly redolence that infused everything associated with the Buddha. The Buddha was said to be pure, the jewel of all living beings, devoid of the literal and metaphorical foul odor of humanity. It is said that even before his birth, the gods created three chambers in his mother's womb, one filled with the precious scent of sandalwood and the other two imbued with the heavenly redolence of perfume. Thus, in life, everything emanating from the Buddha was said to be fragrant, from his presence to his words. The sweetness of incense radiated from him wherever he went and remained long after he departed, like a fragrant memory. After his death and cremation, it is said that the Buddha was transformed into pure fragrance, like transcendent incense infusing the breeze. During his lifetime, the fragrant words of the Buddha were always listened to rather than written down. After his death, they became synonymous with the fragrance of incense, and as such, incense was "listened to" by his disciples rather than smelled.

As Buddhism spread with monks traveling from India to China nearly two thousand years ago, the practice of listening to the fragrance of the Buddha in the form of incense traveled with them. The Chinese used the term *wénxiāng* (聞香) to describe listening to incense. Centered less on the conventional sense of smell, wénxiāng represented *sensing* the presence of the Buddha through incense, listening deeply using all the senses. With the introduction of Buddhism from China to Japan in the sixth century, and as the Japanese ruling classes that favored Buddhism came to power, the Buddhist use of incense entered Japanese life.

But it was the introduction of Zen Buddhism during Japan's Kamakura period (1185–1333 CE), coupled with the samurai's ever-present awareness of life and death, that gave monkō its place in the Japanese appreciation of incense. Much like sitting in meditation, the samurai listened to the fragrance of jinkō for the true nature—known as "Buddha nature"—of the rare fragrant wood. With Zen's emphasis on *kenshō* (見性), flashes of insight into Buddha nature, the meditative use of incense expanded to include all the senses, allowing the samurai to sense their own true nature, if only briefly. Building upon the mysterious and elusive quality of fragrance in which scent was not seen and yet was silently perceived, the samurai derived meaning from the rare fragrance of jinkō, contemplating their own spirituality in the face of death. In time, the Chinese term wénxiāng was translated into Japanese as *kō-o-kiku* (香お聞, hearing incense), and eventually referred to as monkō (listening to incense).

Over time, this practice was elevated by the samurai and cultural elite into the refined art known as Kōdō, the Way of Fragrance. Kōdō invites participants not just to use their sense of smell, but through monkō, to listen deeply to incense, using all the senses and opening to the expression of nature provided by rare fragrant woods. In this way, the senses are free to expand beyond what is accessible in the physical world to the infinite possibilities available in our own true nature, thus allowing "the ears to see and the eyes to hear," as the renowned Rinzai Zen master Daitō Kokushi said. Through monkō, the fragrance of incense transcends fragrance, opening us to the natural world beyond the sense of smell.

To understand the concept of monkō more fully, it is helpful to examine the Buddha's teachings on our view of reality. The Diamond That Cuts through Illusion, more commonly known as the Diamond Sutra, provides a way to perceive the world in wholeness that leads to deeper insights into reality. This famous sutra gives many examples of how our view is limited by the illusion of separateness and reiterates how all things transcend their outward forms. To the Western view based on separateness, where something is itself and not something else, this can be quite confusing. To understand this, let's contemplate a cherry blossom. Although the Buddha recognizes a cherry blossom as anyone would, he first recognizes that a cherry blossom is made entirely of non-cherry-blossom elements: the earth it grew from, the sunlight it drew energy from, the rain that nourished it, the tree it bloomed from, and the effort of the gardener who tended it. This deeper perception leads to greater insight into the true nature of the cherry blossom. The blossom is more than its simple outward form, and with a more complete picture of its true nature, the cherry blossom itself can be more fully appreciated.

This is the heart of listening to incense. By going beyond the sense of smell and listening with our whole being, we recognize a greater holistic view, opening ourselves to appreciating incense with the full awareness of its true nature. We get to experience the non-fragrance elements that make up fragrance—the woods, plants, roots, and resins in the incense—with greater clarity. Going deeper, we can experience the incense manufacturer's knowledge, the centuries-old Japanese tradition of incense making, and the craftsman's skill in preparing the incense. Immersing ourselves further, we can experience the living essence of these materials: the sun they drew energy from, the rains in the jungles the woods grew in, and nature's myriad resources that produced the aromatic materials. We can be transported to the past—to the time when these materials grew in the earth, which, in the case of jinkō, may be centuries ago, or to the centuries during which the incense recipe has been in use.

In this way, we open ourselves to experience fragrance not as fragrance, but as the miracle of creation it is. Through monkō, the echoes of the past are realized in the present and a common experience is shared with Heian aristocrats, samurai nobles, and even emperors. When experienced holistically, without being limited to a single sense, the true nature of incense opens us to insights that may be poetic or deeply moving, or even lead to greater insights into our own experience, our world, or nature itself.

For those in the West, such insights may seem complex and even daunting, if not a little far-fetched. But this attitude comes from focusing on outward forms, from letting the complexity of such a simple concept stand in the way of the holistic experience of immersing oneself in fragrance. The actual practice of monkō is easy for anyone, because when listening to incense, there is no right or wrong. When we quiet our minds and let the fragrance of nature be our guide, we open ourselves to wherever the incense may take us. Regardless of the destination, the goal is always a simple one: the appreciation of fragrance, in whatever form that experience takes for the listener. By being present in monkō, one gains insights that are as unique as the one who listens for them.

Fragrant woods and aromatics are nature's self-expression. They are nature's fragrant works of art. No two expressions of this art will be the same, and no two people will experience fragrance the same way. Listening to incense, like the Buddha's words, can teach us from the purity of nature's wisdom. Our challenge then is to open ourselves to nature's expression and enjoy the fragrant gifts it provides. We do this through monkō, listening to incense with all the senses.

With this in mind, the following are some suggestions for cultivating a deep sense of monkō as we appreciate incense.

Begin with ritual. In Kōdō, the entire listening experience is built around the ritual appreciation of fragrance. Ritual trains the brain to prepare to receive. To be open. To be receptive. When preparing to listen to incense, create your own ritual. This need not be as extensive as a formal Kōdō session. It can be as simple as how the incense is lit, how the incense is placed in the *kōro* (香炉, incense burner), or even just where you sit to listen. Your ritual should be yours, as individual as you are. It should be enjoyable. It should focus the mind on the incense before you. It can be as simple or as complex as you like. But it should signal to your body and mind that you are about to listen to incense.

Close your eyes. In our modern world, we've become dominated by our visual sense, almost to the exclusion of our other senses. We're glued to our phones and digital devices, staring at their altered reality like zombies out of touch with the natural world. This is a recent phenomenon, one that would be unfamiliar to the Heian courtier or the Sengoku warrior, for whom the use of all the senses was completely natural. Much as light beyond the visible spectrum can be felt as heat and unheard sound can be felt as vibration, incense shares the wisdom of nature through all the senses. Closing our eyes expands our universe and amplifies the information available to us. When listening to incense, closing our eyes allows us to go within. To receive more holistically. To experience the fragrant gifts of nature in a natural way.

Be spontaneous. We don't consciously think of lifting each foot as we walk; we just walk. We don't think about breathing. We don't think about our heart beating. Our lungs breathe and our hearts beat spontaneously; they perform their functions as intended without our conscious intervention. When listening to incense, allow yourself to spontaneously react to its fragrance with your whole being. Allow thoughts to come and go. Notice feelings, memories, sounds, and emotions as they spontaneously arise, without grabbing hold of them or trying to force them into being. Allow them to ping-pong, creating a chain reaction that can lead to insights you otherwise might not have found. Trust that insights will occur spontaneously without any help or effort from you.

Be an observer. In our modern way of life, we strive to be the masters of our destiny, controlling our own story through our own unending actions. When listening to incense, this habit often leads to the desire to control or shape the experience. We seek to respond to our experience rather than listen. That's not how nature works. Nature is not rigid, fixed, or permanent. It moves, changes, and flows. When listening to incense, once we stop observing and latch on to our experience, we step out of nature's flow of information. As the saying goes, "The Tao that can be named is not the Tao." When listening to incense, seek to be an observer. Be passive. Be receptive. Be open. Observe. Allow yourself to listen as nature speaks through fragrance.

Be patient. Patience is required for information to be received. Listening to incense isn't like turning on the evening news. Be patient with your listening. It takes time for the information to come through. When it does, it often comes as a hint or a glimpse that sparks a deeper understanding, much like kenshō in Zen represents a flash of insight into our true nature. When listening to incense, we often have our schedules to keep. We press. We become impatient. Be patient with yourself. Just as intuition occurs spontaneously, like the beating of our heart, listening to incense reveals its insights according to its own perfectly chosen schedule.

Embrace nature's rhythm. The Japanese art of incense is tuned to the natural rhythm of the seasons. Nature moves at its own pace and acts spontaneously when the time is right. When it is spring, flowers bloom; in the summer, fireflies light the night; in autumn, leaves paint the forests in vibrant colors before falling to the ground; and in winter, the snow falls and ponds freeze. Incense has been chosen to celebrate, harmonize, and enjoy the seasons for over a thousand years. Such harmony with nature is ancient wisdom that our modern world has largely forgotten as we enjoy fruit out of season and view videos on demand. By tuning into nature's natural rhythm when we listen to incense, we align ourselves with nature's wisdom and open to the insights it provides.

Play. At the heart of listening to incense is the enjoyment of fragrance. Too often we become serious, concerned about getting it right rather than simply enjoying the miracle of nature incense represents. There is a reason that hundreds of *kumikō* (組香, incense games) were developed over the centuries to enjoy through Kōdō. Play was meant to be present when listening to incense. Play is our most creative state. Play is enjoyable. Play exists in the moment. When listening to incense, remember to *enjoy* the journey along the Fragrant Path. Be open to the fragrant gift of nature that incense represents. Make a game of listening to incense. Be delighted. Experience nature's gift of fragrance with childlike wonder, where everything feels new, anything seems possible, and enjoyment is the goal.

CHAPTER 24

一期一会

ICHIGO ICHIE
Once-in-a-lifetime moments with incense

TEA AND INCENSE ARE INDELIBLY LINKED IN JAPAN. BORN OF Zen foundations in the eastern hills of Kyoto during the fifteenth-century Higashiyama culture of Shōgun Ashikaga Yoshimasa, perfected through the *wabi-cha* (侘茶, tea of quiet taste) of revered tea master Sen Rikyū, and taken to unparalleled heights under the reigns of Japan's three unifiers, Oda Nobunaga, Toyotomi Hideyoshi, and Tokugawa Ieyasu, Chadō (茶道, the Way of Tea) rose to form the preeminent *geidō* (芸道, art of refinement) of Japan. Evolving in tandem with the ritual service of tea, Kōdō (香道, the Way of Fragrance) grew into its own distinct refined art. Because Chadō and Kōdō were often taught together as one unit of study by many of the earliest schools of tea, to appreciate Japanese incense, it is helpful to explore the crossover between tea and incense culture. With its origins in the quiet contemplation of Zen practice embodied in the tea ceremony, the Japanese concept of *ichigo ichie* is just as at home in incense culture as it is in the Way of Tea.

Sen Rikyū, the distinguished sixteenth-century tea master whose teachings form the basis for the tea ceremony today, highlighted the importance of hanging *ichigyōmono* (一行物), one-line scrolls highlighting the sayings of Zen masters, in the tearoom *tokonoma* (床の間, alcove) for their meaning as well as the virtue of their calligraphy. Today ichigyōmono featuring the phrase *ichigo ichie* (一期一会) can be found displayed in tea shops and tearooms throughout Japan. Translated variously as "one time, one meeting," "in this moment, an opportunity," and "a once-in-a-lifetime encounter," ichigo ichie highlights the Zen Buddhist concept that each moment is transient, a unique occurrence that can never be repeated and should, therefore, be treasured.

Originally derived from the phrase *ichigo ni ichido* (一期に一度), meaning "one chance in a lifetime," Rikyū taught the importance of treating each tea ceremony as though the gathering would occur only once in the lifetime of both guest and host. The first known written example of ichigo ichie occurs in 1588 in the notes of Yamanoue Sōji, a tea master and student of Rikyū. In his notes, Sōji shortened Rikyū's phrase to *ichigo ichie* in order to highlight the nature of time, emphasizing the importance of each moment's unique, fleeting, and unrepeatable quality. In 1858, the lord of the Hikone Domain (modern-day Shiga Prefecture), Ii Naosuke, elaborated upon this concept further in his book on the tea ceremony, *Chanoyu Ichie Shū* (茶湯一会集, *Collection on the Oneness of Chanoyu*): "Even though the host and guests may see each other often socially, one day's gathering can never be repeated exactly. Viewed this way, the meeting is indeed a once-in-a-lifetime occasion."

Ichigo ichie reminds us that each experience, each gathering, each encounter—from the mundane to the celebrated—takes place in a moment that is unique and will never happen again. Viewed through this perspective, ichigo ichie urges us to treasure each moment by giving our full attention to what we are experiencing, be it washing the dishes, celebrating with friends, playing with our children, or listening to incense. With so many distractions at our fingertips today, it is easy to be physically one place and mentally somewhere else, even when surrounded by others. Ichigo ichie reminds us that each moment is ethereal and transient, and if we are not mindful, the moment will pass us by and be lost forever.

Given the rare nature of fragrant woods prized in the Japanese art of incense, ichigo ichie takes on special relevance. At the heart of Kōdō, jinkō is an especially good illustration of ichigo ichie's teaching. A miraculous gift of nature, it is estimated that only one or two *Aquilaria* trees in a hundred will ever produce the fragrant resin that makes jinkō so highly prized. Even should a tree produce resin, it can take up to one hundred years to produce enough resin to be considered high-quality fragrant wood. The region, country, geography, microclimate, and even which side of the mountain the tree grows on can influence the fragrance of the resinated wood produced, making each and every tree a singular work of fragrant natural art that can never be duplicated. (See chapter 14 for more on jinkō and other fragrant woods.) The use of jinkō is cherished by the Japanese, as they realize each piece represents a unique gift of nature, lost forever once consumed. With this in mind, in Kōdō, jinkō is heated, not burned, and only a small piece—one the size of a grain of rice—is used at a time.

At its essence, ichigo ichie asks two things of us: to treat each moment as unique and special, and to invest fully in each moment as it unfolds. For centuries, the Japanese have embraced these two guiding principles of ichigo ichie through the use of incense. Heian courtiers used incense to scent their clothes and homes to elevate the distinctiveness of each encounter. Samurai used jinkō to purify their armor, focusing their mind upon the moment as they prepared to face death. Japanese elite held gatherings to compare famous pieces of jinkō brought from guests' notable collections, creating highly sought-after events due to the once-in-a-lifetime chance to experience such rare fragrant woods. By understanding how treating every moment as unique and fully investing ourselves in it can enrich our experience, we can use the principles of ichigo ichie to better appreciate Japanese incense.

ONCE-IN-A-LIFETIME MOMENTS

The first aspect of ichigo ichie reminds us to treat every moment as a once-in-a-lifetime occurrence. Given the effect of smell upon memory, incense is uniquely positioned to help us do this. In terms of evolution, our sense of smell is one of our oldest and most mysterious senses. Our earliest developed sense, until approximately age ten, the sense of smell is even more dominant than the sense of sight. Our noses can recall up to ten thousand odors, with certain odors triggering memories back to early childhood. When we find that something tastes really good, it is because our sense of smell detected qualities we regard positively. The sense of smell is so powerful that manufacturers often use fragrance to improve the perception of the quality of a product, increasing our willingness to pay more for it. People even tend to smell in color, for example, associating smells like citrus with the colors orange and yellow, and grassy fragrances with greens and browns.

One of the reasons our sense of smell has such a powerful association with memory has to do with the way our brains store information. Odors are encoded in the brain directly from the olfactory bulb, a rounded mass of tissue in each nasal cavity that is filled with nerve cells connected directly to the limbic system, which includes the amygdala and the hippocampus—regions of the brain related to regulating emotion and memory. Because of this anatomy, certain odors can spontaneously trigger specific memories from emotional moments, positive or negative. We remember the smell of Grandma's house not only because of the fresh-baked chocolate chip cookies she gave us as a child, but also because we felt loved and happy there. As each individual's memories are unique, so too are our associations with odors, so the same odor can trigger different memories in different individuals. There is even a name for this phenomenon: a "Proustian moment." In French author Marcel Proust's 1913 novel *À la recherche du temps perdu* (*In Search of Lost Time*), the narrator describes the spontaneous flood of emotion from a childhood memory triggered by the smell of a French madeleine dipped in tea: "No sooner had the warm liquid, and the crumbs with it, touched my palate than a shudder ran through my whole body, and I stopped, intent upon the extraordinary changes that were taking place. An exquisite pleasure had invaded my senses, but individual, detached, with no suggestion of its origin."

Studies have shown that although memories triggered by odors are not necessarily more accurate, they are more emotionally evocative, and odors experienced infrequently often proved to be the most discernable. With thousands of fragrances and the mutable nature of fragrant woods and aromatics, Japanese incense is exceptionally positioned to trigger memories or help us encode new ones, elevating any experience by highlighting its once-in-a-lifetime nature. And since everyone will have different memories associated with specific fragrances, each individual will form their own associations, further elevating the once-in-a-lifetime nature of our experience with incense.

THE UNIQUENESS OF THE MOMENT

The second aspect of ichigo ichie asks us to invest fully in each moment as it unfolds. At the heart of ichigo ichie is Zen, and at the heart of Zen is the practice of being entirely in the moment with our full being. Written in 1828, the *Zencharoku* (禪茶録, *Zen Tea Record*) explains how even during the tea ceremony, it is investment in the moment that matters most: "The practice of seeking your self-nature through Tea is nothing other than sweeping away all your various thoughts, and concentrating the mind one-pointedly." Directing our attention in this way is not limited to the tea ceremony, however. Zen asks us to be fully present when washing the dishes, driving to work, or lighting incense as well. In doing so, we enter a space free of time, where infinite possibilities lie.

Referred to as the "eternal now," when we focus all our attention upon the activity at hand, something magical happens. Nothing else remains but the moment. Time as we typically perceive it disappears. Our experience of time becomes timeless and infinite, eternally arising in the moment. Most often, we view our lives as a series of events that happen sequentially, the past leading to the present, the present leading to the future, with all events occurring as though time is a river separate from us, always flowing downstream. However, Zen asks us to hold a nondualistic view of time, accepting that time can simultaneously be experienced sequentially and infinitely. In his thirteenth-century masterwork *Shōbōgenzō* (正法眼蔵, *Treasury of the True Dharma Eye*), Dōgen Zenji, the founder of Sōtō Zen, refers to this concept as *uji* (有時, being-time) where time and being are not separate, but two sides of the same experience. For Dōgen, time and being are linked, with each moment capable of expressing all moments simultaneously—past, present, and future existing in each moment.

Dōgen's writings on uji have been studied for centuries, because, like a Zen koan, the concept is difficult to grasp with our dualistic minds. But uji asks us, in this moment, to accept the moment as infinite and interconnected with all other moments. For example, as these words are being written in my "now," I am experiencing the moment that Dōgen described the concept of uji nearly eight hundred years ago. Dōgen experiences my words being written in my "now" as an outgrowth of the same moment of his writing. As you are reading my words, the moment you are experiencing as "now" is both the unique moment of reading them and the moment in which they were written—both in my current "now" and Dōgen's "now" nearly eight hundred years ago. And through our shared "now," I am experiencing the moment of my words being read both in my "now" and yours. When we view our lives sequentially, with one event leading to the next, we overlook the interconnectedness each infinite moment represents. When we embrace the moment fully with all our being, we are freed from sequential time to experience the eternal now.

As Dōgen highlights, in uji, the concept of "now" is much more complex than our sequential view of time allows us to recognize. Einstein, in explaining his theory of relativity, demonstrated how limiting it is to define "now" with a sequential view of time: "When you sit with a nice girl for two hours, you think it's only a minute. But when you sit on a hot stove for a minute, you think it's two hours. That's relativity." What we consider "now" cannot be measured by time as we understand it. As each moment arises, it immediately vanishes, moving inextricably to the next. When the feeling of hunger arises as brain activity in our awareness, the moment hunger itself first arose has already passed. If we wish to express the feeling of hunger in words, the time to process the thought and produce speech is even further removed from the moment hunger first arose. In the time it takes to define the moment, the moment has passed.

Ichigo ichie asks us to keep the awareness of the eternal now at the forefront of our attention. It reminds us that every moment is infinite and unique and that experiencing the moment directly with all our being is experiencing life itself in a timeless state. Given such a gift, ichigo ichie advises us to treasure each moment as the once-in-a-lifetime miracle that it is by focusing all our attention, all our thought, all our being on the experience before us. In much the same way incense can help us encode individual memories, incense offers us a proven method for focusing our mind on the moment. Just as bells in Buddhist monasteries are rung to call attention to mindfulness practice, the act of lighting incense forms a ritual that serves as a call to bring our attention to the moment. The fragrance released thereafter reminds us to remain present in the moment and continues to subtly prompt us to return our focus to the moment at hand as we go about our activities.

THE MOMENT WITH INCENSE

Ichigo ichie provides us with a wonderful model through which to more deeply appreciate Japanese incense. The following are some suggestions for combining the principles of ichigo ichie with Japanese incense to enhance the special nature of each moment and fully invest oneself in it.

When celebrating a special event, include a specifically chosen incense. Promotions, graduations, semester ends, and anniversaries are all once-in-a-lifetime moments to be treasured and remembered. By using incense to trigger the brain's connection between smell and memory, we can enhance these special events to make them more indelible, ensuring memories that are not only distinctive but also recalled more vividly.

Welcome guests with incense. In Chadō, guests arriving for the tea ceremony are greeted with the fragrance of incense to create a unique, welcoming experience. The same practice can be used in our own gatherings by placing incense in areas guests will be welcomed, to increase the event's memorability and once-in-a-lifetime nature. Ichigo ichie reminds us that even if host and guest see each other every day, no matter how casually, each meeting is still unique and can never be repeated. Using incense to welcome friends for a casual get-together celebrates the singular nature of the evening just as much as it would for a special birthday party.

Host an incense gathering. A great way to combine ichigo ichie and incense is to host an incense gathering. In feudal Japan, invitations to gatherings where rare and famous pieces of fragrant wood would be listened to were highly prized for the once-in-a-lifetime opportunity they presented. There are many ways such a gathering can be held today, even without a daimyō's collection of rare incense. For example, invite friends to a special gathering to listen to a specially selected incense, highlighting its unique character and fragrant properties. A variation is to create a group that meets monthly, with a different participant bringing a special incense to share with the group each month. No matter how the gathering is organized, using incense to create a special event is sure to emphasize the once-in-a-lifetime nature that listening to incense represents.

Celebrate the change of seasons with incense. The Japanese expression *mono no aware* (物の哀れ), which can be translated as "awareness of the transience of things," highlights the bittersweet emotion resulting from our awareness of the impermanent nature of the moment. One of the best examples of mono no aware is illustrated by the changing of the seasons. The Japanese have a profound appreciation for the many subtle changes that occur year-round, letting the seasonal changes drive their selection of incense. Auspicious rare woods such as kyara are burned in January to set positive intentions for the year. February highlights the plum blossoms (*ume*) of late winter followed by peach blossoms (*momo*) in March. The star of April's flower viewing (*hanami,* 花见) is the cherry blossom (*sakura*), which is revered nationwide for its potent illustration of mono no aware. Summer season begins in May with the harvests of green tea (*matcha*), and continues with blooms of hydrangea (*agisai*) in June, fields of lavender (*rabenda*) in July, and rose blossoms (*bara*) in August. As the weather cools, the lotus blooms (*hasu*) are celebrated in September, and, symbolizing long life and vitality, cypress (*hinoki*) is highlighted in October. The emblem of the imperial family and the subject of one of Japan's oldest festivals, the chrysanthemum (*kiku*) is celebrated in November. To end the year, in December the fragrance of jinkō is highlighted to convey gratitude for the year's many blessings. Whatever fragrance you choose, try celebrating the seasons with incense meaningful to your experience.

Sit with a single incense. In our modern lives, we often multi-task to get through the things we wish to accomplish in a day. Ichigo ichie asks the opposite of us. Highlighted in the humorous Zen saying "Don't just do something, sit there," ichigo ichie highlights our need to just be. Applied to incense appreciation, this means listening to incense simply to listen to incense and nothing else. Often, we light incense to enhance an aspect of our experience or to dissect its different fragrant notes, short-circuiting our ability to be present with the incense in front of us. Instead, the next time you light incense, try to simply sit with it, with no other purpose. Just being with incense allows it to open to us and creates an experience that transcends fragrance.

Incorporate incense into daily routines. It is easy to go through the start of our day on autopilot, barely awake as we drift through our morning routine. The same can often be true of our evening routines, as the workaday nature of life leads us to miss the unique, once-in-a-lifetime moments that occur each evening, such as tucking our children into bed or being completely present with our partner. Adding incense to our daily routines is an easy way to remind ourselves of the inherent ichigo ichie in even the most ordinary moments and to make those moments more memorable.

CHAPTER 25

EMPTINESS

Space to appreciate incense

THERE WAS ONCE A SCHOLAR OF GREAT INTELLECT, AN EXPERT in many subjects, who, having studied Zen, learned of an acclaimed master known for his teachings. People were said to travel great distances to seek out the master's wisdom and ask for his enlightenment on Zen. Rarely would the master turn them away. The scholar undertook a pilgrimage to visit this famed master. Upon arriving, the scholar asked the master to share his knowledge with him, the master agreed, and the two began a discussion. During their conversation, it became apparent that the scholar was quite full of opinions, often interrupting the master and interjecting his own understandings. As was customary when hosting a guest, tea was served. As the scholar droned on, the master began to pour his guest a cup of tea. But as the cup approached its filling point, the master continued to pour, until the cup overflowed onto the table, dripping onto the scholar's robes. Shocked out of his recitation, the scholar exclaimed, "Stop! Can't you see the cup is already full?" Setting down the teapot, the master said, "You are like this cup. Your mind, too, is already full so that nothing more can be added. I cannot teach you about Zen until your mind has become like an empty cup."

Our experience appreciating Japanese incense can often be like that of the scholar—our minds so full that nothing more can be added, our attention so focused on our own thoughts that we miss the experience of the incense burning right in front of us. Renowned Zen teacher Shunryu Suzuki in *Zen Mind, Beginner's Mind* famously described the need for us to empty our cup: "If your mind is empty, it is always ready for anything; it is open to everything. In the beginner's mind there are many possibilities; in the expert's mind there are few." By emptying our mind when listening to incense, we are better able to genuinely appreciate the incense before us and experience its true nature.

In Kōdō, the most formal setting for the ritual appreciation of incense, the act of listening to incense is performed in complete silence. In the West, such silence is often viewed as uncomfortable or negative. We fill our interactions with small talk from fear of an "awkward silence." We fill our environment with background noise from our electronic devices so we can "keep busy," lest our minds become quiet. To the Japanese, however, silence has a positive association and is viewed as perfectly normal. Silence is something to be appreciated rather than avoided, as silence creates space from which form and meaning emerge; it is in silence that true meaning can be discerned from that which is unspoken. The Japanese refer to such moments of silence and the space created by them as *ma* (間).

The Japanese concept of ma describes silence in terms of its infinite potential in time and space and pervades all aspects of Japanese culture. Ma is expressed in artwork, architecture, calligraphy, and more through an artistic interpretation of empty space that holds as much importance as the subject of the art itself. Ma is physical, implied, and intentional. It is much more than "lack" or "absence" within space; instead, it is a powerful, positive force, invisibly evident. Ma represents the space between musical notes that turns cacophony into melody, the pause between words that creates meaning, and the blank space in a *kakejiku* (掛軸, hanging scroll) that highlights its subject. Ma is empty, yet filled with potential, powerful in its stillness. It represents a complete lack of duality, where no separation exists, and where all is one. In ma lie infinite possibilities from which all things take shape and spring to life. In Buddhist thought, ma is represented as emptiness and all its potential. As Shunryu Suzuki describes it, "Emptiness is the garden where you cannot see anything. It is actually the mother of everything, from which everything will come." The kanji for ma, 間, provides a hint of its profound meaning. By combining the kanji for "gate," 門, with the kanji for "sun," 日, in ma, 間, we see the gateless gate that leads to enlightenment, like sunlight streaming through the gap around a closed door.

By applying the concept of emptiness to the appreciation of incense, we allow ourselves to empty our cup, quieting the mind so we can appreciate Japanese incense as it truly is. Now, this is not to say that every experience with incense needs to be of the deep, meditative, ritualized practice undertaken during Kōdō. Far from it. Relaxation, enjoyment, or background ambience is what most people seek from their experience with incense. At the same time, by emptying our minds as best we can of three common obstacles—expectation, judgment, and attachment—we are better able to truly appreciate the incense before us, however we experience it.

EXPECTATION

The first common obstacle to appreciating incense is expectation. Long before we light incense, we have expectations for it. We read its product description and begin to create a mental picture of what its fragrance will be like before we even purchase it. We then color our mental picture with our previous encounters with incense and project that image onto an experience that has yet to happen. Once we have built up our mental picture, when we light a new sandalwood incense, for example, we expect it to fit into the fictional image we have created, and we are confused and upset when reality does not align with this image. This is especially true when our brand-new sandalwood is not as sweet or as creamy as we expected, or it is quieter and more subtle than we expected. Heaven forbid our new sandalwood incense have unique characteristics like a sour or caramel note. That doesn't match the expectation that we've filled our minds with at all!

There is nothing wrong with having personal preferences, as likes and dislikes are natural and bring comfort and enjoyment to our lives. However, if we allow our minds to be filled by our expectations rather than our experience with the incense in front of us, those expectations color our experience before it even begins. We expect our new incense to behave in a certain way and are distracted from the actual experience when it does not correspond to that expectation. Often, we exaggerate the aspects we like or diminish the aspects we do not to ensure the incense before us conforms to our expected mental picture, missing the truth of the actual incense we are supposed to be appreciating.

Shunryu Suzuki put it this way: "If you received things just as an echo of yourself, you do not really see them, you do not fully accept them as they are." To appreciate incense as it truly is, we must empty our cup of expectation as much as we can and listen to the incense as it is right there in front of us. This is no easy task, as expectation creeps into every experience we have, far beyond incense. But if we can empty our cup of what we are expecting—even a little bit—we may be pleasantly surprised by our experiences with incense. Genuine and unexpected fragrant notes, which might have gone unnoticed to a mind filled with expectation, now have the opportunity to open themselves to us.

JUDGMENT

Another common obstacle to fully appreciating incense is judgment. However, emptying our minds of this obstacle is much more easily said than done. We judge everything continuously. We judge how well we slept, how good our breakfast was, the quality of our commute, our dog's intelligence, our baby's cuteness—neverendingly comparing them all to fictional standards that we have created in our own minds.

When we light incense, our mind is often full of a list of automatic judgments ready to take over our experience before we even have it. How does this incense compare to other incense we've burned before? How does it compare to the last time we burned it? How does the current brand of incense compare to the previous brand? Rather than appreciating incense right in front of us for what it is, we instead compare it to our internal picture of what we believe it should or should not be, passing judgments of good or bad, better or worse, high or low. Our minds are so conditioned for judgment that it happens automatically and in the blink of an eye.

Expectation and judgment often go hand in hand, but where expectation finds us focusing on a fictional picture in our minds of what we expect the incense to be, judgment focuses our experience on making an evaluation of the perceived value of the incense before us. Instead of simply appreciating the incense, we put it on a personal scale based on our past experiences, measuring where it falls short or excels in comparison. With our attention focused on our internal scale, we end up evaluating a picture of what we think the incense should or shouldn't be instead of actually appreciating the incense right in front of us.

Again, this judgment process is natural. In an effort to enhance the comfort and enjoyment of our lives, we all have standards to which we compare our experiences. Our standards are developed over time and practice, and as such, they are not necessarily off the mark. But the difficulty arises in that these types of judgments are focused on our own limited internal pictures, comparing experiences in the past to experiences that have yet to happen, rather than opening us to the limitless potential of the incense experience we are having. When our mind experiences incense from a place of judgment, we view it through a limited perspective: our likes, our dislikes, and the boundaries of our experience. If we can empty our cup of judgment, even a little, we allow ourselves to experience what Suzuki refers to as "absolute value," glimpsing the true nature of the incense before us rather than only the "perceived value" that comes from our limited evaluation of it. In emptying ourselves of judgment, we become able to appreciate incense from a limitless perspective, where its true nature can express itself unfiltered.

ATTACHMENT

A third common obstacle when appreciating incense is fixing our attention on a specific note from the overall fragrance and holding on to just that one note. This tendency commonly arises when we seek to describe the indescribable nature of the fragrance we are listening to. Our minds mentally dissect the incense before us, filling our thoughts with the specific note we've attached to in our attempt to describe the fragrance. When we become so attached to a specific note and fill our attention with it, there is no room left for the other notes to surprise or delight us, and our experience with incense becomes restricted. Just as a finger pointing at the moon is not the moon, our description of a fragrance is not the fragrance itself, but a mental picture we've created. As Dōgen Zenji, the founder of Sōtō Zen said, "We human beings attach to something that is not real and forget all about what is real."

When appreciating incense, what is real is the incense burning right in front of us. If we fixate on a cinnamon note, for example, our mind fills with the cinnamon-ness of the incense, coloring our experience and taking us away from the true nature of the incense we're listening to. We are then less likely to notice non-cinnamon notes and may miss the subtlety of the incense's more refined qualities or how the interplay of its many notes creates something grander. If we have a preference for cinnamon, our preoccupation with its note is even stronger and can lead to the exclusion of not just the other notes present but also the larger experience. In our preoccupation with the cinnamon-ness of the incense, we lose sight of the experience that goes beyond fragrance, like the warmth the full fragrance brings, the soothing calm it imparts, or the peacefulness it provides. This is not to say that we must cease to notice the cinnamon note or refuse to acknowledge it as the dominant note in the incense before us, nor that we should enjoy the cinnamon note any less. We simply want to notice it and then let it go, emptying our cup to make room for all the incense has to offer.

Our preoccupation with specific notes when listening to incense speaks to our desire to describe our experience. There is nothing wrong with this desire, nor is it without merit, as we require methods of cataloging our understanding. Descriptions of incense ingredients and fragrance profiles are helpful, especially when selecting which incense to purchase or deciding which to burn. It is not *describing* incense that limits our experience with it. It is when we *fix our attention* on describing it—holding tightly to a few fragrant notes—that we lose our way and limit our appreciation. When we let go, releasing our attachment, incense is given the freedom to expand, allowing the limitless potential of its fragrant ingredients to open us to insights that often transcend fragrance.

BEYOND INCENSE

The obstacles of expectation, judgment, and attachment go well beyond the appreciation of incense and are familiar obstacles in everyday life. In fact, in Buddhist thought, they are seen as common obstacles to enlightenment. However, while Japanese incense is historically rooted in Buddhism, one does not need a firm foundation in Buddhism, Zen, or meditation to appreciate Japanese incense. Although that type of grounding may be helpful, it is our willingness to empty our minds of the obstacles that stand between us and our genuine appreciation of incense that matters most. Awareness of these obstacles is the first step to emptying our minds of them, even though we will rarely fully overcome them. As Shunryu Suzuki notes, "When you empty your mind, […] then whatever you see you meet yourself." Appreciating incense authentically with an empty mind opens us to its true nature and, thereby, to our own. That, in and of itself, is a wonderful gift that incense can provide, if only we can empty our cup to receive it.

CHAPTER 26

KŌDŌ
The incense ceremony

A T THE PINNACLE OF THE JAPANESE ART OF INCENSE RESTS THE ritual appreciation of Kōdō (香道, the Way of Fragrance). Often referred to as the incense ceremony, Kōdō is one of the three *geidō* (芸道), the Japanese arts of refinement, along with the tea ceremony of Chadō (茶道, the Way of Tea) and the arrangement of flowers of Kadō (華道, the Way of Flowers). Just as Kadō and Chadō surpass the outward manifestations of their art forms, Kōdō transcends fragrance. It invites participants not merely to use the sense of smell but, during a once-in-a-lifetime gathering, to listen deeply to incense with their whole being and experience the ineffable nature of fragrance as expressed through a literary and poetic framework. The result is a comprehensive art form that is a uniquely Japanese expression of art, culture, and spirituality. Like the mysterious nature of the sense of smell, in which fragrance is received inexplicably, invisibly, and silently, Kōdō is redolent, mutable, and timeless. At its most basic, Kōdō is a practice of identifying fragrances, yet it is simultaneously a reflection of the deeper spiritual, cultural, and historical events that forged its refinement. In its purest expression, Kōdō is the enjoyment of fragrance.

THE TWO SCHOOLS OF KŌDŌ

The most comprehensive of the geidō, Kōdō relies not only on a knowledge of the enigmatic nature of fragrant woods, but it also employs a wide range of subjects, including poetry, literature, history, calligraphy, choreography, etiquette, and the influence of Zen, taking up to thirty years to master. With an unbroken tradition spanning more than five hundred years, Kōdō traces its origins to the Higashiyama cultural salons of Shōgun Ashikaga Yoshimasa in the late 1400s. It was there in the eastern hills of Kyoto that the nascent geidō of Kadō, Chadō, and Kōdō developed concurrently under the guidance of Yoshimasa's *dōbōshū* (同朋衆, professional connoisseurs), key among them, Sanjōnishi Sanetaka and Shino Sōshin—the two credited with establishing the Rikkoku (六国), the "Six Nations" framework used extensively to classify aloeswood. (See chapter 15 for more on the Rikkoku.) Sanetaka and Sōshin are also considered the founders of the two oldest schools of Kōdō still in existence today: Oie-ryu (御家流) and Shino-ryu (志野流), the word *ryu* (流) capable of meaning both "school" and "style."

Sanjōnishi Sanetaka is considered the founder of the Oie style initially favored by members of the imperial household and nobility. As Sanetaka was a court noble of rank, originally Oie-ryu was practiced by the imperial household and its courtiers, who had knowledge of the literary references used in its *kumikō* (組香, incense games), but over time, samurai and commoners seeking greater refinement studied Oie-ryu as well. Blending the refined choreography and principles of the tea ceremony with the literary and poetic framework of kumikō, the goal of Oie-ryu is to create a unique experience in an enlightened atmosphere, the essence of which is the enjoyment of fragrance.

Shino Sōshin is considered the founder of the Shino style that initially spread through the samurai and affluent merchant classes. In time, Shino-ryu was practiced by samurai, court nobles, and commoners alike, often taught in conjunction with the tea ceremony. Shino-ryu was founded upon a Zen-inspired ritual appreciation of incense and the meditative nature of monkō. As with Oie-ryu, the gaming aspects of Shino-ryu kumikō are placed within Sanetaka's framework of classical poetry and literature and emphasize the enjoyment of fragrance.

The schools share many commonalities in their forms and, in general, conduct Kōdō in similar settings. Referred to as a *kōseki* (香席), a gathering for Kōdō typically takes place in a Japanese-style room of eight to ten tatami mats in size, approximately the size of an average living room. The kōseki is run by the *kōmoto* (香元), who acts as a combination of incense master, host, and master of ceremonies. The kōmoto is responsible for selecting the specific woods and kumikō for the kōseki, preparing special incense burners known as *kikigōro* (聞香炉) with ash and charcoal, and passing the kikigōro to the participants during the ceremony. The kōmoto is assisted by a recordkeeper known as an *o-shippitsu* (お執筆), who also creates an official written record of the kōseki.

Known as *renshū* (連衆), participants typically number ten or fewer and are seated by social rank. If there is an honored guest, known as *shōkyaku* (正客), that person is the first to receive the kikigōro; if there is no shōkyaku, the most senior participant is first. The lowest-ranking participant, known as *o-tsume* (お詰), is the last to receive the kikigōro. With the kōmoto and o-shippitsu at the front of the room, the renshū sit in a rectangle that allows the kikigōro to be passed from the kōmoto to shōkyaku, and then from one participant to the next, rotating around the room until finally arriving back at the kōmoto. Considered a formal affair, decorum dictates that men wear suit jackets and women wear clothing that goes below the knee; alternatively, either may wear traditional kimono. As the fragrances experienced during Kōdō are often very subtle and intricate, renshū refrain from wearing anything with a fragrance, such as colognes, perfumes, or hand creams. Wearing jewelry such as rings, watches, and bracelets is also discouraged, as it may damage the finish of the often-antique kikigōro that are handled.

The differences between Oie and Shino styles of Kōdō are often subtle. The incense utensils used, known as *kōdōgu* (香道具), tend to be more natural, unadorned, and wabi-inspired in Shino-ryu, whereas in Oie-ryu, kōdōgu tend to be highly ornate, adorned with mother-of-pearl inlay or rich maki-e lacquer decoration. In Oie-ryu, the seasons are often highlighted through the decoration of the kikigōro and utensils. By contrast, Shino-ryu highlights the seasons using a *shino-bukuro* (志野袋), a bag for holding the wrapped packages of jinkō; the bag is decorated with a bow tied in a flower-shaped pattern chosen based upon the seasonal theme of the kōseki, with a specific flower representing each of the twelve months. Subtle differences in form and presentation of kōdōgu are evident as well; for instance, in Oie-ryu, the kikigōro is passed counterclockwise, whereas in Shino-ryu, it is passed clockwise.

The use of fragrant woods also differs slightly; while both schools use the six nations of the Rikkoku, Shino-ryu uses jinkō exclusively, whereas Oie-ryu may also use sandalwood as Sasora and includes a seventh category called Shin-kyara (新伽羅), kyara classified as coming from later than the Edo period. Oie-ryu also uses *waboku* (和木), woods originating from Japan, such as *hinoki* (檜, Japanese cypress); unlike jinkō, which is taken directly from nature, when waboku is used, it is sourced from timbers with a rich history, such as a pillar from a temple.

Regardless of their subtle differences, Oie-ryu and Shino-ryu agree that, first and foremost, Kōdō is centered upon the enjoyment of fragrance.

THE THREE ASPECTS OF KŌDŌ

No matter the school, in practice, Kōdō can be thought of as having three distinct aspects. The first is the poetic and literary framework expressed through the chosen kumikō. At its most fundamental level, kumikō give Kōdō a game-playing aspect where participants try to memorize, recognize, and identify different fragrant woods. But at a more profound level, kumikō provide a poetic form in which fragrance transcends itself and becomes an expression of aesthetic and seasonal themes, illustrating poetry, literature, and history. Filled with a reverence for the seasons that is highlighted within a form prescribed by the kumikō, Kōdō transcends mere gameplay and embodies a rich, comprehensive cultural experience. This aspect of Kōdō is covered in greater depth in chapter 27 on kumikō.

The second aspect of Kōdō is the one most easily overlooked, yet it is often the most profound. During Kōdō, participants do not "smell" or "sniff" fragrance. Instead, Kōdō invites them to go beyond their sense of smell and, through monkō, to "listen" to incense deeply, using all their senses and emptying their minds to fully experience the expression of nature provided by rare and fragrant woods. Although a knowledge of Zen is not required, nor Zen ideals promoted, Zen's influence upon Kōdō's earliest formation is evident in the act of quieting the mind and focusing all the senses upon fragrance. Unlike perfumes or colognes, the scents of the fragrant woods used are ethereal, subtle, and sublime. By approaching them through the meditative practice of monkō, the senses are sharpened and sensitivity to nature's expression is developed. The effort not only hones the mind but also enriches the spirit through the meditative refinement of the inner self.

Monkō trains participants to focus their whole being on the present moment as they experience the subtle fragrance of rare woods from the heart, opening to a dialogue with the natural world. Freed from the distractions of the day and its stresses, the mind is calmed by the soothing enjoyment of fragrance. Kōdō offers participants an opportunity for relaxation and introspection, allowing them to be fully present in the moment, the experience, and the fragrance. This embodies the "Way" that *dō* (道) of Kō-*dō* represents: the lifelong training and refinement of the mind and spirit through the meditative appreciation of fragrant woods.

The third distinct aspect of Kōdō is the social dynamic created during the once-in-a-lifetime gathering of the kōseki. Kōdō as an art form is a social activity of shared experience. It does not occur without the interaction of host and guests. At its most fundamental level, Kōdō is an opportunity to play a game in a social setting and enjoy fragrance with others. As a comprehensive art, Kōdō creates a social environment of harmony, respect, purity, and tranquility, where interest in cultural traditions and art forms is nurtured and developed. Knowledge of Japanese poetry, literature, and history is enhanced, and classical skills such as calligraphy are developed. The refinement of the personality occurs through the practice of manners and etiquette learned during the social gathering. A collective sense of happiness is gained through comparing individual experiences of the excitement of recognizing a fragrant wood or experiencing a fragrance for the first time. When the ceremony ends, regardless of the number of fragrances correctly identified, participants are happy, having enjoyed a sense of togetherness through a shared experience.

On a deeper level, the kōseki embodies the once-in-a-lifetime nature of *ichigo ichie*. (See chapter 24 for a full discussion.) Even should the same participants attend two similar events, the experience would never be the same—from the unique interactions that occur as they arrive, to the way they pass the kikigōro, to the way they enjoy the reporting of the results. The kōmoto's movements, the o-shippitsu's record, the reporting, and the reaction to the outcome all will be different from event to event. The fragrant woods at the center of the event are especially unrepeatable. Even if pieces of the same wood are used at two different events, the fragrance would be subtly different each time, affected by the temperature, humidity, and unique resin within that portion of wood. Through its once-in-a-lifetime nature, Kōdō transcends fragrance, creating a social environment where the appreciation of fragrance is heightened.

THE KŌDŌ CEREMONY

While the details of each kōseki vary, there is a general pattern they follow. The following description depicts a Kōdō ceremony of the Oie style.

Even before the day of the kōseki, the kōmoto puts a great deal of thought into which kumikō to select for the gathering and which specific incense woods to use. Creating a sense of harmony with the seasons and among guests is paramount, as is the creation of an event appropriate for the guests attending. The choice of woods is tailored to the participants' skill level and could range from clearly different fragrances to strikingly similar woods, the number of different woods determined by the chosen kumikō. The selected woods, cut to the size of a grain of rice, are each folded into a paper packet and discretely labeled. Additionally, the kikigōro that will be used are chosen. While *kōro* (香炉) is the general term for an incense burner, kikigōro ("listening incense burner") are special three-footed ceramic incense burners used specifically for Kōdō. They are typically smaller in size, about three inches in diameter and slightly less in height, made to fit in the palm of one's hand. The kikigōro are chosen to highlight both the season and the theme of the kumikō, harmonizing with them through their subtle artistry and natural beauty. The number of kikigōro used varies by kumikō, but two is common.

As the guests arrive, the kōmoto prepares the kikigōro with white ash and odorless, clean-burning charcoal in a process requiring great skill, known as *hai-demae* (灰手前). Using *koji* (火箸), special metal "fire chopsticks," a burning coal is placed in the center of the ash in the kikigōro. Using a *haioshi* (灰押), a flat metal spatula in the shape of a *shaku* (笏, scepter), the ash is lifted over the charcoal to form a cone-shaped mound. A single koji is then used to create a vent hole in the center of the ash mound to channel the heat from the burning coal. A pattern known as a *hashi-me* (箸目, chopstick eye) is then created in the ash using the koji. The hashi-me divides the ash mound visually into five equal sections, with a smaller sixth division facing the front foot of the kikigōro. This sixth section is known as the *kiki-guchi* (聞口) and signifies the "listening line," the position of the kōro where incense is listened to.

In general, there are two patterns of hashi-me, though others may also be used. The most formal pattern has lines drawn in all five divisions, and the kikigōro in which it is used is referred to as the Shin no kōro (真の香炉, True Incense Burner). The less formal hashi-me includes only the division lines without any additional pattern, and the kikigōro in which it is used is referred to as Gyō no kōro (行の香炉, Line Incense Burner). The details of the hashi-me—for example, the number or direction of the lines in a section—may vary depending upon the season and kumikō chosen. Once the ash is prepared, a *habōki* (羽箒, feather brush) is used to remove stray ash, purifying the kikigōro.

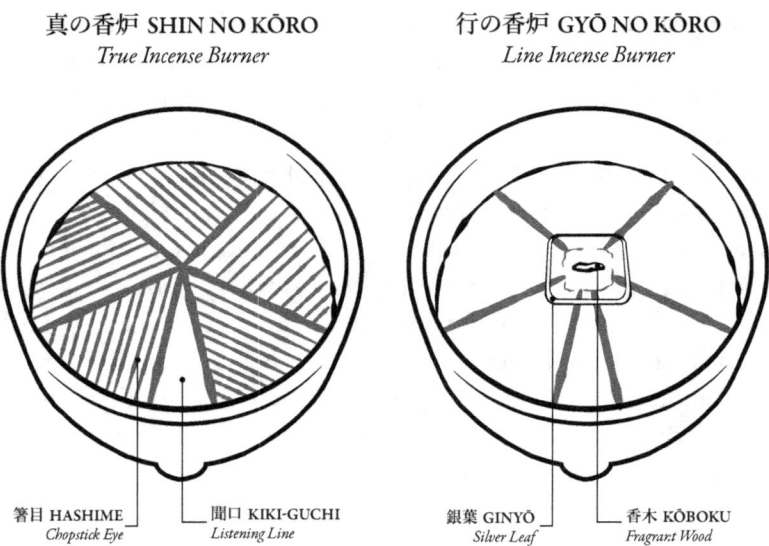

真の香炉 SHIN NO KŌRO
True Incense Burner

行の香炉 GYŌ NO KŌRO
Line Incense Burner

箸目 HASHIME
Chopstick Eye

聞口 KIKI-GUCHI
Listening Line

銀葉 GINYŌ
Silver Leaf

香木 KŌBOKU
Fragrant Wood

Figure 1: Hashi-me

After the renshū are seated in their appropriate places and waiting silently, the kōmoto and recordkeeper enter the room, taking their places at the front, with the kōmoto seated nearest the honored guest. The kōmoto uses a *midarabako* (乱箱), a high-sided tray, to carry the various incense utensils, incense boxes, packets of incense, score sheets, and the kikigōro that will be used for the kōseki. After the kōmoto greets the renshū with the statement "Incense is begun," the renshū bow. Placing the midarabako temporarily to her left, the kōmoto then takes blank recording paper and an inkstone (a stone upon which dry ink and water are mixed for calligraphy) from a utensil stand to her right and presents them to the recordkeeper.

Next, the kōmoto ceremonially spreads an *uchishiki* (打敷), a framed, patterned silk rug, over the tatami in front of her. The designs of the uchishiki are selected according to the kumikō, harmonizing with the theme of the event and the season. Next, a *jishiki* (地敷), a thick paper placemat covered with gold foil on one side and silver foil on the other, is placed on top of the uchishiki. Then, beginning the choreographed process known as *temae* (手前), the kōmoto gracefully places the kōdōgu, incense boxes, and kikigōro in a prescribed formal arrangement on the placemat. After the incense tools have been placed, the kōmoto ceremonially purifies each one, carefully replacing it on the jishiki after it is cleaned.

As this is occurring, the recordkeeper prepares the official record of the kōseki. As a formal document of a once-in-a-lifetime event, the kōseki record is beautifully written in fine calligraphy on quality paper, with the name of the kumikō inscribed in large, bold writing on the top right corner of the sheet. All the information about the kōseki is included—the date and location, the kikigōro used, the names of the fragrant woods, the names of each participant and the honored guest, the names of the kōmoto and recordkeeper conducting the kōseki, and eventually the answers of each participant. After everything has been prepared, folded answer sheets, known as *tegiroku-shi* (手記録紙), are distributed to the renshū, followed by small boxes containing an inkstone and brush for each participant.

Next, using *gin'yō basami* (銀葉鋏), a flat-ended tweezer-like tool, the kōmoto carefully places a *gin'yō* (銀葉, silver leaf) on top of the ash mound of the True Incense Burner, directly above the vent where the heat from the coal rises. After aligning the gin'yō square to the front of the kikigōro, the kōmoto announces, "Heating is begun." The kōmoto then uses a *kōsaji* (香匙), a small spoonlike tool, to place a small piece of fragrant wood on the gin'yō perpendicular to the front of the kikigōro. After the wood is allowed to heat for a few moments, the kōmoto listens to the incense to ensure fragrance is being emitted steadily. Once satisfied, the kōmoto announces, "Sample incense," and then passes the kikigōro to the honored guest, and listening begins. The sample incense is a reference fragrance for participants to commit to memory for comparison to later unknown fragrances in the kumikō; some kumikō have one sample, some have multiple, and some have none.

The incense burner is placed to the right of the guest, with the kiki-guchi, the "listening line," facing away from the listener. The listener carefully picks up the kikigōro and, holding it in the palm of the left hand, uses the right hand to rotate it three times clockwise, 180 degrees total, so that the listening line face them. The right hand then cups the top of the kikigōro, leaving an opening between the thumb and fingers for listening. As the incense is heated rather than burned, no smoke is produced; only pure fragrance is released. This allows the listener to raise the kikigōro directly to their nose, sit up straight, and take a deep breath in to listen to the fragrance. They then turn their head to the side to exhale so as not to disturb the ash or incense. No more than three deep breaths are taken, as using any more time may cause the fragrance to fade by the time the kikigōro makes its way around the room. Once listening is complete, the listener again rotates the kikigōro three times until the listening line is facing away from them. Then the kikigōro is passed to the next participant, carefully setting it on the tatami to their right, and the process is repeated.

As the first kikigōro is passed, the kōmoto prepares the kikigōro for the next sample incense. The second kikigōro passed is the Line Incense Burner, its pattern differentiating it from the True Incense Burner. Once prepared with gin'yō and wood, the second sample is passed around the renshū and listened to in the same manner as the first.

Once a kikigōro has made its way around the entire renshū, it is returned to the recordkeeper, who also listens to the incense. Finally, the kikigōro is returned to the kōmoto, who removes the gin'yō using the gin'yō basami and places it on a *gin'yō-ban* (銀葉盤), an ornate stand with ten to twelve flower-shaped mother-of-pearl pedestals called *kiku-za* (菊座). Afterward, the kikigōro is replaced on the jishiki placemat in preparation for its next use.

After the sample incenses have been passed, the kōmoto announces the start of heating the real (unknown) incense, and ceremonially shuffles the incense packets for the kumikō. Depending upon the kumikō chosen, as few as three packets or as many as twenty-five could be shuffled, with three to ten chosen for listening. The renshū then bow and prepare their inkstones, after which they write their names on their answer sheets. Placing a gin'yō on the True Incense Burner, the first unknown wood is placed upon the gin'yō, and the unfolded packet, discreetly labeled with the name of the wood, is held in place at the lower left of the jishiki using a metal pin known as a *uguisu* (鶯). The kōmoto then announces the first kikigōro, and it is passed around the renshū for listening in the same fashion as the sample incense. As the first kikigōro makes its way around the room, the kōmoto prepares the second kikigōro (the Line Incense Burner), pinning the unfolded incense packets to the uguisu in order before passing the next incense.

As the renshū listen to the unknown incense in each round, they silently compare it to the sample incense and, depending on the goal of the kumikō, try to discern something about it: Is it the same or different from the sample? Is it the same or different from the fragrant woods in prior rounds? Between the arrival of each kikigōro, participants have the opportunity to take notes to help with these questions.

Depending upon the kumikō chosen, the kōmoto prepares the kikigōro with unknown woods three to ten times, using the packets of incense previously shuffled, alternating between the True Incense Burner and the Line Incense Burner. Once all the incense has been passed, listened to by the renshū, and the gin'yō removed and placed on the gin'yō-ban, the kōmoto announces that the kumikō is concluded.

Next, the kōmoto gracefully and ceremonially returns all the kōdōgu to the midarabako. After bowing, the renshū write their answers on their answer sheets, which are collected by the recordkeeper and written in the official record of the kōseki. After all the answers have been recorded, the kōmoto reads to the renshū the name of each wood in the order it was passed, and the recordkeeper scores the answers, giving one point for each correct answer provided. Once scoring is complete, the recordkeeper presents the kōseki record sheet to the kōmoto, who passes it on to the renshū for inspection, starting with the honored guest. Once the record sheet makes its way around the room, the kōmoto rolls it up and formally presents it to the participant with the highest score. In the case of a tie, the record is presented to the most senior of the tied participants. Finally, the kōseki is ended and the silence broken as the renshū all bow and conclude with the phrase *kōmichimashita* (香満ちました), meaning "filled with fragrance."

Although Kōdō is experiencing a resurgence of interest, it is still the least known of Japan's three geidō. Some reasons for this include more than a generation of decline during the reforms of the Meiji Restoration in the late nineteenth century, the high cost and rare nature of the fragrant woods utilized, and a general decline in knowledge of the poetic and literary classics that form the basis of the kumikō at the center of the art. However, both Oie-ryu and Shino-ryu have experienced a rebirth in the last half century, and both schools now offer classes throughout Japan to train a new generation of incense masters in the refined art of Kōdō.

CHAPTER 27

KUMIKŌ
The comprehensive art of incense

IN THE NIGHT SKY ABOVE THE IMPERIAL PALACE, THE EERIE CRY OF the *nue* (鵺) haunted the emperor. The fragrance of incense filled the air as purification rituals were performed to ward off the spell of the winged monster's frightening song, but night after night, the nue returned. Frustrated and fearful and horribly disturbed by such an ill portent, the court discussed what to do to subjugate the unnatural disturbance that threatened the sovereign's well-being. It was decided to call upon Minomoto Yorimasa, a well-known poet, warrior, and skilled archer, to shoot the thrush-monster out of the sky and restore the emperor's peace of mind. Yorimasa was summoned to the palace and informed of his task. Upon learning what was expected of him, Yorimasa's heart grew heavy. The task was daunting, and he wondered if it were even possible. *Even in broad daylight, shooting such a difficult target is too much to ask of a man, but it is unthinkable, black as the night is, in the cloudy sky of the Fifth Month when the rains come.*

Yet as the night darkened and the clouds rolled in, Yorimasa did as he was asked. When the nue's cry rang out, he turned his bow to the night sky, prayed to the patron deity of archers, and let his arrow fly. As the assembled court looked on, his prayers were heard: the arrow struck its mark, and the nue fell from the sky, mortally wounded. All were terrified to see such an unnatural creature: it had the head of a monkey, the legs of a tiger, the tail of a snake, and the body of a *tanuki* (化け狸, shape shifter). With the nue conquered, the emperor and all the court were filled with praise for Yorimasa. He was gifted robes, and poems were recited in his honor, comparing him to the legendary heroes of antiquity.

Recorded in the *Taiheiki* (太平記, *Chronicles of the Great Peace*), tales such as "Yorimasa and the Nue" were well known to the Imperial Court and samurai aristocracy of Japan. Just as a classical education in the West includes the study of humanistic works of literature and poetry such as Homer's *The Iliad* and *The Odyssey*, for centuries the classical education of the Japanese nobility was not complete without a thorough knowledge of the *gunki monogatari* (軍記物語, war tales) such as the *Taiheiki*, fluency in royal anthologies of poetry such as the *Kokin Wakashū* (古今和歌集, *Collection of Poems Ancient and Modern*), and examination of classical literature such as *Genji Monogatari* (源氏物語, *The Tale of Genji*). Arising from the *miyabi*-infused incense comparison games of the Heian period, the rowdy guessing games of samurai *tōkō* (闘香, incense battles), and Sanjōnishi Sanetaka's refinement of those forms, *kumikō* (組香, incense games) blend the ritual appreciation of incense with the poetic, literary, and historic knowledge that was a prerequisite for the Japanese elite. From its start in the cultural salons of Shōgun Ashikaga Yoshimasa, Sanetaka's poetic and literary framework was infused into hundreds of kumikō created at the height of Kōdō's popularity during the Edo period (1603–1868).

At their most fundamental level, kumikō introduce a game-playing aspect to Kōdō, where participants try to memorize, recognize, and identify different fragrant woods. Answers are recorded; the score is kept; the kōseki record is awarded to the participant with the highest score. It is easy to understand how a novice might view kumikō as a game of olfactory competition, with winners and losers. But this perspective captures only the simple, outward form of kumikō.

Instead, it is the poetic and literary framework credited to Sanjōnishi Sanetaka that provides the true spirit at the heart of kumikō. Rather than being simple competitive guessing games, kumikō offer a literary form within which incense is free to transcend fragrance and become an expression of aesthetic and seasonal themes that illustrate poetry, literature, and history. In fact, the idea of competition is not only minimized but often discarded completely, instead placing the emphasis on the poetic and literary form's expression of the enjoyment of fragrance. Drawing upon a knowledge of the classics, kumikō create a form in which poetry is brought to life through fragrant woods, the miyabi of Heian courtiers is experienced through passing a kikigōro, and the spirit of ancient history is experienced through the kōseki. It is this transcendence of fragrance that kumikō provides, elevating Kōdō beyond a simple guessing game to a rich, comprehensive cultural experience unique to Japan.

To best understand how kumikō illustrates poetry and literature with fragrance, it is helpful to think of kumikō as a play. William Shakespeare wrote *Hamlet* around 1600, and many kumikō had their forms established around this time as well. Over the centuries, *Hamlet* has been performed thousands of times following the form Shakespeare created over four hundred years ago; similarly, kumikō continue to be performed today following the forms established during the Edo period. Plays like *Hamlet* are interpreted by a director, just as kumikō are interpreted by the kōmoto. Costuming, art direction, and set design are all carefully chosen by the director, giving each production of *Hamlet* a unique flavor while still remaining true to the form Shakespeare created. The same is true of kumikō, as the kōmoto interprets its form and selects the tools, kikigōro, and setting to complement it. Just as an actor is cast in the role of Hamlet, providing their own interpretation of Shakespeare's famous character, the kōmoto goes to great lengths to select specific woods that take on the roles of lines of poetry or literary events, each providing its own fragrant interpretation. When it comes to casting actors, a director may cast a specific actor in a role for their expertise or reputation, just as the kōmoto may choose from fragrant woods for their specific characteristics or from famous *meikō* (名, named aloeswood) for their reputation.

The director also stages a production of *Hamlet* differently depending upon the type of audience and the venue. The same consideration is taken with kumikō, as the kōmoto selects the kumikō to create harmony with the seasons and a sense of tranquility among participants. Like a performance of *Hamlet*, a kumikō allows the listeners a reprieve from their day-to-day lives and stresses. It provides an oasis of tranquility, where the hectic pace of life is left behind, allowing the listeners to relax and enjoy the elegant art of incense in the calm peacefulness of silent lucidity. Finally, just as each performance of *Hamlet* is unique, each kumikō performed is an expression of ichigo ichie and can never be repeated exactly, the fragrant woods consumed and lost forever at the close of the kōseki.

One of the earliest recorded kumikō is known as Jūshūkō (十種香, Ten Types of Incense). Although Jūshūkō preceded Sanetaka's poetic and literary framework, it was one of the first recorded kumikō to emphasize its social underpinnings. During Jūshūkō, fragrant woods are used to illustrate the custom of courtiers being recognized by their personal fragrance, a practice highlighted in the literary classic *The Tale of Genji*. To perform Jūshūkō, the kōmoto carefully selects four different woods to play the parts of four courtiers circulating at a lavish banquet. Care is taken to select woods whose distinct fragrances illustrate the unique personality of each courtier. Before the kōseki, the kōmoto prepares three packets each of three fragrant woods to represent three introduced guests, and one packet to represent a mysterious, unintroduced guest, for a total of ten packets of incense.

During the kōseki, three courtiers are introduced once to the renshū—that is, the woods representing them are sampled for memorization. However, the fourth wood, representing a mysterious courtier the renshū have yet to meet, is held in reserve. After the fragrances of the three introduced guests have been sampled and committed to memory, the kōmoto ceremonially shuffles the remaining seven packets of incense, and a kikigōro is prepared and passed for each one. During these seven rounds, the renshū listen to each fragrance, trying to discern the courtier it belongs to and identify the mysterious unknown courtier.

The earliest kumikō, such as Jūshūkō, were often competitive events filled with gambling and rowdiness, lacking the etiquette and refinement Sanetaka would add more than two centuries later. Despite this, Jūshūkō serves as one of the earliest examples of how kumikō could use fragrant woods to transcend fragrance, taking on roles like actors in a play.

Sanetaka's poetic and literary framework elevated kumikō from a rowdy, competitive game to one centered upon the rich, comprehensive nature of a refined art form. At the height of Kōdō's popularity during the middle of the Edo period, hundreds of kumikō were created, covering a wide variety of themes based on events from ancient history, poems from royal anthologies, and characters of classical literature. Weaving a reverence for the seasons into an experience centered on classical literature and poetry, emphasis was placed on the enjoyment of fragrance rather than on competition. Much like the organization of the *Kokin Wakashū*, kumikō emphasized a heightened sense of the passing seasons, employing specific kumikō like a fragrant embodiment of *kigo* (季語), the seasonal words used in waka poetry.

The following are examples of kumikō that might be chosen for each of the four seasons.

SPRING KUMIKŌ: RISSHUN-KŌ

The first day of spring in the traditional Japanese calendar is known as Risshun (立春). To celebrate spring's return, the kumikō Risshun-kō (立春香) uses as its poetic framework the first poem from the *Kokin Wakashū*, attributed to Ariwara Motokata, a waka poet of the early Heian period:

> *Springtime has arrived*
> *While the old year lingers on.*
> *What then of the year?*
> *Are we to talk of "last year"?*
> *Or are we to say "this year"?*

In our modern world, this poem may be difficult to understand, as New Year's Day falls long before the start of spring. However, rather than using a fixed-date calendar like our current Gregorian calendar, the ancient Japanese embraced the seasons through a flexible lunar-solar calendar. The traditional Japanese calendar identified twenty-four seasons, with each season split further into three microseasons, for a total of seventy-two microseasons, each of which was tied to a particular solar or lunar event. In the case of spring, the first day occurred each year around February 4. However, the lunar new year was tied to the second new moon after the winter solstice, which could happen over a wide swath of time—anywhere from January 21 to February 20. Under the ancient Japanese calendar, spring could arrive while the previous year still lingered!

In performing Risshun-kō, each of the four lines of the poem is played by a fragrant wood. The first two lines, "springtime arrives" and "old year lingers on," are played by fragrant woods that are passed to the renshū as samples to be enjoyed and memorized. Then, randomly, the last two woods are passed, fragrantly representing the last two lines of the poem, "last year" and "this year." For these fragrant woods, "last year" uses the same sample as "old year lingers on," whereas "this year" is a new incense. In total, three incense woods are used and four kikigōro are passed—two as known samples and two at random. After listening, the renshū decide the answer to the poem, seeking to recognize the new year from the old based upon fragrance.

SUMMER KUMIKŌ: AYAME-KŌ

In the kumikō Ayame-kō (菖蒲香), we visit the rainy season of early summer and return to the tale of "Yorimasa and the Nue" recounted in the Taiheiki. At the court of the emperor resided a beautiful courtesan named Lady Ayame, from whom the kumikō takes its name. *Ayame* (菖蒲) is the Japanese word for iris, the May flower that grows during the rainy season on the edges of flooded rice fields. One day, several years prior to slaying the nue, Yorimasa had seen the Lady Ayame but only ever so briefly, as imperial courtesans remained behind screens and were rarely ever seen. Yorimasa was smitten by her elegance and grace on sight. Falling hopelessly in love, he wrote to the Lady Ayame for years, with no reply. Due to the duration of the one-sided correspondence, the emperor was aware of Yorimasa's feelings. After Yorimasa slew the nue, the emperor sought to reward him with the Lady Ayame as a bride. But the emperor was wary that Yorimasa was merely infatuated with her beauty, having only caught a glimpse of her.

To assuage his concern, the emperor decided to test Yorimasa to see if it was just her beauty or true love that drove his affections. To do so, he had the Lady Ayame and four other courtiers of similar age and appearance dress in the same kimono and appear together. He then asked Yorimasa to identify the Lady Ayame. This proved too difficult a task for Yorimasa, as he had only briefly seen the Lady Ayame years earlier. Concerned that guessing incorrectly might tarnish his character and family name as well as those of the Lady Ayame, Yorimasa hesitated to choose. When the emperor insisted, Yorimasa composed the following poem, in the moment, as his answer:

> *The fifth-month rains*
> > *swamp the water oats along the shore,*
> *making it hard to tell*
> > *irises from one another*
> *and pull just one.*

The emperor was so impressed with Yorimasa's poem that he immediately relented and gave the Lady Ayame to Yorimasa, who was lauded not only for slaying the nue but also for his poetic ability. It is Yorimasa's poem that serves as the framework for the kumikō Ayame-kō.

To perform Ayame-kō, five fragrant woods are chosen to play each of the five lines of Yorimasa's poem, the fourth line representing the Lady Ayame as it specifically names irises. The goal is to identify the fragrance representing Lady Ayane, so to adjust the kumikō to the experience of the participants, the kōmoto may pick five very similar fragrant woods or only one or two that are similar to the fragrant wood representing the Lady Ayame. A total of six packets of incense are prepared: one packet of incense for each of the four lines representing the four courtesans chosen by the emperor and two packets representing the Lady Ayame.

The kumikō starts by passing a sample of the fragrant wood playing the part of the Lady Ayame for the renshū to commit to memory, just as Yorimasa's brief glimpse of her stirred his feelings. Next, the remaining five packets are ceremonially shuffled and a kikigōro for each is prepared and passed to the renshū. Experiencing Yorimasa's conundrum firsthand, participants attempt to identify the Lady Ayame from memory, bringing the tale from the *Taiheiki* to life through fragrance.

AUTUMN KUMIKŌ: KIKU-AWASE-KŌ

Known as *kiku* (菊) in Japanese, the chrysanthemum is a sign of nobility used by the Imperial Court and symbolizes the harvests of autumn. The practice of *kiku-awase* (菊合わせ), the comparison of chrysanthemums, is centuries old and continues to this day in the *kikatenran-kai* (菊花展覧会, chrysanthemum exhibitions) that take place throughout Japan in the fall. Celebrating a royal chrysanthemum viewing, the kumikō Kiku-awase-kō (菊合わせ香) uses as its framework a poem attributed to Sugawara no Ason, a noted poet, scholar, and high-ranking noble of the Heian period. Composed upon viewing chrysanthemums planted in a garden representation of Fukiage Beach, known for its beautiful sands and large dunes, the poem is number 272 in the *Kokin Wakashū*:

> *White chrysanthemums*
> *growing at Fukiage*
> *   where autumn winds blow:*
> *are they in truth flowers,*
> *or might waves be rolling in?*

To perform Kiku-awase-kō, two types of fragrant wood are chosen, one to represent "white chrysanthemum" and the other "autumn winds." Three packets of "white chrysanthemum" and four packets of "autumn winds" are prepared, for a total of seven packets of incense.

First, the kōmoto prepares a kikigōro using one of the packets of "autumn winds" as a sample and passes it to the renshū for them to enjoy and commit to memory. Once the sample has been passed, the kōmoto ceremonially shuffles the remaining six packets of incense; then two packets are removed and set aside. A kikigōro is prepared for each of the remaining four woods and passed in random order to the renshū. As participants listen to each incense, they try to discern whether the fragrance is "white chrysanthemum" or "autumn winds." In this way, the renshū take the place of Sugawara no Ason viewing the chrysanthemum display, unsure of whether it is white chrysanthemums or the white caps of waves.

For each of the four woods listened to, participants record their answers on their answer sheet as either "white chrysanthemum" or "autumn winds." The recordkeeper includes the answers in the official record of the kōseki, and uses them to decide the answer to the poem's question. If the majority of the renshū wrote "white chrysanthemum," the recordkeeper declares the poem's answer "chrysanthemum." If the number is equal between "white chrysanthemum" and "autumn winds," the recordkeeper declares the answer as "flower." If a majority of the renshū answered "autumn winds," then the recordkeeper declares the answer as "waves." Thus, the meaning of the poem is expressed through fragrance and the group's effort to discern the answer to its question.

WINTER KUMIKŌ: GENJI-KŌ

The most famous kumikō of all, Genji-kō (源氏香), illustrates Lady Murasaki's Heian classic *Genji Monogatari* through fragrance. Developed during the height of Kōdō's popularity in the Edo period, Genji-kō uses five fragrant woods chosen at random, the identification of which creates a pattern known as a *Genji-mon* (源氏紋). There are fifty-two possible Genji-mon, each of which corresponds to a specific chapter of *The Tale of Genji*. (See the chart in on page 303.) Famous throughout Japan, Genji-mon are widely used as a classic design motif, appearing on kimono, on lacquerware, on buildings as architectural elements, and even on *wagashi* (和菓子) confections. Unlike kumikō that focus upon a specific poem or event as their literary framework, Genji-kō uses fragrance to highlight *The Tale of Genji* as a whole. Each time Genji-kō is performed, any of the fifty-two Genji-mon patterns is a possible outcome. Because *The Tale of Genji* has fifty-four chapters, the first chapter, "Kiritsubo" (桐壺), and the last chapter, "Yume no Ukihashi" (夢浮橋), are not used.

To perform Genji-kō, five unique fragrant woods are selected, and five packets of each prepared, for a total of twenty-five packets of incense. During the kumikō, the packets are ceremonially shuffled by the kōmoto, and five packets are chosen at random. The five selected packets are then shuffled; a kikigōro is prepared for each one and passed among the renshū. As each incense is listened to, participants attempt to discern which of the five woods are alike and which are unique. Answers are recorded using five vertical lines to represent the five woods, from right to left. Horizontal lines are then used to link together vertical lines of woods believed to be the same, resulting in a Genji-mon, a fragrant image of a specific chapter of *The Tale of Genji*.

| *All unique* | *1 and 3 unique, 2,4,5 the same* | *All the same* |

Figure 2: Three Sample Genji-mon

When finished, the renshū compare their answer to a chart of Genji-mon, after which the kōmoto reveals the correct answer. If a participant answers correctly, their answer is marked by the recordkeeper as *tama* (玉), meaning "jewel," in reference to Prince Genji, who was referred to as a shining jewel among men. With twenty packets of incense remaining, Genji-kō can be repeated up to four times in the same fashion. Regardless of whether one answers correctly or not, it is the enjoyment of fragrance that is paramount, with incorrect answers considered nothing more than the reading of a different chapter of Lady Murasaki's beloved classic.

CHART OF GENJI-MON 源氏紋

46	37	28	19	10	1
椎本 SHIIGAMOTO *At the Foot of the Oak Tree*	横笛 YOKOBUE *The Transverse Flute*	野分 NOWAKI *An Autumn Tempest*	薄雲 USUGUMO *A Thin Veil of Clouds*	賢木 SAKAKI *A Branch of Sacred Evergreen*	UNUSUED 桐壺 KIRITSUBO *The Lady of the Paulownia- Courtyard Chambers*
47	38	29	20	11	2
総角 AGEMAKI *A Bowknot Tied in a Maiden's Loops*	鈴虫 SUZUMUSHI *Bell Crickets*	行幸 MIYUKI *An Imperial Excursion*	朝顔 ASAGAO *Bellflowers*	花散里 HANACHIRUSATO *The Lady at the Villa of Scattering Orange Blossoms*	帚木 HAHAKIGI *Broom Cypress*
48	39	30	21	12	3
早蕨 SAWARABI *Early Fiddlehead Greens*	夕霧 YŪGIRI *Evening Mist*	藤袴 FUJIBAKAMA *Mistflowers*	乙女 OTOME *Maidens of the Dance*	須磨 SUMA *Exile to Suma*	空蝉 UTSUSEMI *A Molted Cicada Shell*
49	40	31	22	13	4
宿木 YADORIKI *Trees Encoiled in Vines of Ivy*	御法 MINORI *Rites of the Sacred Law*	真木柱 MAKIBASHIRA *A Beloved Pillar of Cypress*	玉鬘 TAMAKAZURA *A Lovely Garland*	明石 AKASHI *The Lady at Akashi*	夕顔 YŪGAO *The Lady of the Evening Faces*
50	41	32	23	14	5
東屋 AZUMAYA *A Hut is the Eastern Provines*	幻 MABOROSHI *Spirit Summoner*	梅枝 UMEGAE *A Branch of Plum*	初音 HATSUNE *First Song of Spring*	澪標 MIOTSUKUSHI *Channel Markers*	若紫 WAKAMURASAKI *Little Purple Gromwell*
51	42	33	24	15	6
浮舟 UKIFUNE *A Boat Cast Adrift*	匂宮 NIOU MIYA *The Fragrant Prince*	藤裏葉 FUJI NO URABA *Shoots of Wisteria Leaves*	胡蝶 KOCHŌ *Butterflies*	蓬生 YOMOGIU *A Ruined Villa of Tangled Gardens*	末摘花 SUETSUMUHANA *The Safflower*
52	43	34	25	16	7
蜻蛉 KAGERŌ *Ephemerids*	紅梅 KŌBAI *Red Plum*	若菜上 WAKANA *Early Spring Greens Part 1*	螢 HOTARU *Fireflies*	関屋 SEKIYA *The Barrier Gate*	紅葉賀 MOMIJI NO GA *An Imperial Celebration of Autumn Foliage*
53	44	35	26	17	8
手習 TENARAI *Practicing Calligraphy*	竹河 TAKEKAWA *Bamboo River*	若菜下 WAKANA *Early Spring Greens Part 2*	常夏 TOKONATSU *Wild Pinks*	絵合 E-AWASE *A Contest of Illustrations*	花宴 HANA NO EN *A Banquet Celebrating Cherry Blossoms*
54	45	36	27	18	9
UNUSUED 夢浮橋 YUME NO UKIHASHI *A Floating Bridge in a Dream*	橋姫 HASHIHIME *The Divine Princess at Uji Bridge*	柏木 KASHIWAGI *The Oak Tree*	篝火 KAGARIBI *Cresset Fires*	松風 MATSUKAZE *Wind in the Pines*	葵 AOI *Leaves of Wild Ginger*

303

CHAPTER 28

香の十徳

KŌ NO JITTOKU
The Ten Virtues of Incense

THE POEM "KŌ NO JITTOKU" (香の十徳), PASSED DOWN IN Japan since the fifteenth century, extols the virtues of using incense. Attributed to the influential and eccentric Zen monk Sōjun Ikkyū, who transcribed and distributed it among the merchants, literati, and nobles of the time, "Ten Virtues of Incense" was originally written in the eleventh century by Huang Tingjian, a master poet and calligrapher from China's Song dynasty. "Ten Virtues of Incense" is still widely cited today for its description of the beneficial qualities attributed to Japanese incense.

感格鬼神

IT BRINGS COMMUNICATION
WITH THE TRANSCENDENT

Incense has been used for centuries in spiritual practices
in both Eastern and Western religions. Fragrant offerings
are used as universal expressions of communication with
the divine, with the smoke from incense often viewed as
carrying prayers to the heavens. The Japanese reverence for
the seasons, combined with the fragrant woods used in the
art of incense, creates a dialogue with the natural world,
opening our perception and allowing us to experience the
true nature of the woods, thereby revealing our own.

清浄心身

IT PURIFIES BOTH MIND AND BODY

The Japanese have used incense for over a thousand years to purify the body, mind, and spirit. For centuries, it has been believed that the pure natural woods and aromatic ingredients used in Japanese incense possess healing and psychotropic properties, and recent scientific studies confirm many of these beliefs. Whether using frankincense for a calming influence, lavender for relaxation, or cypress for stimulating concentration, the Japanese art of incense has provided these beneficial properties for generations.

能払汚穢

IT REMOVES
IMPURITY

Japanese incense is often used to purify the spaces where

ceremonies and rituals are performed. Many of its ingredients

have proven antimicrobial and antibacterial properties

that have been used for centuries to neutralize odors and

purify and cleanse spaces. For example, *hinoki* (檜, Japanese

cypress) contains hinokitiol, which is known to absorb

toxins and to possess strong antibacterial properties capable

of inhibiting the growth of fungi, bacteria, and viruses.

能覚睡眠

IT IMPARTS ALERTNESS

Aromatic ingredients commonly used in Japanese incense, such as camphor, cinnamon, and clove, have been recognized for their ability to increase mental awareness, gently stimulate the brain, increase concentration, and improve cognitive function. Fragrant woods like jinkō and sandalwood are well known for their calming properties, yet also are used for their ability to increase focus and concentration and are popular with Japanese students studying for entrance exams.

静中成友

IT IS A COMPANION
IN SOLITUDE

Incense is well known for its association with meditation and

mindfulness practices that cultivate inner focus. Jinkō and

sandalwood, the two most prominent fragrant woods used in

Japanese incense, have been employed for centuries to deepen

the meditative state. Aromatics such as frankincense have

been used since antiquity for their calming effects on the mind.

塵裏愉閑

IN THE MIDST OF BUSY AFFAIRS, IT BRINGS A MOMENT OF PEACE

There is something timeless about lighting a stick of Japanese

incense and enjoying the tranquil beauty of its rising smoke

and the way the soft fragrance fills a space with serenity. The

act of listening to incense transports us out of our routine,

allowing us to focus on the simple beauty of fragrance and

enjoy a moment of peace in the midst of our busy lives.

多而不厭

WHEN IT IS PLENTIFUL, ONE NEVER TIRES OF IT

Our brains are wired to link memories and emotions to scents. The rare fragrant woods and aromatics found in Japanese incense are powerful triggers for the mind, eliciting feelings and evoking memories. Incense can be used for an endless number of reasons, from heightening the once-in-a-lifetime nature of an event to celebrating the change of seasons to simply enhancing our daily routines.

募而知足

WHEN THERE IS LITTLE, STILL ONE IS SATISFIED

The high-quality natural ingredients used in Japanese incense easily fill a space with luxurious fragrance. Even small sticks of high quality jinkō are capable of scenting a room for many hours after they are consumed. Yet Japanese incense never seeks to overpower or overwhelm with its fragrance. Instead, Japanese incense builds gently and consistently over time, creating a fragrant environment in which to exist.

久蔵不朽

AGE DOES NOT CHANGE ITS EFFICACY

One of the greatest qualities of the rare and fragrant woods used in Japanese incense is that, much like fine wines, they often improve with age. Unlike lower-quality incense dipped in chemical scents, Japanese incense uses primarily natural ingredients that retain their fragrant properties, many of which deepen over time. If a piece of the famous Ranjatai, first presented as a tributary gift to Empress Suiko in 595 CE and still preserved in the treasure repository at Tōdai-ji, were to be listened to today, the same exquisite fragrance Empress Suiko experienced over a millennium ago would be shared with those fortunate enough to enjoy it now.

常用無障

USED EVERY DAY,
IT DOES NO HARM

Of all the virtues of incense, this is the one modern-day consumers need to be most aware of. Unlike many incense sticks made by adhering a binder to a bamboo core and dipping it in synthetic scent, Japanese incense is composed primarily of natural ingredients. However, all incense, even reduced-smoke varieties, produces smoke. With modern, environmentally "tight" building techniques and closed spaces, burning incense without sufficient ventilation can have negative health effects. However, by taking simple precautions, Japanese incense can be enjoyed safely.

(See chapter 19.)

GLOSSARY

Amai (甘): Sweet; one of the five taste categories of the *Gomi*.

ansokukō (安息香): Benzoin.

aragoto (荒事): Rough; "wild warrior" *Kabuki* acting style.

ashigaru (足軽): Foot soldier.

ayame (菖蒲): Iris flower.

Ayame-kō (菖蒲香): Name of a *kumikō*.

Baika (梅花): Plum Blossom; one of the six seasonal themes in the *Mukusa no Takimonō*.

bakufu (幕府): "Tent government"; refers to the center of the shōgunal government.

basara (婆娑羅): Extravagant samurai during the Northern and Southern Courts period.

bonita: Board for collecting extruded incense during manufacture.

Buke Shohatto (武家諸法度): Various Points of Laws for Warrior Houses, which defined the samurai role, behavior, and so on.

bushi (武士): Warriors; precursor of *samurai* class.

Bushidō (武士道): The Way of the Warrior.

butsudan (仏壇): Buddhist altar.

byakudan (白檀): Sandalwood.

byōbu (屏風): Folding screen.

Chazen Ichimi (茶禅一味): A saying meaning "Zen and tea have one taste."

Chadō (茶道): The Way of Tea; the tea ceremony.

chanoyu (茶の湯): Hot water with tea; tea ceremony.

chashitsu (茶室): Tearoom.

chidori (千鳥): Plover, a type of coastal bird.

Chidori-kōro (千鳥香爐): A famous celedon *kikigōro* featuring a plover on the lid.

chonmage (丁髷): Topknot hairstyle of the *samurai*.

chōji (丁子): Clove.

chōku (長句): In *renga*, the long verse (first three lines). See also *tanku*.

chōnin (町人): Townsman class of merchants and artisans.

Chūshingura (忠臣蔵): *The Treasury of Loyal Retainers*, or *The Tale of the Forty-Seven Rōnin*.

dai kunkō (大薫香): Great- or large-size incense sticks.

Daibutsu Kaigan Kuyo-e (大仏開眼供養): Eye-Opening Ceremony.

Daibutsu-den (大仏殿): Great Buddha Hall.

Daijōten-nō (太上天皇): Retired Emperor (formal title).

daimyō (大名): Feudal lords; heads of clans who controlled *hans* (domains).

Daimyō-kōji (大名小路): Daimyō Alley; land near Edo Castle where the *daimyō* maintained residences.

Dainichi Nyorai (大日如来): Vairocana Buddha; Great Sun Buddha.

daisu (臺子): A simple two-tiered portable shelf used in the tea ceremony.

daisu kazari (臺子飾): Utensil stand decoration.

daiuikyō (大茴香): Star anise.

Dajō-daijin (太政大臣): Grand Minister of State (formal title).

Dondon-yake (どんどん焼け): "Quick-quick burning"; a fire that nearly destroyed Kyoto in 1864.

dō (道): The "way," as in the Way of the Warrior or the Way of Fragrance.

dōbōshū (同朋衆): Professional connoisseurs with extensive knowledge of the arts.

e-awase (絵合): The comparison of pictures; picture games/contests.

Engaku-kyo (円覚経): Sutra of Perfect Enlightenment.

ensuikeikō (円錐型香): Cone incense.

fudai daimyō (譜代大名): "Insider" *daimyō*; *daimyō* who were hereditary Tokugawa vassals prior to the Battle of Sekigahara (in 1600). See also *tozama daimyō*.

"Fukoku kyōhei" (富国強兵): "Enrich the country, strengthen the military"; slogan adopted by the Meiji government to replace "*Son'nō jōi!*"

fushimono (賦物): Thematic device or rules for *renga*.

gago (雅語): Words of elegance used in Japanese poetry.

gaijin (外人): Term meaning "foreigner not of Asian descent."

geidō (芸道): Art of refinement.

gekokujō (下克上): "The low overturning the high," a phrase related to the upheaval of the social classes.

Genji Monogatari (源氏物語): *The Tale of Genji* by Lady Murasaki Shikibu; written in the eleventh century.

Genji Monogatari Emaki (源氏物語絵巻): Famous twelfth-century scroll of *The Tale of Genji*.

Genji-kō (源氏香): A *kumikō* based on *The Tale of Genji*.

Genji-mon (源氏紋): Five-line design motifs representing specific chapters of *The Tale of Genji*.

gin'yō (銀葉): Silver leaves; small, silver-leaf plates used when warming *jinkō*.

gin'yō basami (銀葉鋏): Silver-leaf tweezer-like incense tool.

gin'yō-ban (銀葉盤): Ornate stand with ten to twelve pedestals on which to place *gin'yō*.

Gokaidō (五街道): The Five Highways; a series of national highways.

Gokajō no Goseimon (五箇条の御誓文): Charter Oath issued in 1868 that spelled out the government's Westernization aims.

Gomi (五味): Five Tastes; a system of fragrance categorization based on the five basic tastes of sweet, bitter, sour, spicy, and salty. See also *Rikkoku* and *Rikkoku-Gomi*.

gunki monogatari (軍記物語): Military chronicles.

Gyō no kōro (行の香炉): Line Incense Burner; name for the *kikigōro* in which the less formal pattern of *hashi-me* is used.

habōki (羽箒): Feather brush; incense tool.

Hagakure-kikigaki (葉隠聞書): *Dictations Given Hidden by Leaves*; a famous book on *Bushidō*.

hai-demae (灰手前): The process of preparing ash and burners for the incense ceremony.

Haibutsu-kishaku (廃仏毀釈): "Abolish Buddhism and destroy Shākyamuni"; slogan/name of a violent anti-Buddhist movement.

haijin (海禁): Chinese sea bans.

haikai no renga (俳諧の連歌): Comic linked verse. See also *renga*.

haioshi (灰押): Ash press.

Haitō-rei (廃刀令): Sword Abolishment Edict; banned the wearing of swords for all but former *daimyō*.

haka (墓): Family grave.

han (藩): The feudal system of *daimyō* domains; a domain controlled by a *daimyō*.

Hana no Gosho (花の御所): The Flower Palace; center of the Ashikaga *shōgunate*.

Hana no Hana (花の花): Flower of Flowers; first Japanese floral incense from 1911.

hana-awase (花合せ): The comparison of flower-arranging; flower-arranging games/contests.

hanami (花見): Flower viewing.

hashi-me (箸目): "Chopstick eye"; patterns/lines made in the ash of an incense burner.

Hatsuhana (初花): One of the *katatsuki* considered the three great tea caddies of the world, along with Narashiba and Nitta.

He Xian Fang (和香方): *Blended Incense Recipes*; earliest known text on the use of incense; Chinese, approximately 430 CE.

Heike Monogatari (平家物語): *The Tale of the Heike*.

hicha (非茶): Non-tea, or lesser tea.

hie (冷え): Chill; relating to *chanoyu* (tea ceremony).

hinoki (檜): Japanese cypress.

hiragana (平仮名): A popular *kana* syllabary.

hokumen no bushi (北面の武士): Private armies of retired emperors.

honcha (本茶): Real tea, or true tea.

Hōmon hyakushū (法門百首): *One Hundred Poems of the Dharma Gate*; twelfth-century *waka* collection.

Hōōden (鳳凰殿): Phoenix Hall; constructed at the 1897 Chicago World's Fair.

hyakuin (百韻): One hundred rhymes; the standard length of a *renga* competition.

Hyakunin Isshu (百人一首): *One Hundred Poets, One Poem*; *waka* anthology from the Nara and Heian periods.

ichibokudaki (一木薫): One-wood burning.

ichigo ichie (一期一会): A once-in-a-lifetime encounter; derived from *ichigo ni ichido*.

ichigo ni ichido (一期に一度): One chance in a lifetime.

ichigyōmono (一行物): One-line scroll highlighting the sayings of Zen masters.

ichiza konryū (一座建立): A feeling of group unity and harmony.

iemoto (家元): The house head of a school of refined arts.

ikebana: Another name for *Kadō*, or the Way of Flowers.

Ikenobō (池坊): The honorific given to the *iemoto*, the head of those in charge of flower arrangement for the temple.

iki (粋): A unique sense of style developed by *chōnin* that was fresh, youthful, and chic.

Ikkō-ikki (一向一揆): Warrior monks during the Sengoku period.

Ikokusen Uchiharai-rei (異国船打払令): Edict to Repel Foreign Vessels issued in 1825.

In no chō (院庁): Name for the courts of the retired emperor.

insei (院政): Cloistered rule; a practice in which emperors abdicated their formal duties and retired from public life.

jakō (麝香): Musk.

ji ji muge (事事無礙): Buddhist concept of interdependence.

Jijū (侍従): Chamberlain; one of the six seasonal themes in the *Mukusa no Takimonō*.

jikōban (常香盤): Incense clock.

jinkō (沈香): Rare and fragrant aloeswood; shortened form of *jinsuikōboku*.

jinsuikōboku (沈水香木): Sinking incense wood; aloeswood; often shortened to *jinkō*.

jishiki (地敷): Thick paper placemat covered with gold or silver foil placed on top of the *uchishiki* during the incense ceremony.

Jōi Chokumei (攘夷勅命): Edict to Expel the Barbarians issued in 1863.

Jūshichijō Kenpō (十七条憲法): Seventeen Injunctions; Chinese-influenced constitution.

Jūshūkō (十種香): Ten Types of Incense; one of the earliest examples of *kumikō*.

Kabuki (歌舞伎): A form of theater that was bold, energetic, and dynamic. See also *Noh*.

Kadō (華道): The Way of Flowers; *ikebana*.

kaidan (戒壇): Buddhist ordination platform.

kaikō (貝甲香): Onycha; shell fragrance.

kaisho (会所): Reception hall.

kakejiku (掛軸): Hanging scroll.

kakkō (藿香): Patchouli.

Kamakura Shin Bukkyō (鎌倉新仏教): Kamakura New Buddhism.

kami (神): Gods, deities.

kamikaze (神風): Divine wind.

kana (仮名): System of writing; Japanese syllabary attributed to Buddhist monk Kūkai.

kanazōshi (仮名草子): Printed books written in *kana* with little or no *kanji*; Edo period.

kanji: Japanese writing system that uses Chinese characters; characters.

kanshō (甘松): Spikenard.

kanso (簡素): Simplicity and purity.

Kao irai no Kadensho (花王以来の花伝書): The oldest known manuscript of *Kadō*.

Karai (辛): Spicy; one of the five taste categories of the *Gomi*.

karamono (唐物): Imported works of rare and eloquent Chinese art and culture.

kare (枯れ): Withered; relating to *chanoyu* (tea ceremony).

kata (型): Prescribed form or way of an artform.

katatsuki (肩衝): Square-shouldered tea caddy.

Kayō (荷葉): Lotus Blossom; one of the six seasonal themes in the *Mukusa no Takimonō*.

keihi (桂皮): Cinnamon.

Kenmu-Shikimoku (建武式目): The Kenmu Code; a code developed to rein in the *basara* lords' outlandish exhibitions of wealth and consumption.

kenshō (見性): Flash of insight into Buddha nature/enlightenment.

kigo (季語): Seasonal words used in *waka* poetry.

kikatenran-kai (菊花展覧会): Chrysanthemum exhibitions that take place throughout Japan in the fall.

kiki-guchi (聞口): Listening line; the position in the incense burner from which the incense is listened to.

kikigōro (聞香炉): Incense burner for listening to incense during *Kōdō*.

Kikka (菊花): Chrysanthemum; one of the six seasonal themes in the *Mukusa no Takimonō*.

kiku-awase (菊合わせ): The comparison of chrysanthemums; chrysanthemum games/contests.

Kiku-awase-kō (菊合わせ香): Name of a *kumikō*.

kiku-za (菊座): Flower-like pedestals on the *gin'yō-ban*.

"Kimigayo" (君が代): The Japanese national anthem.

Kinchū Narabi ni Kuge Shohatto (禁中並公家諸法度): Laws for the Imperial Court and Court Nobles; *shōgunate* action that relegated the role of the Imperial Court to ceremony, scholarship, and the arts.

kiri (桐): *Paulownia* wood.

Kissa Yōjō-ki (喫茶養生記): *Record of Drinking Tea for Health*; book written in 1214 by Myōan Eisai.

koji (火筋): "Fire chopsticks"; incense tool.

Kojiki (古事記): *Record of Ancient Things*; the oldest written record of Japanese history.

Kokin Wakashū (古今和歌集): *Collection of Poems Ancient and Modern*; famous book of poetry published in 920 CE; nicknamed the *Kokinshū*.

Kokinshū (古今集): Shortened name for the *Kokin Wakashū*.

"Kokoro no fumi" (心の文): "Letter of the Heart"; a letter written by Jūko describing the tea ceremony aesthetic.

koku (斛): A unit of currency; enough rice to feed five thousand people for one year.

kokubun-ji (国分寺): Buddhist temple system originally created by Emperor Shomū in 741 CE.

kokugaku (国学): National learning.

kokutai (国体): The strict defining of a Japanese national identity.

Kokutai no Hongi (国体の本義): *Cardinal Principles of the National Entity of Japan*; published in 1937 by the Japanese ministry of education.

kō (香): Incense.

"Kō no Jittoku" (香の十徳): "Ten Virtues of Incense"; a poem or poetic verse originally from the eleventh century.

kō-awase (香合せ): The comparison of aloeswood.

kō-o-kiku (香お聞): Hearing incense.

kōboku (香木): Fragrant wood.

Kōdō (香道): The Way of Fragrance; the incense ceremony.

kōdōgu (香道具): Incense utensils.

kōgō (香合): Small incense container.

kōjū (講中): Official in charge of incense for purification and ceremony at the Imperial Court.

kōmoto (香元): Incense ceremony host; the person in charge of the incense ceremony.

kōro (香炉): Incense burner.

kōsaji (香匙): Small, spoonlike tool for placing incense wood.

kōseki (香席): Incense gathering; a gathering for *Kōdō*.

Kōzen gokokuron (興禅護国論): *The Promotion of Zen for the Protection of the Country*; an 1198 treatise by Eisai that was based on the Prajnaparamita Scripture for Humane Kings Who Wish to Protect Their States.

Kōzuke no Suke (上野介): Title of a high-ranking court official of protocol.

kubi-jikken (首実検): A viewing ceremony of heads taken in battle.

kumikō (組香): Incense games.

kun'yomi reading (訓読み): A reading of *kanji* that used the native Japanese pronunciation. See also *on'yomi reading*.

Kundaikan-sōchōki (君台観左右帳記): An instruction manual for the display of tea implements.

Kunshū Ruishō (薫集類抄): A twelfth-century compilation of takimonō recipes attributed to Jakuren.

Kurobō (黒方): Black; one of the six seasonal themes in the *Mukusa no Takimonō*.

kurofune (黒船): Black ships of the West; named such due to their blackened wooden exteriors, which were treated with pitch.

kyara (伽羅): Generally considered the highest grade of aloeswood.

Kyara (伽羅): One of the six nations of the *Rikkoku*; *jinkō* found in a very small geographic area in present day central and southern Vietnam.

ma (間): Moments of silence and the space they create, in which form and meaning emerge.

maeku (前句): In *renga*, the preceding verse. See also *tsukeku*.

mainichi-kō (毎日香): Everyday incense; used as an incense category; also Mainichikoh as a product name. See also *tokusen*.

maki-e (蒔絵): Literally "sprinkled design"; a decorative technique in which powdered gold or silver is sprinkled onto wet lacquer to create landscapes, patterns, or symbols.

makkō (抹香): Incense powder.

Makura no Sōshi (枕草子): *The Pillow Book*; written in approximately 1002 CE.

Manaban (真南蛮): One of the six nations of the *Rikkoku*; today generally considered to be *jinkō* imported from Cambodia.

Manaka (真那伽): One of the six nations of the *Rikkoku*; the name is thought to be a lingual adaptation of Malacca, the former capital and port city in present day Malaysia.

Mańyōshū (万葉集): *Collection of Ten Thousand Leaves*; the oldest Japanese anthology of waka poetry.

meibutsu (名物): Famous, highly prized objects.

meibutsu-gari (名物狩り): The compulsory collection of *meibutsu*.

meikō (名香): Named pieces of *jinkō*.

Mibun Tōsei Rei (身分統制令): Social Status Control Order; also known as the Separation Edict. This law permanently froze the social classes of all Japanese, establishing a rigid class order based on the Confucian *shi-nō-kō-shō* system.

midarabako (乱箱): High-sided tray to carry the various incense utensils.

Ming Shi (明史): Book that contains the official history of the Ming.

mini sun (ミニ寸): Mini-size incense sticks.

mitsu-gusoku (三具足): Incense, flowers, and light; offerings present at Buddhist altars.

miyabi (雅): Courtly refinement; elegance.

mokkō (木香): Costus.

monkō (聞香): Listening to incense.

mono no aware (物の哀れ): Bittersweet awareness of the transience of beauty and the passage of time.

mono-awase (物合せ): The comparison of things (Heian period), such as poetry, flower-arranging, or incense.

monogatari (物語): Narrative tales.

mu (無): Nothingness; used to denote an indescribable combination of tastes, as relates to the *Gomi* in particular.

Mukusa no Takimonō (六種の薫物): Six Kneaded Incenses; a framework that organized incense into six seasonal themes: Baika (梅花, Plum Blossom); Kayō (荷葉, Lotus Blossom); Rakuyō (荷葉, Fallen Leaves); Kikka (菊花, Chrysanthemum); Jijū (侍従, Chamberlain); Kurobō (黒方, Black).

mushin (無心): The Zen state of "no-mind."

nagare-zukuri (流造): Streamlined roof architectural style.

nanban (南蛮): "Southern barbarians"; initially used to describe traders from southern China, but came to refer to Westerners, as in the nanban trade.

Nanboku-chō jidai (南北朝時代): Northern and Southern Courts period; a fifty-year period during the 1300s in which two courts vied for superiority.

nerikō (練香): Kneaded fermented incense.

Nigai (苦): Bitter; one of the five taste categories of the *Gomi*.

Nihon Shoki (日本書紀): *Chronicles of Japan*; the second oldest written record of Japanese history.

Nihon-ga (日本画): A Japanese-style of painting that incorporated Western techniques.

Nihonkokuō (日本国王): King of Japan; a title that made Japan subservient to Ming China.

nikki bungaku (日記文学): Poetic diaries.

nioi-bukuro (匂い袋): Sachet incense.

Noh (能): A style of theater that was formal, stoic, and restrained. See also *Kabuki*.

nue (鵺): A mythological flying monster with the head of a monkey, the legs of a tiger, the tail of a snake, and the body of a *tanuki* (shape shifter).

nyūkō (乳香): Frankincense.

o-chanoyu-goseido (御茶湯御政道): Tea-ceremony government.

O-kazari-sho (御飾書): Companion volume to *Kundaikan-sōchōki*.

o-shippitsu (お執筆): Recordkeeper for the incense ceremony.

o-tsume (お詰): Lowest-ranking guest at the incense ceremony.

Obon (お盆): Annual Buddhist holiday commemorating family ancestors.

ogi-awase (荻合わせ): The comparison of fans; fan games/contests.

Oie-ryu (御家流): Oie School of Kōdō; one of the two main schools of incense; Sanjōnishi Sanetaka is considered to be the founder. See also *Shino-ryu*.

on'yomi reading (音読み): A reading of kanji that approximated the original Chinese pronunciation in Japanese. See also *kun'yomi reading*.

onnade (女手): "Woman's hand"; refers to *hiragana*, a *kana* syllabary.

Ōjuku-kō (黄熟香): Original name of the famous incense wood *Ranjatai*.

Rakoku (羅国): One of the six nations of the *Rikkoku*; generally refers to *jinkō* originating from Thailand.

Rakuyō (荷葉): Fallen Leaves; one of the six seasonal themes in the *Mukusa no Takimonō*.

rangaku (蘭学): Dutch studies.

Ranjatai (蘭奢待): Famous incense wood that washed up on Awaji Island in 595 CE.

renga (連歌): A poetic form using the *tanka* form and consisting of linked verses created by two or more poets.

renshū (連衆): Participants at the incense ceremony.

rikka (立花): A style of standing flower arrangement.

Rikkoku (六国): The "Six Nations" framework used extensively to classify aloeswood. See also *Gomi* and *Rikkoku-Gomi*.

Rikkoku-Gomi (六国五味): Six Countries, Five Tastes; a framework that combines the *Rikkoku* and *Gomi* frameworks to classify aloeswood.

risshi (律師): Buddhist precepts master.

Risshun (立春): Name for the first day of spring.

Risshun-kō: Name of a *kumikō*.

rōnin (浪人): Masterless *samurai*.

ryōtō tetsuritsu (両統迭立): A pattern of succession alternating between the junior and senior branches of the imperial family.

ryu (流): School, or form.

ryū-nō (龍脳): Borneol.

sabi (寂): An ineffable quality that could be likened to the patina achieved with age; a deep tranquil beauty that emerges through the passage of time and that reminds us of the fleeting nature of things.

Sakoku-rei (鎖国令): The Closed Country Edicts, or Sakoku Edicts; these edicts were intended to quarantine Japan from the influence of the West.

Sakyamuni: Chinese name for the Buddha.

samurai (侍): The warrior aristocracy class.

sankin-kōtai (参勤交代): Alternate attendance; decree from 1635 that said all *daimyō* were required to spend alternating years living in Edo (rather than in their domain).

sanna (山奈): Galangal.

Sasora (佐曽羅): One of the six nations of the *Rikkoku*; the nation this classification represents is believed to have been either a region in India or the western portion of Southeast Asia near Myanmar and Bangladesh.

satori (悟り): Enlightenment.

Seii Taishōgun (征夷大将軍): Supreme Military Commander (formal title); often shortened to *Shōgun*.

Sen'ō Kuden (専応口伝): The documented oral traditions of *Ikenobō Kadō*.

Sengoku Jidai (戦国時代): The Warring States period of Japan.

senkō (線香): Stick incense.

seppuku (切腹): Ritual suicide.

shakkyōka (釈教歌): Buddhist poetry.

shaku (笏): Scepter.

shariden (舎利殿): Buddhist relics hall.

shi-nō-kō-shō (士農工商): The four social classes of warrior, farmer, artisan, and merchant in the Confucian system.

shikimoku (式目): Cohesive literary rules for *renga*.

shikken (執権): Shōgunal regents.

Shin Kokin Wakashū (新古今和歌集): *New Collection of Poems Ancient and Modern*; *waka* anthology commissioned by the emperor in 1201.

Shin no kōro (真の香炉): True Incense Burner; name for the *kikigōro* in which the most formal pattern of *hashi-me* is used.

Shin-kyara (新伽羅): *Kyara* classified as coming from later than Edo period.

Shinbutsu bunri (神仏分離): Separation of Shintō and Buddhism; a series of edicts that restricted Buddhism.

shino-bukuro (志野袋): Bag for holding packages of *jinkō*.

Shino-ryu (志野流): Shino School of Kōdō; one of the two main schools of incense; Shino Sōshin is considered to be the founder. See also *Oie-ryu*.

Shiokarai (塩辛): Salty; one of the five taste categories of the *Gomi*.

shishi (志士): Men of high purpose; young, ambitious, anti-Western *samurai* in favor of restoring the emperor to power in the mid-1800s.

Shishu Jippukucha (四種十服茶): Four Kinds of Tea in Ten Cups; name of a game.

shoin (書院): A type of Zen study used as a reception hall.

shoin kazari (書院飾): Reception hall ornamentation.

Shoin-zukuri (書院造): Architecture style that emerged at Higashiyama.

shōen system (荘園公領制): A system of private, tax-exempt landed estates.

Shōgun: Shortened form of the title *Seii Taishōgun*, Supreme Military Commander.

shōgunate: The government of the *shōgun*.

shōkō (焼香): Burning incense; granulated incense.

shōkyaku (正客): Honored guest at the incense ceremony.

Shōsō-in Repository: The imperial treasure repository.

shuin-jō (朱印状): Red-seal edicts, or red-seal letters.

shuinsen (朱印船): Red-seal ships; ships granted trading licenses under the official protection of the *shōgunate*, named such due to the vermillion seal on the license.

shukuba (宿場): Post stations along the *Gokaidō*.

"Son'nō jōi" (尊皇攘夷): "Revere the Emperor, expel the barbarians" was a saying used by the *shishi*; it was also the name for the movement to restore the emperor.

sonaekō (供香): Burned directly upon hot coals.

soradaki (空薫): "Empty burning"; burning incense for pleasure.

Sumatora (寸門多羅): One of the six nations of the *Rikkoku*; the name is an alliteration of Sumatra, an island just south of the Malay Peninsula in the present-day island nation of Indonesia.

Suppai (酸っぱい): Sour/acidic; one of the five taste categories of the *Gomi*.

sutra: Sacred Budhist scripture.

tabu-no-ki (栴の木): Powdered bark of the Japanese Bay tree that is used as a binder in incense.

Taiheiki (太平記): *Chronicles of the Great Peace*; a forty-volume chronicle of the Northern and Southern Courts period.

Taiko no katana-gari (太閤の刀狩り): Taiko Sword Hunt; a red-seal edict that forbade the possession of weapons by any class other than the *samurai*.

takigumikō (たき組香): Linked incense; a type of *kumikō*.

takimonō (薫物): Incense for pleasure; the name given to *nerikō* during the Heian period.

takimonō-awase (薫物合せ): The comparison of incense; kneaded incense games/contests.

tama (玉): Jewel; used in *Genji-kō* to denote the correct answer.

tama: Ball; single mass of clay-like raw incense during incense manufacturing.

tan sun (短寸): Short-size incense sticks.

tanegashima (種子島): Portuguese *teppō* (rifles) manufactured by the Japanese.

tanka (短歌): Japanese poetic form with thirty-one sound units in 5-7-5-7-7 pattern; in English, usually described as thirty-one syllables in five lines of 5-7-5-7-7 syllables.

tanku (短句): In *renga*, the short verse (last two lines). See also *chōku*.

tansu (箪笥): Chest of drawers.

tanuki (化け狸): Shape shifter; the *nue* had the body of a shape shifter.

tatehana (立花): Standing flower arrangement.

tegiroku-shi (手記録紙): Answer sheets used for *kumikō* during the incense ceremony.

temae (手前): The choreographed actions of the *kōmoto* during the incense ceremony.

tenka fubu (天下布武): Rule by military force; slogan of Oda Nobunaga.

tensu (天守): Main keep of a castle.

teppō (鉄砲): Iron cannon; early matchlock rifles.

teppō ashigaru (鉄砲足軽): Foot soldiers armed with *tanegashima*.

tokonoma (床の間): Alcove in a tearoom or Japanese-style room where items are displayed.

tokusen (特撰): "Special" or "select." See also *mainichi-kō*.

tozama daimyō (外様大名): "Outsider" *daimyō*; *daimyō* who became Tokugawa vassals after the Battle of Sekigahara (in 1600). See also *fudai daimyō*.

tōcha (闘茶): Tea battle; tea-tasting competition.

tōjin yashiki (唐人屋敷): The Chinese quarter at Nagasaki.

Tōkaidō (東海道): The Eastern Sea Route that connected Edo to Kyoto.

tōkō (闘香): Incense battle.

tsukeku (付句): In *renga*, the responding verse. See also *maeku*.

Tsukubashū (菟玖波集): *The Tsukuba Anthology*; the first imperial anthology of *renga*.

tsukumogami (付喪神): An object over one hundred years old, believed to be given a soul for its service, thus becoming almost supernatural.

uchishiki (打敷): Framed silk rug spread over the *tatami* during the *Oie* form of *Kōdō*.

uguisu (鶯): Metal pin used to hold opened packets of incense during the incense ceremony.

uji (有時): "Being-time"; the concept defined by Dōgen that time and being are one.

ukiyo (憂世): The Buddhist term referring to the world of illusion and suffering; a homophone for *ukiyo*, 浮世 (note the difference in the first character).

ukiyo (浮世): To float; a homophone for *ukiyo*, 憂世 (note the difference in the first character) and play on words to define "the floating world."

Ukiyo Monogatari (浮世物語): *Tales of the Floating World*; a famous book written in 1666 by Asai Ryōi.

ukiyo-e (浮世絵): "Pictures of the floating world"; a form of woodblock printing featuring scenes of Edo.

ukiyo-zōshi (浮世草子): "Books of the floating world"; often written entirely in *kana* and using colloquial language.

Urasenke Chadō: Urasenke School of Tea.

uta-awase (歌合わせ): The comparison of poetry; poetry games/contests.

uzumakisenkō (渦巻き線香): Coil incense.

wabi: A nuanced term that could represent the beauty found in simplicity, quiet contentment, humility, or a combination.

wabi-cha (侘茶): The tea of quiet taste.

waboku (和木): Fragrant woods originating from Japan.

wagashi (和菓子): Elegant sweets paired with tea.

waka (和歌): Song or verse; poetry.

wénxiāng (聞香): Chinese term to describe listening to incense.

wokou (倭寇): Chinese term for Japanese pirates.

xiāng (香): Chinese word for incense.

xiāng wán: Chinese medicine (fragrant pills) taken internally or burned to release fragrance.

Yamato-e (大和絵): A style of classic Chinese narrative illustration gilded with gold.

yojohan chashitsu (四畳半茶室): Four-and-a-half tatami mat tearoom.

Yoshiwara (吉原): The Edo pleasure quarters.

yūsoku kojitsu (有職故実): Knowledge of ancient wisdom and refined practices of the Imperial Court.

zashiki kazari (座敷飾): A style of interior decoration.

Zuiroku-san (瑞鹿山): Auspicious Deer Mountain; a name given to the temple Engaku-ji.

zukō (塗香): Powdered incense.

REFERENCES

Al Jazeera English. *Scent from Heaven.* Documentary. Posted
February 25, 2016, by Al Jazeera English. YouTube.
https://www.youtube.com/watch?v=jv69pYSm2oo.

Awajishima no Koshi. "Awaji Island." Awaji Island Koshi, accessed
April 15, 2024.
https://www.awaji-kohshi.com/en/top.html.

Baieido Co., Ltd. "History of Baieido." Baieido, accessed March 22,
2024.
https://www.baieido.co.jp/jp/about/.

Barzun, Jacques, ed. *The Taiheiki: A Chronicle of Medieval Japan.*
Translated by Helen Craig McCullough. Columbia University
Press, 1959.

Boston University Pardee School of Global Studies. "Room
No. 2: Art at the Fair – The Japanese Pavilion at the 1893
World's Columbian Exposition in Chicago." Asia at the World's
Fairs, accessed March 22, 2024.
https://asiaworldsfairs.org/room-no-2-at-the-fair/
(site discontinued).

Buck-Albulet, Heidi. "From 'Task' to 'Title'? Japanese Linked Poetry
and the Fushimono." In *Exploring Written Artefacts*, edited by
J. B. Quenzer. Berlin: De Gruyter, 2021.

Business Insider. "Why Sandalwood Is So Expensive." March 12,
2022. YouTube video, 9:38.
https://www.youtube.com/watch?v=QPRpWg_wU0A.

Campbell, Gavin. "Japanese World War II Art History: From 1931–
1945." Virtual lecture, Context Learning, December 19, 2023.
https://www.contexttravel.com/.

Campbell, Gavin. "Kyoto Japan: A Tour Through the Seasons."
Virtual lecture, Context Learning, December 12, 2023.
https://www.contexttravel.com/.

Campbell, Gavin. "The Opening of Japan." Virtual lecture, Context
Learning, June 21, June 28, July 5, 2023.
https://www.contexttravel.com/.

Campbell, Gavin. "Tokyo's Edo Past: The Birth of Japanese Cool."
Virtual lecture, Context Learning, November 21, 2023.
https://www.contexttravel.com/.

Castellanos, Kenia M., Judith A. Hudson, Jeanette Haviland-Jones,
and Patricia J. Wilson. "Does Exposure to Ambient Odors
Influence the Emotional Content of Memories?" *The American
Journal of Psychology* 123, no. 3 (2010): 269–79.

Chaplin, Danny. *Sengoku Jidai. Nobunaga, Hideyoshi, and Ieyasu:
Three Unifiers of Japan*. CreateSpace Publishing, 2018.

Coleridge, Henry James, ed. *The Life and Letters of St. Francis Xavier*.
2nd ed. 2 vols. London: Burns & Oates, 1890.

Corbett, Rebecca. "Women and Tea Culture in Early Modern Japan."
Chapter 1 in *Cultivating Femininity: Women and Tea Culture in
Edo and Meiji Japan*. University of Hawai'i Press, 2018.

Dōyo, Sasaki, Kyoko Selden, and Lillian Selden. "'Renga' by Sasaki
Dōyo Selected from the *Tsukubashū* (*Tsukuba Anthology*)."
Review of Japanese Culture and Society 27 (2015): 55–62.

García, Héctor, and Francesc Miralles. *The Book of Ichigo Ichie:
The Art of Making the Most of Every Moment, the Japanese Way*.
London: Quercus Editions Ltd, 2020.

Gatten, Aileen. "A Wisp of Smoke: Scent and Character in *The Tale
of Genji*." *Monumenta Nipponica* 32, no. 1 (1977): 35–48.

Genuine Japan. "Genuine Japan Channel No. 2: The Shino School
of Incense 'Kōdō.'" January 12, 2018. YouTube video, 13:17.
https://www.youtube.com/watch?v=y27tnZdcQDU&t=733s.

Grossberg, Kenneth A. "From Feudal Chieftain to Secular Monarch:
The Development of Shogunal Power in Early Muromachi
Japan." *Monumenta Nipponica* 31, no. 1 (1976): 29–49.

Hall, Kenneth R. "Local and International Trade and Traders in the
Straits of Melaka Region: 600–1500." *Journal of the Economic
and Social History of the Orient* 47, no. 2 (2004): 213–260.

Hanh, Thich Nhat. *Awakening of the Heart: Essential Buddhist Sutras
and Commentaries*. Parallax Press, 2012.

Hanh, Thich Nhat. *Zen Keys: A Guide to Zen Practice*. Double Day
Random House, 1973.

Haskel, Peter. *Zen Master Tales: Stories from the Lives of Taigu, Sengai, Hakuin, and Ryōkan.* Shambhala Publications, 2022.

Hata, Masataka. *Koh Senshū: A Cultural History of Japan as Seen through Incense.* Translated by Mark Jamentz. Shoyeido Incense Co., 2023.

Hiroyuki, Jinbo. *Kōdō no Rekishi Jiten* [Historical Encyclopedia of Kōdō]. Tokyo: Kashiwa Shobō, 2003.

Horiguchi, Satoru, and Dinah Jung. "Kōdō—Its Spiritual and Game Elements and Its Interrelations with the Japanese Literary Arts." *Journal of the Royal Asiatic Society,* 23 no. 1 (2013): 69–84.

Ito, Kiyoshi. "Revival Attempt of Incense Ceremony in the Modern Ages." *Journal of the International Center for Cultural Resource Studies.* Kanazawa: International Center for Cultural Resource Studies, Kanazawa University, 2015.

Iwasaki, Mawaya. *"The Three Ways of Tea • Flower • Incense,"* Lecture, Japanese Traditional Culture, Kogakkan University, Osaka, Japan. November 2, 2019.

Jansen, Marius B. *The Making of Modern Japan.* The Belknap Press of Harvard University Press, 2002.

Japanese Civilization Institute. "Making Full Use of the Five Senses." *Japanese Civilization Institute Newsletter* 13, no. 3 (2018): 2–8.

Jung, Dietrich. "The Cultural Biography of Agarwood—Perfumery in Eastern Asia and the Asian Neighbourhood." *Journal of the Royal Asiatic Society* 23, no. 1 (2013): 103–125.

Kaufman, Cathy. "A Simple Bowl of Tea: Power, Politics, and Aesthetics in Hideyoshi's Japan, 1582–1591." Dublin Gastronomy Symposium, 2018.

Keene, Donald. *Emperor of Japan: Meiji and His World, 1852–1912.* New York: Columbia University Press, 2002.

Keene, Donald. *Yoshimasa and the Silver Pavilion: The Creation of the Soul of Japan.* New York: Columbia University Press, 2003.

Koek, E. "Portuguese History of Malacca." *Journal of the Straits Branch of the Royal Asiatic Society* 17 (1886): 117–149.

Konishi, Jin'Ichi, Karen Brazell, and Lewis Cook. "The Art of Renga." *Journal of Japanese Studies* 2, no. 1 (1975): 29–61.

Lillehoj, Elizabeth. "Tōfukumon'in: Empress, Patron, and Artist." *Woman's Art Journal* 17, no. 1 (1996): 28–34.

Lim, Ivy Maria. "From Haijin to Kaihai: The Jiajing Court's Search for a Modus Operandi along the South-Eastern Coast (1522–1567)." *Journal of the British Association for Chinese Studies* 2, no. 1 (2013): 1–26.

Lockard, Craig A. "'The Sea Common to All': Maritime Frontiers, Port Cities, and Chinese Traders in the Southeast Asian Age of Commerce, ca. 1400–1750." *Journal of World History* 21, no. 2 (2010): 219–247.

López-Sampson, Arlene, and Tony Page. "History of Use and Trade of Agarwood." *Economic Botany* 72, no. 1 (2018): 107–129.

Masanori, Kikuchi. "Nippon Kōdō: Bringing Japan's Incense Traditions to the World." Nippon.com, June 29, 2016. https://www.nippon.com/en/features/c02502/.

McCullough, Helen C., translator. *Kokin Wakashū: The First Imperial Anthology of Japanese Poetry: With "Tosa Nikki" and "Shinsen Waka."* Stanford University Press, 1985.

Minsky, Laurence, Colleen Fahey, and Caroline Fabrigas. "Inside the Invisible but Influential World of Scent Branding." *Harvard Business Review*, April 11, 2018. https://hbr.org/2018/04/inside-the-invisible-but-influential-world-of-scent-branding.

Moeran, Brian. "Making Scents of Smell: Manufacturing and Consuming Incense in Japan." *Human Organization* 68, no. 4 (2009): 439–450.

Morita, Kiyoko. *The Book of Incense: Enjoying the Traditional Art of Japanese Scents*. Kodansha USA, 1992.

Musashi, Miyamoto. *The Book of Five Rings*. Translated by William Scott Wilson. Shambhala Publications, 2002.

Nippon Kodo. "Incense Ceremony and Culture." Nippon Kodo, accessed September 12, 2024. https://www.nipponkodo.com/ceremony/.

Nobuo, Takeda. "Ornament (Kazari): An Approach to Japanese Culture." *Archives of Asian Art* 47 (1994): 35–45.

Ooms, Herman. "The Religion of the Household: A Case Study of Ancestor Worship in Japan." *Contemporary Religions in Japan* 8, no. 3/4 (1967): 201–333.

Oyler, Elizabeth. "The Nue and Other Monsters in *Heike Monogatari*." *Harvard Journal of Asiatic Studies* 68, no. 2 (2008): 1–32.

Pitelka, Morgan. "Warriors, Tea, and Art in Premodern Japan." *Bulletin of the Detroit Institute of Arts* 88, no. 1–4 (2014): 20–33.

Reider, Noriko T. "'Menoto no sōshi' (A Tale of Two Nursemaids): Teaching for the Women of High Society in the Medieval Period." *US-Japan Women's Journal* 42 (2012): 62–83.

Roberts, Shinshu. *Being-Time: A Practitioner's Guide to Dōgen's Shōbōgenzō Uji*. Wisdom Publications, 2018.

Roemer, Michael K. "Thinking of Ancestors (and Others) at Japanese Household Altars." *Journal of Ritual Studies* 26, no. 1 (2012): 33–45.

Sanjonishi, Giyousui. *Rekishi kara sahō made kōdō yoku wakaru kaori no sekai o fukameru* [Kodo: Deepen your understanding of the world of fragrance, from history to etiquette]. Tokyo: Mates Publishing Company, 2022.

Schopen, Gregory. "The Fragrance of the Buddha, the Scent of Monuments, and the Odor of Images in Early India." *Bulletin de l'École Française d'Extrême-Orient* 101 (2015): 11–30.

Sheldon, Charles D. "Merchants and Society in Tokugawa Japan." *Modern Asian Studies* 17, no. 3 (1983): 477–488.

Shiba, Ryotaro. *The Last Shogun: The Life of Tokugawa Yoshinobu*. Translated by Juliet Winters Carpenter. Kodansha International, 2004.

Shikibu, Murasaki. *The Tale of Genji, Unabridged*. Translated by Dennis Washburn. W. W. Norton, 2015.

Shinada, Yoshikazu. "*Man'yōshū*: The Invention of a National Poetry Anthology." Translated by Kevin Collins. In *Inventing the Classics: Modernity, National Identity, and Japanese Literature,* ed. Haruo Shirane and Tomi Suzuki. Stanford University Press, 2000.

Shoyeido. "The History of Shoyeido." Shoyeido, accessed March 22, 2024. https://www.shoyeido.co.jp/about/history.html.

Shūhō, Zuikei, and Charlotte von Verschuer. "Japan's Foreign Relations 1200 to 1392 A.D.: A Translation from 'Zenrin Kokuhōki.'" *Monumenta Nipponica* 57, no. 4 (2002): 413–445.

Sonoda, Hidehiro. "The Decline of the Japanese Warrior Class, 1840–1880." *Japan Review* 1 (1990): 73–111.

Sōshitsu, Sen, XV. *The Japanese Way of Tea: From Its Origins in China to Sen Rikyū*. Translated by V. Dixon Morris. University of Hawai'i Press, 1998.

Surak, Kristin. "From Selling Tea to Selling Japaneseness: Symbolic Power and the Nationalization of Cultural Practices." *European Journal of Sociology/Archives Européennes de Sociologie*, 52 no. 2 (2011): 175–208.

Suzuki, Shunryu. *Not Always So: Practicing the True Spirit of Zen*. Edited by Edward Espe Brown. HarperCollins Publishers, 2002.

Suzuki, Shunryu. *Zen Mind, Beginner's Mind: Informal Talks on Zen Meditation and Practice*. Shambhala Publications, 1970.

Toby, Ronald P. "Why Leave Nara?: Kammu and the Transfer of the Capital." *Monumenta Nipponica* 40, no. 3 (1985): 331–347.

Tsunetomo, Yamamoto. *Hagakure: The Secret Wisdom of the Samurai*. Translated by Alexander Bennett. Tuttle Publishing, 2014.

Vaporis, Constantine N. "Lordly Pageantry: The Daimyo Procession and Political Authority." *Japan Review* 17 (2005): 3–54.

Vaporis, Constantine N. "To Edo and Back: Alternate Attendance and Japanese Culture in the Early Modern Period." *Journal of Japanese Studies* 23, no. 1 (1997): 25–67.

von Verschuer, Charlotte. "Ashikaga Yoshimitsu's Foreign Policy 1398 to 1408 A.D.: A Translation from 'Zenrin Kokuhōki,' the Cambridge Manuscript." *Monumenta Nipponica* 62, no. 3 (2007): 261–297.

Walsh, Colleen. "What the Nose Knows: Experts Discuss the Science of Smell and How Scent, Emotion, and Memory Are Intertwined—and Exploited." *The Harvard Gazette*, February 27, 2020. https://news.harvard.edu/gazette/story/2020/02/how-scent-emotion-and-memory-are-intertwined-and-exploited/.

Watts, Alan. *The Way of Zen*. Vintage Books, Random House, 1957.

Williams, Duncan Ryūken. *The Other Side of Zen: A Social History of Sōtō Zen Buddhism in Tokugawa Japan*. Princeton University Press, 2005.

Yamada, H. *Kōboku no ki hon zukan surui to tokuchō ga hitome de wakru* [Illustrated guide to the basics of fragrant wood. Understand the types and characteristics at a glance]. Kyoto: Yamada-Matsu Co. Ltd., 2019.

Yunjun, Chen. "The Perfume Culture of China and Taiwan: A Personal Report." *Journal of the Royal Asiatic Society* 23, no. 1 (2013): 127–130.

ABOUT THE AUTHOR

Michael J. Cousineau is the founder of Kikoh Incense, one of the largest retailers of Japanese incense in North America. An award-winning design teacher, he left the classroom after nearly three decades to dedicate himself to his passion for Japanese incense. His writing on the subject has made his website a popular resource that attracts nearly seventy-five thousand visitors annually. When not immersed in the world of incense, Cousineau enjoys playing guitar, exploring arboretums and Japanese gardens, and taking walks with his wife, Linda. Visit his website at kikohincense.com.